LOCUS OF CONTROL

Current Trends in Theory and Research

SECOND EDITION

LOCUS OF CONTROL

Current Trends in Theory and Research

SECOND EDITION

HERBERT M. LEFCOURT
University of Waterloo

LEA LAWRENCE ERLBAUM ASSOCIATES, PUBLISHERS
1982   Hillsdale, New Jersey   London

Lawrence Erlbaum Associates, Inc., Publishers
365 Broadway
Hillsdale, New Jersey 07642

Library of Congress Cataloging in Publication Data

Lefcourt, Herbert M.
  Locus of control.

  Bibliography: p.
  Includes index.
  1. Control (Psychology) 2. Personality. 3. Helpless-
ness (Psychology) 4. Psychology, Pathological. I. Title.
BF532.5.L43   1982   153   82-8793
ISBN 0-89859-222-4   AACR2

Printed in the United States of America
10   9   8   7   6   5   4   3   2   1

Contents

Preface

Since the publication of the first edition of this book, much research has been reported that is pertinent to if not directly concerned with the locus of control construct. In research focused upon attribution processes and helplessness, there have been enough publications to make the review process exceedingly difficult. At the same time, research with locus of control as an individual difference variable has continued apace. Investigators have been exploring a variety of areas such as health, work, affiliative behavior, etc., using novel measuring devices to assess locus of control beliefs pertinent to their specified criteria.

In the attempt to update and expand upon the first edition, I have tried to draw attention to the new directions currently surfacing in the literature. Some of these new directions derive from research concerned with locus of control as an individual difference variable, some from studies dealing with situational determinants of perceived control, and others from studies concerned with rather specific causal attributions used to explain life's experiences.

The purpose of this new edition is to help researchers keep abreast of the widespread developments in this field while retaining an understanding of the sources and major assumptions from which this research endeavor has evolved.

Herbert M. Lefcourt
University of Waterloo

Preface to the First Edition

In this book readers will find a detailed description of research investigations and discussions of the social and personal ramifications of the findings reported. It will become evident to the reader that psychological research can be addressed to larger philosophical questions regarding the nature of man, and this may prove to be of interest for graduate and advanced undergraduate students in psychology who express cynicism about the relevance of psychology for understanding the human condition.

Most generally this book will be of interest to psychologists and other behavioral and social scientists who are concerned with personality and psychopathology. The approach taken in this book derives directly from the excellent working example of the Boulder-model orientation in clinical psychology that was presented by the Ohio State University Clinical Psychology faculty of the late 1950s. The congruence between research and clinical activity, which is at the core of the Boulder model, was convincingly illustrated among that faculty. Consequently, the writer can express appreciation to Julian B. Rotter, and the late George A. Kelly, Alvin Scodel, and Shephard Liverant. In addition, I note my appreciation of the late Vaughn Crandall who first introduced this writer to social learning research during my undergraduate years.

Finally, this writer would like to offer appreciation to each of several individuals: to my wife Barbara who helped me to develop an "internal critic" for evaluating my own writing, to Elizabeth Hogg and Carol Sordoni, my research assistants, who performed an assortment of roles that facilitated the process of book writing, and to the wonderful University of Waterloo secretaries who somehow or other were able to familiarize themselves with some woeful handwriting.

Herbert M. Lefcourt
University of Waterloo

LOCUS OF CONTROL

Current Trends in Theory and Research

SECOND EDITION

1 Locus of Control: Understanding the Concept

INTRODUCTION

Man has reached a stage in his history that surrounds him with challenges to his very survival. Faced with problems of overpopulation and the consequent overcrowding, discomfort, and environmental pollution, he can easily come to feel overburdened, irritable, and hopeless. The title of the Broadway musical "Stop the World I Want To Get Off" is a common distillation of the thoughts of many an urban dweller. One of the most disturbing accompaniments of population density has been the sharp increase in incidents of violence, with the resulting insecurity to which urban dwellers have become accustomed. Robberies, assaults, murders, and rape, sometimes with no apparent purpose, have become commonplace in sections of many large cities. Citizens purchase weapons for protection of their homes and certain communities establish protective wire or electronic screening devices with guarded entrances to protect themselves against marauders. In New York City, the number of large guard dogs is said to be enjoying such an increase that a street sanitation problem has developed.

If it were not so serious, much of the world today could be construed as a bad joke. When we consider the repeated evidence of man's cruelty to man throughout history, it is possible to question whether man is likely to survive in the relatively free state within which he lives today, crowded closer together with others and dependent upon some belief in the ephemeral good will or conscience within himself and others for his daily feelings of safety.

Writers such as Arthur Koestler (1967) and Hannah Arendt (1963), and psychological researchers such as Stanley Milgram (1963), lead us to believe that man is indeed a creature strange enough that he might be capable of destroying

1

himself and his planet for what would seem to be trivial reasons: a desire for social approval or loyalty to one's in-group, for example. Given these negative views of man's nature, some commentators have stressed the need for man to surrender his myths of freedom and sovereignty. Norman Cousins, editor emeritus of *Saturday Review,* has repeatedly called upon nations to acknowledge the fruitlessness of national sovereignty and to submit to world law and order. Sovereignty is said to be an anachronism in a time of accelerating speed of communication, travel, and weapons development, and with the consequent increasing rate of crisis occurrence.

On the more personal level, the behaviorist B. F. Skinner argues that man must surrender his myths of freedom and will (Skinner, 1971). Despite the oppressive tone of Skinner's book, *Beyond Freedom and Dignity,* it has become a best seller, something unusual for the writings of psychologists. Whereas Norman Cousins' formulations of world order seem appealing to persons of liberal sensibilities, Skinner's derogation of free will does not. Carl Rogers, Rollo May, Arthur Koestler, and others view these Skinnerian pronouncements as totalitarian in nature (Time, 1971).

In Skinner's thinking, man must relinquish his belief in freedom and self-determination and come to accept the fact that he is controlled by forces outside himself. With such acceptance, Skinner believes, man will become more responsive to those controlling forces that reinforce what is more naturally acceptable to humans. Today's relatively random world, in which normlessness and unpredictability prevail, would thus cease to be, as man would avail himself of rewards for more orderly and mannerly behavior. The chance elements of childhood and social experiences that can come to produce psychotic assassins and deviates of all manner would be eliminated and most men would become altruistic and pleasant to one another. Would that such a world could be!

The thesis of this book is that uncertainties and variations in personal experience sometimes *produce* deviates but also *produce* ingenious and creative individuals. Unique and innovative minds grow among those who can come to perceive differences between others and themselves, and who continue to hold the assumption that they are free agents, the makers of their own fates.

This book will focus upon research that has been conducted in psychological laboratories and in field settings concerning the effects of an individual's perception of control. Whether people, or other species for that matter, believe that they can determine their own fates, within limits, will be seen to be of critical importance to the way in which they cope with stress and engage in challenges. In other words, what Skinner believes to be an irrelevant illusion will be shown to be a very relevant illusion, one that seems to be central to man's ability to survive and to enjoy life.

The position presented in this book is not offered with the enthusiasm engendered by confident rebuttal and refutation. Skinner's wish for a more orderly and mannerly world is shared by many if not most individuals. It is paradoxical, however, that the very surrender of the *belief* in free will advocated by Skinner as a step in the direction of a less violent world can be viewed as a source of increased violence, especially that of prosocial kind. Although the data and arguments presented in this book are generally counter to Skinner's position regarding the myth of individual freedom, they are presented with an awareness that the maintenance of the belief in individual freedom is not without considerable cost.

Man must come to be more effective and more able to perceive himself as the determiner of his fate if he is to live comfortably with himself. It is through the very abnegation of self-direction and the surrender to indomitable forces that man commits horrendous acts upon dissimilar others. On the other hand, as we encourage individualism and privacy, we generate more loneliness, discontent, and personal misery among the less advantaged and beget more antisocial criminality. Ecologists have made us aware that whichever way man turns he creates disorder, if not of one sort then of another.

EMPIRICAL DEMONSTRATIONS OF THE CONCEPT

A series of psychological experiments that have immediate relevance to urban malaise will serve to introduce the concept of perceived control. David Glass, Jerome E. Singer, and their colleagues (Glass, Reim, & Singer, 1971; Glass & Singer, 1972; Glass, Singer, & Friedman, 1969; Reim, Glass, & Singer, 1971) conducted a series of investigations concerned with the effects of noise on tasks requiring persistence and attention to details. In several of these experiments, subjects had to complete a set of simple tasks: number comparisons, addition, and letter finding. In the number comparisons task, subjects were asked to indicate whether the multidigit numbers in each set of a series of pairs were the same or different. The addition task simply required subjects to add sets of one- and two-digit numbers. The letter finding task required that subjects find the letter A in five words out of a column of 41 words. These tasks, simple enough in themselves, were administered under four conditions of noise distraction (Glass, Singer, & Friedman, 1969).

An aversive noise was created by combining the sounds of two people speaking Spanish and one person speaking Armenian simultaneous with the sounds of a mimeograph machine, a desk calculator, and a typewriter, all producing a composite, nondistinguishable roar. No doubt the roar was a good replica of general urban mayhem. The authors, all New York residents, were quite experienced with such stimuli. However, it was not simply noise and its impact upon persons working at simple tasks that was of interest. Rather, the concern was with the effects of the predictability and controllability of the noise. In this study, each of four groups received a different combination of stimuli. One group was subjected to a loud noise (110 db) for 9 seconds at the end of every minute of the session. Another group received the loud noise but at random intervals and for random lengths of time. Two other groups received fixed and random noises, but at a softer volume (56 db).

As might have been expected, the initial bursts of noise were effective in distracting most subjects. However, as the session progressed, subjects adapted to the noise, improving in performance on the simple tasks, and exhibiting lesser responsivity to the noise as assessed by physiological measurements. After the session, subjects were engaged in two further tasks during which there was noise or similar interference. One task was designed to evoke frustration. The second task, although routine, required caution and attentiveness.

The frustration task consisted of design copying. Subjects had to trace all the lines in each of four designs with certain restrictions: Subjects were not to lift the pencil from the paper at any time and were not to trace any line twice. Several copies of each design were available so that a subject could make as many attempts to succeed as he desired. Two of the diagrams were insoluble. Therefore, no matter how many times the subject attempted them, he failed.

The dependent variable measured in this task was the number of times that subjects attempted to solve the insoluble designs. Subjects who had received noise at fixed intervals did not differ from a control group that had not been subjected to noise at all. Those subjects who had suffered the noise on a random schedule made considerably fewer attempts, and this was most pronounced when the random noise had been of the higher intensity.

The second task was a proofreading job. Ten errors were included on each of seven pages of an essay. Misspellings, grammatical errors, etc. were to be located during a 15-minute period. Performance on the proofreading task was measured in terms of the percentage of omitted errors. The results were somewhat less significant than for the tracing task, but subjects who experienced random noise made more omissions than those who received fixed interval noise. Loud, random noise was associated with the highest percentage of omitted errors, whereas the softer fixed interval noise was associated with the best proofreading performance.

Although the intensity of noise had some effect on the subjects' performances, it paled in comparison to the effects of predictability. The implications of these results regarding predictability deserve close attention. If noise, or any aversive stimulus for that matter, is unanticipated, the shock value of the stimulus is augmented. Who has not found himself startled by soft but unexplainable sounds occurring in the night? The state of alertness and arousal thus engendered in the individual would probably be continuous if one were in a strange place where the meaning of noises and inferences to be drawn from them were uncertain. In other words, if we do not know the significance of a noise, it will become arousing; the perceiver will feel a need to become alert and ready for anything. The limits of anticipation and apprehensiveness depend upon the perceiver's imagination.

What is the relationship between the meaning of a noise and the predictability of that noise? If we recognize a sound, such as the starting of a furnace motor, we know from where it originates and what consequences may be expected from it. The sequence is predictable; nothing untoward is anticipated. The sound will not change in pitch or intensity. If unusual changes do occur we become suspicious. In the case of the furnace, we would summon a repairman. In short, predictability is a major facet of knowing something. The consistency and reliability of noise in the investigation described above instructs the subject that subsequent changes in volume and timing of the noise are unlikely; there need be little apprehension about a sudden increased intensity. As regularity is perceived, the subject can also ready himself, slowing down in his work efforts when he anticipates the onset of noise. He can, therefore, avoid interruptions by not letting himself be caught unaware and thus be distracted in the midst of an activity.

Implicit in this discussion of predictability is the element of control. If we know the ordinary sounds of the furnace, then we know what must be done to it and when. If another person is predictable, then we have a good idea of how one must act with him to cause certain effects. In being forced to hear predictable noise, we may stop work and wait until it ceases, or steel ourselves for the onset, minimizing our own responses to the noise. It is this perception of the ability to "do something" that gives rise to the concept of perceived control.

In a second investigation reported by Glass et al. (1969), the effect of perceived control was more directly examined. All of the subjects received loud, randomly occurring noise, the most aversive and debilitating condition found in the first study. The major difference between the first and second studies was that, in the second investigation, half of the subjects were provided with a button that would enable them to terminate the noise. These subjects were instructed as to the use of the button, but were encouraged to use it only if the noise became too much for them to bear. In essence, the subjects were provided with a modern analog of control—the off switch.

Subjects with access to the off switch tried almost five times the number of insoluble puzzles and made significantly fewer omissions in proofreading than did their counterparts who were given no such option for controlling the aversive stimulation. These differences were obtained despite the fact that none of the subjects who had potential control actually used it. The mere knowledge that one can exert control, then, serves to mitigate the debilitating effects of aversive stimuli.

From the investigations reported by Glass et al. (1969) it may be concluded that when an aversive event is predictable, its effects are minimized. This may result from the opportunity that regularity creates for us either to schedule our efforts so as to avoid interruption, or to prepare our sensory apparatus so as to be less sensitive to the disturbing event. In addition, control of the termination of the aversive stimulus diminishes the impact of that stimulus, perhaps, by eliminating the fear that "things can get worse" and even beyond endurance. Conceivably it is *fear of unendurable pain* that is debilitating to the cognitive processes of individuals undergoing the experience of unpredictable and uncontrollable but only mild to moderate levels of pain and irritation.

Extrapolation from these conjectures regarding fear of pain to the suffering of anxiety may provide an explanation of well-known clinical phenomena. Would an individual experience anxiety if he had ways of avoiding events that threatened him? Perhaps, "la belle indifference," the beautiful indifference of hysterical women toward their functional disabilities during the Victorian era, was derived from a sense of inner content. Conversion reactions, through which neurologically impossible paralyses occur, often created "secondary gains" for patients in that they would be allowed to avoid "aversive experiences" such as sexual intercourse. It is tempting to suggest that, for many hysterical patients who frequented psychoanalysts' offices during the first decades of this century, hysterical symptoms were an "off switch," a device by which it became possible to terminate threatening events. Similarly, therapy as it is practiced today often seems directed toward helping a patient find a better "off switch," one that enables him to more comfortably approach and cope with threats.

Such conjecture would seem premature if it were not for the reliability and consistency of research on perceived control. Glass, Reim, and Singer (1971) were able to replicate the "access to a button" phenomenon described above when subjects themselves were not in direct control, but could ask a partner to press the button and terminate the noise for them. With shock as the aversive stimulus, Staub, Tursky, and Schwartz (1971) found that subjects who were allowed to administer shock to themselves and to select the level of intensity of that shock reported less discomfort at higher levels of shock and endured stronger shocks than did paired subjects to whom shocks were administered passively. However, when all subjects were given a second series of shock trials administered without subject control, the group that previously experienced control declined in their tolerance for the shocks, rated lower intensity levels as being more uncomfortable, and endured less shock than previously. On the other hand, no changes were found among subjects who had not experienced control.

The Glass and Singer experiments exhibit the effects of control on task performance under aversive conditions. The investigation by Staub et al. (1971) reveals similar shifts in self-reports in that the reported aversive quality of a stimulus decreased when subjects exercised control over that stimulus. These results are congruent with findings reported by Pervin (1963) that subjects preferred predictable, self-controlled conditions. Parallel findings with regard to acknowledged anxiety in each condition were obtained. Other investigations (Corah & Boffa, 1970; Haggard, 1943) have found that stress, as measured by physiological changes, was reduced when subjects were able to control the onset and termination of aversive stimulation.

Yet further support for the assumed importance of perceived control in predicting responses to aversive stimuli can be found in a number of reported studies. Glass, Singer, Leonard, Krantz, Cohen, and Cummings (1973), for instance, found that both the subjective ratings of the painfulness of electric shocks, and the aftereffects of those shocks, diminished when subjects believed that their behavior could effectively reduce shock duration. Glass, and his colleagues then, have been able to demonstrate generality of their results across types of aversive stimuli (noise and shock) and types of aftereffect tasks (maze tracing, proofreading, and Stroop test performance). On the other hand, autonomic responses were not affected by the perceived control manipulations.

Other investigators (Bowers, 1968; Houston, 1972) have reported similar findings: that physiological states monitored during experiments in which electric shocks have been administered have not varied with differences in perceived control. At the same time, however, these investigators have found that reported tolerance of shock levels and statements of anxiety shifted in the anticipated directions with controllability. Golin (1974) has likewise reported that uncontrollable shock has more deleterious effects upon complex learning task performances than controllable shock, though this was most particularly so among highly anxious individuals. On the other hand, when controllability of the shocks was emphasized, the predicted ameliorative effects upon performance were also found, but largely among the less anxious individuals. Only in two studies thus far, (Geer, Davison, & Gatchel, 1970; Hokanson, DeGood, Forrest, & Brittain, 1971) have physiological responses been reliably altered with the perception of control. In the Hokanson et al. (1971) study, systolic blood pressure was reduced among those who could instigate rest periods from a shock avoidance task. Geer et al. (1970) found lower skin conductance among subjects who believed that they could control shock onset, compared to those who did not believe that they could exercise such control.

More recent investigations have replicated some of the earlier research by Glass and Singer (1972). Blechman and Dannemiller (1976), for example, found that subjects who ordinarily were very distractible were able to improve in proofreading accuracy, despite the onset of loud noise, if they had been previously led to believe that they could control the onset of silent periods. A similar set of findings have been reported by Sherrod (1974), Sherrod and Cohen (1978), and Sherrod, Hage, Halpern, and Moore (1977), in their studies of the impact of crowding upon attention maintenance and performance on complex tasks. Although these researchers found that crowding has the anticipated adverse effects upon cognitive functioning, those effects were modifiable by beliefs regarding the subject's ability to leave the crowded settings if he so desired. The beliefs alone were apparently enough to lessen the negative impact of crowding; subjects rarely if ever took advantage of their options.

Other investigators such as Baum, Aiello, and Calesnick (1978) have found that the structures of given settings can induce internal states analogous to those associated with perceived control or helplessness. These researchers have found that students residing in dormitory rooms arrayed in long corridors come to dislike their college experience more than those who live in rooms along short hallways. This difference is thought to derive from traffic patterns that alter the likelihood of unpredictable and uncontrollable intrusions that can interfere with ongoing activities. Long corridor residents were found to dislike their peers more, and most significantly reported a lesser rate of studying than short corridor students. This impact of unpredictable social interchange bears similarity to the findings reported by Schulz (1976), who found that elderly residents of a senior citizens' home were happier and more active if they could determine the timing of visits to them by youthful volunteers.

It seems evident that the belief that one can exercise some degree of control and can predict the occurrence of aversive stimuli has an ameliorating effect upon persons experiencing such stimuli. Pain-producing stimuli such as noise and crowding have proven to be less disruptive to individuals who can predict and control the occurrence of those stimuli. Such findings have been obtained with various types of response measures, performances, self-reports, or physiological responses.

Despite this congruence of findings, some reservations have been expressed (Averill, 1973; Wortman & Brehm, 1975) regarding the pervasiveness of the impact of perceived control. Questions have been raised regarding the ameliorative influence of perceived control. Averill (1973) notes that man must accomodate to many circumstances where a realization of helplessness would be the wiser choice and where belief in one's ability to control the situation could prove to be detrimental. Wortman and Brehm (1975), on the other hand, have questioned whether performance deterioration might result from anger or a lack of concern that develops when subjects are subjected to uncontrollable aversive stimuli during experiments. In other words, the provision of control could be viewed as a courtesy to which subjects respond by becoming more willingly involved in the investigator's tasks.

Though these critics have offered reasonable suggestions regarding the limitations of perceived control as a moderator of aversive situations, there has been enough research conducted using a variety of approaches and species to assure this writer that beliefs regarding control do have an important and assessable effect upon the ways in which persons encounter their experiences. To further document the significance and pervasiveness of the effects of perceived control, we will now examine research findings among other species.

The Response to Aversive Stimulation Among Nonhumans

A classic study concerned with the ramifications of control was reported by Mowrer and Viek (1948). In this seminal and theoretically prophetic experiment,

Mowrer and Viek were able to show that rats exhibited less fear of an aversive stimulus when they could exercise control in terminating it. For each of 15 days, 20 food-deprived rats were offered a bit of food after they had been placed in an experimental cage. Ten seconds after the food was taken by the rat, a shock was delivered through a grid at the floor of the cage.

For half of the sample, the shock was left on until the rat leaped into the air. If the rat did not eat within 10 seconds after food was presented, this failure to eat was regarded as an inhibition. The food was subsequently withdrawn and the shock applied 10 seconds later. One group of 10 animals could terminate the shock through leaping; a second group of 10 were passively yoked to the first group. That is, each member of what was referred to as the "shock-uncontrollable" group was paired with one rat from the shock-controllable group, and received shock for whatever length of time his controlling "partner" received it on each respective day. The crucial dependent variable in this study was the number of inhibitions recorded in each group, for each of the 15 successive days.

The 10 rats in the shock-controlling group had an overall total of only 16 inhibitions [$M = 1.6$] throughout the experiment. In contrast, the shock-noncontrolling or helpless animals produced 85 inhibitions [$M = 8.5$], a difference that was strongly significant. In addition, the helpless group notably increased in the incidence of inhibition from the first 3 days (0,1,3) to the last 3 days (8,8,8), whereas the shock-controlling group did not inhibit at all until the third day, at which time only one inhibition was noted. Only on 4 days did more than one inhibition occur for the shock-controlling group, and there were but two inhibitions on three of these days, and three were obtained on the other day. The helpless group, on the other hand, produced five or more inhibitions on 12 of the 15 days.

These results support the hypothesized effect of control rather well. When the rats could terminate the shock, they exhibited less fear-related behavior. Since all of the animals were hungry, the shock-controlling rats can be said to have been acting more in their own interests in continuing to eat the proffered food. The inhibition of eating in the helpless rats, on the other hand, can be construed as a maladaptive response. Frozen with fear, these animals were unable to eat despite their hunger. One might say that the helpless rats "lost their will" or the active response of defending their self-interest. Though such terms often inspire a facetious response from psychologists, constructs such as hope, helplessness, and will have been recently resurrected in a number of works to help account for the persistence of human activity despite sometimes overwhelming adversity (Menninger, 1963; May, 1969).

Mowrer (1950) seemed keenly aware of some of the far-reaching ramifications of his work: "Perhaps we have isolated here, in prototype, one of the central reasons why human beings so universally prize freedom and why threats to freedom, under a totalitarian regime, are anxiety-producing [p. 472]."

Mowrer also extrapolated from his results to the rather mundane but human experience of concern with illness:

> One is ill and suffering from pain and inconvenience. The physician arrives, diagnoses the difficulty, prescribes treatment, and intimates that in a day or two one will be quite hale again. It is unlikely that the examination or the ensuing exchange of words has altered the physical condition of the patient in the least; yet he is likely to 'feel a lot better' as a result of the doctor's call. What obviously happens in such instances is that initially the patient's physical suffering is complicated by concern lest his suffering continue indefinitely or perhaps grow worse. After a reassuring diagnosis, this concern abates; and if, subsequently, the same ailment recurs, one can predict that it will arouse less apprehension than it did originally. [pp. 472–473].

Not to be caught anthropomorphizing, Mowrer attempted to explain the shock-controlling rat's relief as deriving from anticipatory motoric movements associated with leaping, the shock-terminating response. Later investigators examining the effect of control among animals have been less hesitant to employ concepts such as hopelessness and futility in discussing the behavior of animals.

Among the more dramatic investigations concerned with the loss of control among infrahumans is a study reported by Curt Richter (1959). Richter observed some unanticipated sudden deaths among his laboratory rats as they underwent different procedures. For example, after whisker-cutting, an occasional animal would display a strange corkscrewing motion that eventually ended in death. Richter did not initially draw any inferences from the strange occurrences until these unexplained deaths became more frequent in later experimentation.

In a study concerned with swimming endurance at varying water temperatures, Richter found that a few animals whose whiskers had been trimmed would swim around excitedly for a few seconds in a turbulent bath, dive to the bottom apparently in search of escape, and then, after swimming around for a short time below the surface, would suddenly stop and die. Most fascinating were the autopsy results that revealed the animals had not drowned. Richter had found rats capable of swimming for up to 81 consecutive hours under ideal conditions. Consequently, the short-lived attempt at swimming and sudden death presented a mysterious challenge.

Up to this point, Richter had found whisker-trimming to be a major determinant of this sudden death phenomenon. Although whisker-trimming produced sudden death among wild rats (street- and farm-bred), it seemed less deleterious to the tame laboratory-bred variety. Additionally, several wild rats whose whiskers were not trimmed died suddenly after being placed in the swimming jars, so that whisker-trimming was obviously not the sine qua non determinant of this strange occurrence. Ultimately, Richter concluded that handling per se seemed to be the primary cause of death among wild rats. Handling, which produced arousal among wild rats, also prevented any instrumental activity that could result in escape from the aversive experience. But if the rats were allowed to escape just once, the sudden death phenomenon was eliminated. Richter (1959) observed:

> Interesting evidence showing that the phenomenon of sudden death may depend on emotional reactions to restraint or confinement in glass jars comes from the observation that after elimination of hopelessness the rats do not die. On several occasions we have immersed rats in water and promptly removed them. The animals quickly learned that the situation was not actually hopeless and so became aggressive and tried to free themselves or escape and showed no signs of giving up. Such conditioned rats swam on the average 40 to 60 hours or more. Once freed from restraint in the hand or confinement in the glass jar, speed of recovery is remarkable. A rat that would certainly have died in another minute or two becomes normally active and aggressive in only a few minutes [p. 309].

Richter concluded that neither restraint nor whisker-trimming alone kills a rat. Rather, death results from a combination of responses to various stresses occurring in rapid succession that generate a sense of hopelessness in the animal. Richter expressed this in the following manner:

> This sudden-death phenomenon may however be considered also as a reaction at a much higher level of integration. The situation of these rats is not one that can be resolved by either fight or flight—it is rather one of hopelessness: being restrained in the hand or in the swimming jar with no chance of escape is a situation against which the rat has no defense. Actually, such a reaction of apparent hopelessness is shown by some wild rats very soon after being grasped in the hand and prevented from moving. They seem literally to give up [pp. 308-9].

In other words, the wild animal whose repertoire of behavior consists of rapid movements such as biting, running, and jumping is suddenly bereft of any adequate and ready response for coping with stressful demands. And yet, if rescued once, the animal seemed to learn that if it only persevered all was not hopeless—torture was not infinite. Richter's rats did not learn an instrumental response. Rescue was a fortuitous event and the animal could not have learned what it could do to prevent a recurrence of his bad fortune.

Some learning theorists, such as Guthrie, might suggest that removal from the swimming jar would be a reward for the last response made at the time of rescue. Expectancy theorists, on the other hand, might contend that the animal enjoyed a revival of hope through learning that there was an end and limit to the aversive stimulation. Consequently, if the rat were able to persist in swimming for rather lengthy periods of time, then survival was possible. Because swimming itself could not terminate their duress, the animals may simply be said to have learned to endure while waiting for the end of confinement.

Though Richter's work is compelling, other investigators have, in recent years, raised questions about the interpretations of the sudden death phenomenon. Richter's findings have been replicated (Binik, Theriault, & Shistack, 1977) though with some variation. Binik et al. found that domestic rats were as subject to sudden death as were wild rats. On the other hand, Hughes and Lynch (1978) and Hughes, Stein, and Lynch (1978) have contended that the inferences drawn from the manner in which Richter's rats died are in error.

These investigators have reviewed relevant physiological data and offered their own data that suggest that Richter's rats may well have drowned rather than having suffered from a vagal or "giving up" death. Bradycardia, the slowing of the heart rate, thought to indicate a passive succumbing to stress, has been found to be an oxygen-conserving reflex that commonly occurs when animals dive into water. Therefore, one of the signs used to implicate helplessness in the swimming deaths noted by Richter may have been misinterpreted. As Hughes, Stein, and Lynch (1978) conclude, Richter's interpretations may have been "anthropomorphism for experimentally induced drownings [p. 399]."

In response to Hughes and Lynch (1978), Binik and Seligman (1979) have acknowledged skepticism about the role of helplessness in explaining sudden swimming death. However, these latter investigators decry the "naive reductionism" that suggests that evidence implicating physical mechanisms obviates the need for examining psychosocial influences. Although Richter's original study of sudden death can be faulted, given the nature of the induced stress and possibly misinterpreted observations, Binik and Seligman (1979) contend that this should not preclude further study of the effects of psychosocial influences in life-threatening situations. There have been enough data reported with infrahuman species to reinforce the assumption that helplessness can be involved in both sudden death and depression deficits.

Hopelessness in Psychiatric Settings

Endurance stimulated by hope of relief is familiar in medical settings. Patients must often wait as wounds heal, sometimes with little or no certainty that therapeutic healing will actually occur. While waiting for recovery, patients must often amuse themselves and keep actively engaged enough so that the desire to regain health is maintained. Deaths have been ascribed to a lessened will to live or to giving up in the face of improbable recovery.

The writer was witness to one such case of death due to a loss of will within a psychiatric hospital. A female patient who had remained in a mute state for nearly ten years, was shifted along with her floor-mates to a different floor of the building where she lived while her unit was being redecorated. The psychiatric unit where she had been living was known among the patients as the "chronic/hopeless" floor. In contrast, the first floor to which the patient was moved was most commonly occupied by patients who held privileges, including the freedom to come and go on the hospital grounds and the surrounding streets. In short, the first floor was an exit ward from which patients could anticipate discharge fairly rapidly.

Patients temporarily moved from the third floor, the "chronic/hopeless" floor, were given medical examinations prior to the move, and the patient in question was judged to be in excellent medical health, though still mute and withdrawn. Shortly after moving to the first floor, the patient surprised the ward staff by becoming socially responsive and, within a two-week period, she ceased being mute and was actually becoming gregarious. As fate would have it, the redecoration of the third floor unit was soon completed and all previous residents were returned to it. Within a week after she had been returned to the "hopeless" unit, the patient collapsed and died. The subsequent autopsy revealed no pathology of note, and it was whimsically suggested at the time that the patient had died of despair.

Cases such as this could be cast aside as selected and unrepresentative anecdotes if they were not so commonplace. Richter cited a variety of determinants of sudden, unexplained death that have included voodoo, hexes, fright, the sight of blood, and hypodermic injections. Unaccountable deaths have been reported among persons in good health who have attempted to commit suicide, though they had barely scratched the surface of their skin or had only ingested a few aspirin tablets. Richter (1959) concluded: "Some of these instances seem best described in terms of hopelessness—literally a giving up when all avenues of escape appeared to be closed and the future holds no hope [p. 311]."

Kobler and Stotland (1964) have reported upon the outbreak of a series of suicides within a psychiatric hospital in which staff conflicts had resulted in the patients losing hope that they could ever improve. Although this example could be interpreted as an instrumental response for terminating a hopeless situation, the "passive" surrender of chronically ill patients may also be viewed as a determined act. The patient gives in to what he sees as his inevitable decline and becomes apathetic, which then results in lessened responsiveness to his felt needs. The positive contribution of self-participation and involvement in medical healing has been examined with some success by Rue Cromwell and his colleagues (1977).

We will return to a discussion of some of these investigations in later chapters. At present, we shall give our attention to two other groups of investigations that have demonstrated the importance of control among other nonhuman primates.

Perceived Control of Shock and Escape Behavior in Dogs

Seligman, Maier, and Solomon (1969) have summarized the findings from a series of studies in which they investigated the effects of inescapable shock upon subsequent escape behavior of dogs. In most of these experiments (Overmier & Seligman, 1967; Seligman, 1968; Seligman & Maier, 1967; Seligman, Maier, &

Geer, 1968), inescapable shock was administered by placing the dog in a cloth hammock-like harness so that the dog's legs hung below his body through four holes. A shock source was applied to the dog through electrodes that were taped to the footpads of the dog's hind feet. The dog was given a series of shocks, varying in duration and frequency in each experiment.

A second experimental procedure placed dogs in a two-way shuttlebox in which escape- or avoidance-responding could be observed. In this unit the animal was exposed to a conditioned stimulus (often light-dimming), after which an unconditioned stimulus (an electric shock) was administered through the grid floor. Whenever the animal crossed the shoulder high barrier in the center of the box, the shock was terminated. In contrast to the harness procedure in which an aversive stimulus was administered and the animal could do nothing that would alter the situation, the shuttlebox situation offered immediate control in that the shock could be eliminated altogether if the animal responded to the conditioned stimulus or warning signal by crossing the barrier.

Overmier and Seligman (1967) compared three groups of dogs that had received inescapable shock of varying frequency and duration with a group receiving no such treatment before entering the shuttlebox unit. Comparisons were made in the latency of escape responses, the number of failures to escape shock, and the overall percentage of subjects that never escaped shock. The authors summarized their data as follows:

> Not only do statistical differences appear between the performances of Ss exposed to inescapable shock and those of unshocked Ss during subsequent instrumental avoidance training 24 hours later, but large qualitative differences also appear. The phenomenon we have reported is dramatic to observe. Whenever a S, which was not treated with inescapable shock, first received shock in the course of instrumental training, it typically barked, yelped, ran and jumped until it escaped. An S previously exposed to inescapable shock *initially* reacted to the first shock during instrumental training in much the same way. In contrast, however, it soon typically stopped vocalizing and moving in an agitated fashion and would remain silent until shock terminated. On succeeding trials, Ss would typically continue in a maladaptive pattern of behavior—not necessarily the same on each trial—and passively "accept" the severe pulsating shock [p. 30].

After experimenting with other relevant conditions, the authors posited that the source of interference in learning to escape from the shock in the shuttlebox derived from helplessness learned in experiencing the inescapable shock. Subsequent experiments replicated the finding that inescapable shock interfered with learning instrumental behaviors for eliminating shock in the shuttlebox and offered some clues as to how learned helplessness may be overcome. Prior experience with escapable shock immunizes dogs against the negative effects of later inescapable shock (Seligman & Maier, 1967). That is, dogs who received a sequence of escapable and inescapable shock trials behaved very similarly in the shuttlebox unit, as did animals that had only received escapable shock. In contrast, both of these groups differed greatly from those animals that received only inescapable shock. Seligman and Maier (1967) describe their results as follows:

> Subjects which have had prior experience with escapable shock in the shuttlebox show more energetic behavior in response to inescapable shock in the harness. This contrasts with the interference effect produced by inescapable shock in Ss which have had no prior experiences with shock or in Ss which have had prior experiences with inescapable shock. Thus, if an animal first learns that its responding produces shock termination and then faces a situation in which reinforcement is independent of its responding, it is more persistent in its attempts to escape shock than is a naive animal [pp. 7–8].

The passivity-engendering effect of inescapable shock was apparently eliminated in animals who previously had some successful experience with controlling shock. In a later quasi-therapy experiment, Seligman, Maier, and Geer (1968) attempted to overcome the interference effect of inescapable shock by encouraging successful behavior in the shuttlebox. The barrier between sections of the shuttlebox was removed and the experimenter called out "Here boy!" to the dog through an open window on the side of the box opposite the side upon which the dog sat. If the dog responded to the call and crossed the lowered barrier, shock would have terminated and the dog would therefore have "fortuitously" learned of the escape route. One of the four subjects did respond to this treatment and began to escape shock in the shuttlebox. The other three, however, had to be subjected to more strenuous approaches. With leashes attached to their collars, the dogs were pulled across to the "safe side" on each trial of shock. The rationale was, of course, to force the subject to be exposed to the response-reinforcement contingency. The dog that responded to the simpler calling procedure began to escape reliably after 20 such trials. Dogs that had to be pulled across the barrier required 20, 35, 50 such trials before escape became a reliable phenomenon. In short, resistance to learning the simple contingencies of the shuttlebox was marked.

Seligman (1967, 1968) concluded that the inappropriate passive acceptance of aversive stimuli among their canine subjects could be construed in terms of perceived lack of control over reinforcements. Further research with "learned helplessness" has served to substantiate previous results reported by Seligman and his colleagues. Hiroto (1972; 1974) reproduced Seligman's experimental paradigm utilizing inescapable aversive stimuli (loud tones) with human subjects to create "learned helplessness." Hiroto contrasted the subsequent escape/avoidance learning of subjects who had been exposed to pretreatments of either inescapable or controllable aversive stimulation versus those with no pretreatment at all, and in so doing replicated Seligman's learned helplessness phenomenon. Those who received pretreatments of inescapable aversive stimulation exhibited the longest latencies before making avoidance responses in a subsequent aversive task. Hiroto had also obtained measures of his subjects' beliefs about control and varied the instructions to the criterion task as to the degree of skill required for successful avoidance. In congruence with what one might anticipate if one were extraordinarily optimistic, Hiroto obtained a series of interactions implicating each element of causal perception as an effective determinant of escape and avoidance behavior. Subjects who believed that they could affect their outcomes were more apt to make avoidance responses and were quicker to learn these responses than were those who were more fatalistic regardless of instructions or pretreatments. Likewise, subjects receiving 'skill' instructions were superior to those who had been provided ''chance'' instructions; and fatalistic persons were more ''retarded'' with respect to escape latencies than were those who believed in their effectiveness when both had been subjected to the most debilitating inescapable aversive pretreatment. Since the publication of these earlier studies there has been a voluminous amount of research reported, much of which has been reviewed in three separate volumes (Seligman, 1975; *Journal of Abnormal Psychology*, 1978, *Volume 87 No. 1*; and Garber & Seligman, 1980).

Although learned helplessness—the perceived independence of actions and outcomes—has also been found to have a decided impact upon human functioning, its assumed linkage with depressive deficits has been less than clear and consistent. Seligman and his colleagues (Abramson, Garber & Seligman, 1980; Abramson, Seligman, & Teasdale, 1978) have attempted to reformulate their conceptualizations about learned helplessness to better account for human responses to noncontingent aversive stimuli. In brief, they contend that noncontingent aversive events will have an impact only when the specific outcomes or reinforcements at stake are important to the organism. Depression is more likely when the state of helplessness is perceived to be stable so that improvement is unlikely. The generality of depressive deficits should be associated with the globality of helplessness. That is, the more global the reason for helplessness (being retarded rather than being poor in math, for example), the more pervasive the effects of helplessness will be. In addition, Seligman and colleagues argue that the more internal the attribution for helplessness (the acceptance of responsibility for failure), the more likely self-esteem will suffer, with its possible concomitant of depression.

Although learned helplessness research is in a state of flux and reformulation, the overall conclusions remain: The perceived lack of control over valued reinforcements can help to create the passive acceptance of aversive stimulation among a range of species from cats, rats, and fish to humans (Abramson, Garber & Seligman, 1980). Further evidence in support of these conclusions is presented in the following section.

The Development of Ulcers

Among the investigations discussed thus far, the phenomenon of perceived control of aversive stimuli would seem to be a central determinant of the manner in which one responds to these stimuli. Among humans, rats, and dogs, to have some instrumental response at one's disposal, and to be able to perceive contingency between one's actions and the termination of an aversive stimulus, seems to be a good and necessary thing. It serves us well, then, to refer to one investigation in which perceived effective control proved to be disadvantageous for the subject, whereas the passive recipient of aversive stimuli seemed to survive experimental treatment more adequately.

Brady, Porter, Conrad, and Mason (1958) found that monkeys pressing levers at a fast rate to avoid shocks developed ulcers. For this research, Brady devised a procedure whereby monkeys were yoked in an apparatus. One subject, euphemistically called the executive monkey, was trained to press a lever that would terminate a shock delivered to the animal's feet. Another monkey was connected electrically in series with the "executive" so that any shock received by one would also be received by the other. The "executive" could exercise control; the other subject was a passive recipient. In this way both animals of a pair were subjected to the same shocks but one had "the button" and the other didn't.

After a number of days in this procedure, death occurred to each of four "executives" whose autopsies revealed extensive gastrointestinal lesions with ulceration. Sacrificed partners did not reveal any indications of such gastrointestinal complications. The findings in this study would encourage us to be a bit more temperate in judging the value of perceived control. However, in an elaborate replication of the "executive monkey" study, Weiss (1971) found evidence that ulcers were both more common, and the ulcerous lesions more extensive, among animals deprived of control.

Although Weiss used a different species (rats) than Brady et al. (1958), the major reason for the reversal in findings was attributed to the method of selection of "executive" and "yoked" subjects by Brady et al. Subjects were *not* randomly selected for these roles. Rather, each pair of monkeys was administered a two- to four-hour avoidance pretest, and the monkey responding at the higher rate was always chosen as the executive.

The Weiss investigation was an improvement on the Brady study in several ways. First, Brady et al. employed a subject sample of only four pairs of monkeys; Weiss used 180 male rats. In addition, Weiss varied the manner in which the rats were to be cued to the onset of shock. From his overall findings, Weiss (1971) concluded:

> The present experiment showed that regardless of whether electric shock was preceded by a warning signal, by a series of warning signals forming, so to speak, an external clock, or by no signal at all, rats that would perform coping responses to postpone, avoid, or escape shock developed less severe gastric ulceration than matched subjects which received the same shocks but could not affect shock by their behavior. . . . The present results, in combination with earlier experiments, serve to establish that the beneficial effect of coping behavior in stressful situations is of considerable generality [p. 8].

Subsequent to these studies, Weiss and a number of other investigators have re-explored the ulceration process. In a chapter summarizing the research, Weiss (1977) concluded that ulceration seemed to be associated with activity levels and the production of relevant feedback. That is, if an animal were to flail about randomly in response to aversive stimulation, the probability of his developing ulcerative lesions could be greater than for a more quiescent animal. On the other hand, if the activity produced a noticeable change or information pertinent to change, the likelihood of lesion development would be lowered dramatically. As Weiss (1977) notes: "It is evident that very little of the variability is attributable to the presence or absence of shock; most of the variability is attributable to differences in controllability and predictability, psychological variables in the situation [p. 267]."

CONCLUSION

On the basis of the evidence reviewed in this chapter on the response to aversive stimulation, perceived control seems to make a great difference. Pain or anxiety are not simply responses to aversive stimuli impinging upon our senses. Reactions to aversive stimuli are evidently shaped and molded by our perceptions of these stimuli, and by perception of our ability to cope with these stimuli. Although these conclusions are far from unique, it is remarkable that the findings appear similar across different species, with different aversive stimuli and response measures. Behaviorists have often attempted to reduce differences between species through invoking universal principles such as reinforcement, but it is also possible to conclude that there are remarkable similarities among diverse species without reducing complex cognitive-perceptual systems to simple reinforcement assimilators. The perception of control would seem to be a significant determinant of the response to aversive events, regardless of species.

2 The Perception of Control as an Enduring Attitude

INTRODUCTION

In the previous chapter, most of the investigations that were reviewed dealt with the effects of perceived control within circumscribed tasks or situations. For the most part, one would not anticipate that such effects would rapidly generalize to a variety of other tasks, nor that the organism under study would form some general self-conception on the basis of that limited experience. Nevertheless, the intractability of the dogs in Seligman's research (1968) and the surrender to death among Richter's animals (1959) do suggest that, for many organisms, the loss of perceived control is not taken as a simple isolated incident, but rather as a pervasive and profound reaction, holding implications for the creature's judgment of his potential for survival.

When one acquaints oneself with the massive literary outpourings regarding the lives of impoverished peoples, displaced persons, and of members of denigrated minority groups, a common characterization is that of abject helplessness and a sense of despair. To people who live in continuously adverse circumstances, life does not appear to be subject to control through their own efforts. Only through some outside intervention do events seem to be alterable, and such intervention is a rare occurrence. A most poignant example of fatalism is recorded by Oscar Lewis (1961). Manuel, one of the Sanchez family about whom Lewis writes, ruminates about the failure of his brief venture as a shoe manufacturer:

> To me, one's destiny is controlled by a mysterious hand that moves all things. Only for the select, do things turn out as planned; to those of us who are are born to be

tamale eaters, heaven sends only tamales. We plan and plan and some little thing happens to wash it all away. Like once, I decided to try to save and I said to Paula, "Old girl, put away this money so that some day we'll have a little pile." When we had ninety pesos laid away, pum! My father got sick and I had to give all to him for doctors and medicines. It was the only time I had helped him and the only time I had tried to save! I said to Paula, "There you are! Why should we save if someone gets sick and we have to spend it all!" Sometimes I even think that saving brings on illness! That's why I firmly believe that some of us are born to be poor and remain that way no matter how hard we struggle and pull this way and that. God gives us just enough to go on vegetating, no? [p. 171].

Manuel's fatalistic view is prototypic of the outlook of deprived individuals. In fact, it would seem to be foolish and intropunitive for many individuals to view themselves as active and self-controlling.

This position has been advanced by Gurin, Gurin, Lao, and Beattie (1969), who found that Negroes who blamed "the system" for their difficulties were more likely to exhibit innovative behavior than their more self-blaming counterparts. These authors contend that to belong to an economically deprived and socially denigrated minority means that one must inevitably experience difficulties and assaults upon his sense of dignity, and that it is to be expected that a person will not therefore blame himself for his fate. The important element to be considered for the present purpose, though, is the manner in which individuals come to terms with their difficulties and, more specifically, how they explain their difficulties to themselves.

In a compelling description of his odyssey through the Southeastern United States disguised as a Negro, John Howard Griffin (1962) explained the manner in which Negroes naturally learn to attribute causality to external rather than internal factors:

The Negro's only salvation from complete despair lies in his belief, the old belief of his forefathers, that these things are not directed against him personally, but against his race, his pigmentation. His mother or aunt or teacher long ago carefully prepared him, explaining that he as an individual can live in dignity, even though he as a Negro cannot. "They don't do it to you because you're Johnny—they don't even know you. They do it against your Negro-ness." [p. 48].

From the foregoing discussion one might infer that the development of external attributions for one's failures and difficulties is both veridical and functionally useful. The belief that one operates "the buttons" when in fact many of the more important environmental reinforcements are beyond one's own capability of control could seem delusional, and would, no doubt, incur some personal anguish. As indicated previously, however, to feel helpless, as if one were not an actor but merely a pawn, is likewise costly in terms of psychological well-being. Kurt Lewin (1940) wrote of the costs and benefits of externality in discussing the problems encountered by Jews as they emerged from a ghetto existence:

Using a term of dynamic psychology, we can say that the individual insofar as his Jewishness is concerned, becomes to a higher degree a separated whole than he was in the time of the Ghetto. At that time he felt the pressure to be essentially applied to the Jewish group as a whole. Now as a result of the disintegration of the group he is much more exposed to pressure as an individual. The weakening of the pressure against Jews as a group since the Ghetto period has been accompanied by a development which has shifted the point of application of external forces from the group to the individual. . . . This, shows the extent the previous behavior was due to the previous situation, a situation in which the individual was uncertain whether a disparagement of his work was attributable to its lack of merit or to the fact that its creator was a Jew. Even though the occasions for this uncertainty might have been rare, they could have the lasting effect of depriving the person of standards by which to measure the extent and limits of his ability, and in this way make him unsure of his own worth [p. 83].

In other words, when an individual is deprived of his sense of self-determination, he is less able to learn about himself from his own experiences; he is less able to develop a definite measure of his own worth. It should come as no surprise, therefore, to discover that Negroes, whose socialization encourages a fatalistic outlook on life, have often been found to hold aberrant self-assessments. E. Franklin Frazier (1962), in his study of the Negro middle class, wrote of the tendency among middle-class Negroes to develop a world of fantasy in which delusions of wealth, power, and prestige in white society were of paramount importance.

An Anecdotal Description of the Stability of Perceived Control

One of the more engaging descriptions of the inner life of the denigrated and depersonalized individual was contained in a letter to the Editor of *Harper's Magazine* (Scott, 1962). The letter was a rebuttal to an editorial by the late John Fischer, then editor, who had written of his despair at the rising rate of visible violence and apathy in Negro slum neighborhoods. Mr. Fischer had contended that blacks should organize into citizens' groups that would promote responsibility and self-control among themselves. The rebuttal reprinted below, artfully presents the effects of pawn status upon an individual and emphasizes the inertia of such an adaptation.

The Negro and the Enlisted Man: An Analogy

Once in a while some of my friends who became commissioned officers in the service will sigh, shake their heads, and ask why I, who was born as proud as they, wasted three years as an Army GI. By now I've learned to shrug and feign puzzlement. For I know that soon enough—when the conversation turns to other topics and becomes sufficiently relaxed—they will reveal a total ignorance of certain experiences denied any middle-class American white except the peacetime Enlisted Man.

I was reminded of this in the July *Harper's* when Editor John Fischer wrote of the Negro's need to assume the responsibilities of first-class citizenship. About Mr. Fischer's service record I know nothing, but in that article he wrote as an officer. I too am a Northern liberal often discouraged by the refusal of Brother Tom to shape up. But as an ex-EM, I understand. In every dirty alley of Harlem, in every missed job of South Philly, I see myself lurking fatigue-clad behind Ft. Dix furnace rooms, relentless in my quest for the bonum minimum; the right to be bored in the way I choose.

Surely no other life open to the American white so closely resembles the Negro's—the world of Them and Us. They with their money, handsome uniforms, knowledge, organization, and (O God) their power. We with our anonymity ("D'ja ever notice how all EM look alike?"), dirt, encouraged stupidity, and uselessness. In such a world, only one weapon is available, but it is mighty: The Resolve to Live Up to Our Reputation. We are clods? dolts? animals? Very well. We shall be the cloddiest, most doltish animals on earth.

The discovery of this moral principle was for me the equivalent of Rousseau's glimpse of the Social Contract. Once I had found it, I could even divide all the EM I ever met into two camps—those who lived by The Resolve and those who rejected it. The former flourished; the latter (and maddeningly enough for me, a large number of these were fellow college boys) remained miserable whiners, petition passers, and demanders of their nonexistent rights—in short, second-rate citizens instead of first-rate slaves.

How did the Resolve operate? The details where so subtle and multitudinous as to defy codification. In fact, you had to be there. But if I had to say it in one sentence, this would do: Stay Out of the stockade, but barely. Obey the letter, but defy the spirit. Rake leaves? All right, one leaf at a time. Sweep the floor, but sweep it with the somnambulant majesty of one who walks under water. Salute like a cheerful idiot. And, whether raking, sweeping, or saluting, give the appearance of doing your wretched, pathetic best.

Such incompetence will endear you to most officers, by confirming their prior notions of you as a comic stereotype; even better, it will make them feel necessary—an almost miraculous accomplishment. Only a few officers will penetrate the disguise, and from these you have nothing to fear. The truly wise will be amused and keep your secret. The merely clever will be maddened because they are helpless; the Army depends too heavily upon enlisted stupidity to risk punishing it.

I received dramatic proof of this very early—in my last week of basic training. Several thousand of us were slowly filing through a wooden shed, having our papers stamped and receiving our orders for permanent assignment. It was a gorgeous day. After all, perhaps the worst was over, and at the least we were going home for a week's leave. So with face shining and heart swelling, I passed through several stations without event.

It happened while I was standing in front of a warrant officer.

"Scott?" he said without looking up.

"Yes sir."

"Where are your glasses?"

Sudden, animal instinct told me something had gone wrong, but I took off my horn-rims and handed them to him.

"Negative. Where are your government issues?" He still hadn't looked at me.

"These are the only ones I have, sir."

Now he looked at me. "Where were you in the third week?"

I saw. In the third week I had been in the hospital with arthritic ankles; my boots had been a size too small. After returning to the company, I had noticed men wearing thick glasses with steel rims, almost like welders' goggles. Like a fool, I had sneered, thinking they had turned gung ho and bought PX glasses. Now with my stomach sliding into my shoes I could only repeat, "These are the only glasses I have, sir."

He wasn't looking at me any more. He was stamping my paper HOLD! "You'll be delayed a week. Your leave's cancelled. Get out of line. Next!"

I stumbled outside and saw my Field First leaning against a wall, looking bored. "Sergeant," I stammered, "what happens to someone held over a week?"

As always, at the prospect of inflicting pain, his boredom vanished. "Oh we got a lotta nice things. Strippin' rifles . . . sandin' tables . . . KP . . ."

All around, my comrades were jostling and swearing and hinting at how their leave-time would be spent. I made my choice.

Turning to a member of my platoon, I whispered, "Let me have those damn steel glasses for a minute." I grabbed them, ran back and put on the glasses.

My God! They were for astigmatism. My myopia was as bad as ever, and now the floor was about fifteen feet below and slightly slanting up toward the right. But I could see well enough to know I was now standing in front of the officer.

"Jackson?" he said, not looking up.

"No sir," I said in my best dirt-farmerese. I ain't Jackson. Scott. You got m' over thur'n the HOLD pile."

He looked up at me and remembered. "You didn't have government-issue glasses."

"Well, sir, you got m' all confused"—chuckle—"I didn't know you mean' *Army* glasses. I got muh Army glasses. I got'm on raht *here*."

I could see him glaring up at me from ten feet below. He was trying to decide whether I was a criminal or a moron. All he had to do, of course, was to ask me to read something. (Read! I couldn't even walk!)

Then, still deciding, he looked behind me and saw the endless stream of cattle with serial numbers to be stamped. He glared at me once more and decided I was insignificant—very likely a moron, but definitely insignificant. He grabbed a pen as though it were a scalpel, scratched out HOLD!, threw my papers at me, and looked away.

"Next!"

I was free. A free moron.

Do I hear protests from officers and civilians that this was civic irresponsibility? Do they believe that EM should prove themselves with honorable behavior and work well done? Then they ignore the implications of a social structure as rigid as a bear trap, where no truly compensatory rewards or punishments exist and where work is infinite in magnitude and infinitesimal in worth. You finish Job A only to have Job B created especially for you. And should you finish Job Z, no one will make you General, or Lieutenant, or even Corporal.

No. The irresponsibility is not civic, but private and psychological. The price you pay for the joyful security of pretending to be what you are not, is to become what you pretend to be.

As a pre-Army undergraduate, I assumed that campus Veterans were merely more sardonic than I toward the Ivory Tower—and more sardonic because they were acquainted with Reality. Only later, myself a Vet in graduate school, did I know that our "cynicism" was the undirected nihilism of someone emerging from years of deception. We no longer knew ourselves. Our conditioned responses, once so useful and amusing in the Army, were now inappropriate. Our new situations demanded action, not endurance and sensual torpor; they demanded perceptions beyond the smug categories of four-letter expletives; they demanded, ultimately, that we remake ourselves in an almost forgotten image. Most of us did it, of course, suffering only the temporary pangs of rehabilitation. But we were left with an understanding that made it worthwhile.

Mr. Fischer is quite right. Every day the Negro's "irresponsibility" becomes more and more inappropriate. But before the Negro will see it, he needs an unequivocal, legal "discharge". And even then it will not be easy. The man who is *born* an EM cannot be rehabilitated. He needs metamorphosis. And unlike the fellow in Kafka, he can't do it overnight [pp. 16–21].

SOCIAL OBSERVATIONS

The letter from Mr. Scott well illustrates how an individual may be reduced to a bumbling, if vigilant, serf, and describes approximately the accomodation to slavery and imprisonment. Stanley Elkins (1961) writes of the characteristics inherent in the American experience with slavery, and in the European experience with Nazi concentration camps, that result in the childlike, irresponsible behaviors of which Mr. Scott writes. Elkins defined the "Sambo" personality of southern lore as an admixture of docility, irresponsibility, loyalty, laziness, humility, and dishonesty. The dominant plantation Negro was said to be "full of infantile silliness and his talk inflated with childish exaggeration [p. 244]." Elkins also reviews the available literature regarding concentration camp life and concludes that, there too, childlike dependence was in evidence. In searching for the common ingredients that would create such infantilelike qualities, Elkins notes that total control of the slave or inmate lay directly in the hands of a master or guard. No alternative authorities existed and decisions regarding life or death resided in that one immediate authority. Elkins (1961) states:

Everything—every vital concern—focussed on the SS: Food, warmth, security, freedom from pain, all depended on the omnipotent significant other, all had to be worked out within the closed system. Nowhere was there a shred of privacy; everything one did was subject to SS supervision. The pressure was never absent. It is thus no wonder that the prisoners should become "as children" [p. 257].

A more recent and overwhelming description of the concentration camp experience (DesPres, 1976) provides much in the way of corroboration for earlier reports. Victims of the random violence so common in concentration camps often became what were called "Musselmanner", the "moslems", or "walking dead." Such persons behaved as though they were not thinking or feeling and, in essence, were said to have died inwardly.

One notable feature of Elkins' discussion centers on the loss of a sense of being a differentiated individual, a subject or actor: "A more exquisite form of pressure lay in the fact that the prisoner had never a moment of solitude; he no longer had a private existence, it was no longer possible, in any imaginable sense, for him to be an individual [p. 250]." The process through which the individual becomes depersonalized is described from firsthand observation by Bettelheim (1943):

> The Author has no doubt that he was able to endure the transportation and all that followed, because right from the beginning he became convinced that these horrible and degrading experiences somehow did not happen to 'him' as a subject, but only to 'him' as an 'object' [p. 431].

This split between subject and object as a device for maintaining oneself in the face of severe shock and strain is similar to the attributive processes mentioned previously by Griffin (1962), Lewin (1940), and Gurin et al. (1969). In brief, when one is the recipient of shocking brutality, one experiences an unbelievable, that is, unpredictable and uncontrollable aversive event: the stuff of nightmares. Hence, one becomes, like the dreamer, at once the seer and the seen. The visible person is tortured while the active person retreats into a position of distant observer. Though neither the South, as portrayed by Griffin (1962), nor the Ghetto, by Lewin (1940), is equivalent in intensity to the total horror of early slavery or concentration camps, the parallels and similarities are obvious. Daily happenings were unpredictable and potentially dangerous, and the victims learned to be inconspicuous and overly responsive or acquiescent to external demands. Man the actor, the master of his fate, or simply the holder of the "button," absented himself and in his place was left the defensive pawn for whom good times were fortuitous and bad times inescapable.

EMPIRICAL FINDINGS

If these prosaic descriptions are as true as they would seem to be, then empirical data should substantiate the assumed link between deprivation, denigration, and perceived control. A contention of each of the authors discussed above is that helplessness, a perceived inability to effect one's fate meaningfully, is the natural response to deprivation and denigration, and, in turn, is a source of immature and poor coping behavior. Among a number of investigations, one study conducted by this writer and a colleague (Lefcourt & Ladwig, 1965a) provides support for these contentions regarding black-white differences.

Lefcourt and Ladwig asked black and white reformatory inmates to respond to a questionnaire, referred to subsequently as the Internal-External Control of Reinforcement Scale (I–E Scale), that had been developed by Julian Rotter and his colleagues at Ohio State University (Rotter, 1966; Rotter, Seeman, & Liverant, 1962; see Appendix). The scale consists of 23 forced-choice items along with six filler items designed to make the test purpose less obvious. Illustrative items are as follows:

I more strongly believe that:
  6. a. Without the right breaks one cannot be an effective leader.
     b. Capable people who fail to become leaders have not taken advantage of their opportunities.
  9. a. I have often found that what is going to happen will happen.
     b. Trusting to fate has never turned out as well for me as making a decision to take a definite course of action.
 23. a. Sometimes I can't understand how teachers arrive at the grades they give.
     b. There is a direct connection between how hard I study and the grades I get.

From a perusal of the test it is evident that the subject describes his own viewpoint by choosing between alternatives that reflect a fatalistic, external-control viewpoint and those indicating a belief in one's own ability to affect and control the events in one's life. In the first comparison, the mean score for 60 black inmates was 8.97 [$SD = 2.97$] and for 60 white inmates the mean was 7.87 [$SD = 3.03$]. The resulting t test was significant [$t = 2.00$, $p < .05$], indicating that blacks acknowledged more external control than did whites. Although the magnitude of the difference was not great, the fact that such a reliable difference could be obtained among a population that was homogeneous with regard to socioeconomic class and antisocial history indicates the meaningfulness of the obtained difference.

A second test of perceived control, Dean's Powerlessness Scale (Dean, 1969; see Appendix), was also administered to the same subjects. The Powerlessness measure consists of nine Likert scale items to which subjects indicate their degree of agreement or disagreement. Illustrative items are as follows:

There is little or nothing I can do towards preventing a major "shooting" war.
We're so regimented today that there's not much more room for choice even in personal matters.

On the Powerless scale, as with the I–E scale, a higher score indicates greater externality or fatalism. Again, the mean for black inmates [$M = 17.30$, $SD =$

5.02] was higher than the mean for white inmates [M = 14.63, SD = 4.98], and the difference was a reliable one [t = 2.89, p < .01]. The extremity of the black's mean score on the Powerlessness measure is underscored by comparison with Dean's norms (Lefcourt & Ladwig, 1966). Based on a stratified sample of 384 males from Columbus, Ohio, the mean Powerlessness score was 13.65 [SD = 6.10]. The black's mean was significantly higher than the normative mean [t = 4.42, p < .001]. In contrast, the mean score for white inmates did not differ appreciably from the norm [t = 1.20, p > .10].

Another investigation by Esther Battle and Julian Rotter (1963) reported similar findings for black and white children with different measuring devices. A group of 80 sixth- and eighth-grade children selected on the basis of sex, social class, and race were tested on two measures of perceived control. One was the Bialer Locus of Control Questionnaire (Bialer, 1961: see Appendix), a 23-item "yes" or "no" questionnaire in which the subject attributes causality to himself or others. Examples of Bialer's items are as follows:

Do you really believe a kid can be whatever he wants to be?
When people are mean to you, could it be because you did something to make them be mean?
When nice things happen to you, is it only luck?

A second measure was a "projective" device, a six-item cartoon test in which the child states what he would say in a series of lifelike situations involving attribution of responsibility. The items pictured in the six cartoons portrayed interactions to which the child had to respond. In the cartoons, another figure addressed the "subject" as follows:

1) How come you didn't get what you wanted for Christmas?
2) Why is she always hurting herself?
3) When you grow up do you think you could be anything you wanted?
4) Whenever you're involved something goes wrong!
5) That's the third game we've lost this year.
6) Why does her mother always "holler" at her? [p. 485]

Performance on the cartoon test indicated that lower-class black children produced more responses coded as external [M = 18.3, SD = 3.4] than did either middle-class blacks [M = 15.8, SD = 3.5], or middle-class (M = 15.0, SD = 4.4) or lower-class white pupils [M = 16.4, SD = 3.5]. The differences were significant between lower-class blacks and all of the other groups, whereas no differences were obtained among the other groups.

The Bialer scale was found to be correlated with the cartoon test [r = −.47, p < .01], which supported the belief that the cartoon test was providing a measure of perceived control. In addition, lower-class children expressed more externality on the Bialer scale than did middle-class children.

In general, then, the double derogation of class and caste was related to the expression of external control beliefs. These findings have been replicated with other populations, measuring devices, and procedures. Strodbeck (1958), for example, has found that Jewish middle- and upper-class subjects express more of a sense of mastery than lower-class Italians. Most of the variance on Strodbeck's mastery scale was attributed to social class. Franklin (1963) also reported a significant relationship between higher socioeconomic class and internality on the basis of a stratified national sample. For another example, Nelsen and Frost (1971) found that the rural poor were more cynical and fatalistic than comfortable urbanites. The latter were found in interviews to be more likely to believe that life events could be controlled through effort. With specific regard to race, blacks have been found to be more external or fatalistic in orientation than have whites with but few exceptions. Lessing (1969), Owens (1969), Shaw and Uhl (1969), Strickland (1972), Zytkoskee, Strickland, and Watson (1971) have found such differences using ad hoc perceived control scales and published scales pertaining to control such as the Bialer, the I–E, and the Nowicki-Strickland (1973) scales (see Appendix).

A more recent study reported by Duke and Lewis (1979) used a special form of the Preschool and Primary Nowicki-Strickland Locus of Control Scale (PPNSIE). This test, which presents youngsters with cartoon representations of interactions between children, was altered so that the figures were all obviously black. The child's task is to select a yes or no answer offered as one cartoon child's answer to a question from another cartoon child. Examples of the questions are: "Do people blame you for things you didn't do?" "Can wishing make good things happen?" Using the black form of the test for blacks and the white form for whites, Duke and Lewis found that, contrary to the expected pattern of decreasing externality with increasing ages of the children, older blacks were found to be more external, whereas whites showed the anticipated decrease with age. In addition, internality was found to be reliably correlated [$r = .54$, $p < .01$] with preference for delayed reinforcements.

On the other hand, a few studies have been reported in which class and race groupings were not reflected in measures of perceived control. Gore and Rotter (1963) failed to obtain social class differences on the I–E scale in a group of southern Negro college students. Likewise, Katz (1967), and Solomon, Houlihan, and Parelius (1969) found no race differences in response to the Intellectual Achievement Responsibility scale (Crandall, Katkovsky, & Crandall, 1965: see Appendix), which measures perceived control in the academic settings of childhood. These investigators attributed their failure to obtain race–related differences to the fact that classroom achievement situations may seem more amenable to control for blacks than the wider range of situations represented in other scales pertaining to control.

In one negative study in which the I–E scale was employed. Kiehlbauch (1968) found no differences between black and white reformatory inmates. This finding was obtained approximately six years after the investigation by Lefcourt and Ladwig (1965a), who also utilized reformatory inmates. Differences between these studies may reflect the rise and fall of Martin Luther King, Malcolm X, the Kennedy brothers, and the tumultuous changes in race relations in the United States, and therefore represent a real shift from fatalism to militancy, to the belief that one must act in one's own behalf or perish. Despite the occasional failure to obtain differences between racial groups on measures of locus of control, and recent evidence to the effect that blacks may be shifting in their perception of control, it is notable that whenever differences are found, the black sample is more likely to espouse external-fatalistic expectations. Likewise, members of the lower socioeconomic class never exceed the more fortunate middle- and upper-class persons in statements of internality.

In addition to racial and socioeconomic comparisons, a number of investigators have attempted to compare cultures where differences in locus of control orientations might be expected to emerge. Reimanis (1977) obtained locus of control scores using Rotter's scale from a sample of Northeastern Nigerians enrolled in Teacher's College as well as U.S. students enrolled at a community college. Given that the Nigerians lived in a physical environment where short range outcomes were relatively unpredictable, and long range outcomes originated from familial lineage and comprised a carrying out of assigned roles, Reimanis predicted more external control orientations among the Nigerians compared to U.S. students. The Nigerians did prove to be decidedly more external.

McGinnies, Nordholm, Ward, and Bhanthumnavin (1974) compared locus of control scores from Rotter's scale across five cultures (Australia, Japan, New Zealand, Sweden, and the U.S.). Across all cultures females were found to be more external than males, a finding that may reflect the perceived opportunities of the sexes. Secondly, the three countries most similar in language, customs, and values—Australia, New Zealand, and the U.S.—produced the most internal locus of control scores, whereas Sweden and Japan, considered to be the more paternalistic nations where fitting in is viewed as more important than autonomy, produced the more external locus of control scores. As a subscript, Boor (1976) used data from the McGinnies et al. (1974) study and another study and found that the locus of control scores characterizing each country were associated with the suicide rates of those countries. Thus, Sweden and Japan were found to produce the most external scores on locus of control scales and had the highest suicide rates.

The most extensive investigation regarding group membership and the perception of control is indubitably a field study conducted by Jessor, Graves, Hanson, & Jessor (1968). These researchers explored, in detail, the relationship among economic and social factors contributing toward the development of deviant behavior. Rather than relying on a simple measure of socioeconomic status, the investigators explored the objective access to opportunity for three groups that comprised a community in the Southwestern United States. Objective access was defined by the position of a subject on eight measures including age, marital status, language spoken in the home, occupation, education, religion, between generation mobility, and social participation. Each position was conceptually linked to a location in the opportunity structure. An example from Jessor et al. (1968) follows:

> A young person has more objective access than an older one since he still has a chance to achieve presently unobtained goals in the future and since youth itself is responded to socially as an asset in socio-occupational life, whereas the older person's chances are diminishing, and age tends to be seen as a limitation in many areas of social life. Those elderly persons who have never married or who have lost their spouses have even less access to such life goals as successful child-rearing, family participation, social involvement with others, and even occupational success [p. 126].

The total of the items, then, indicate the degree to which a person is in a position to secure valued ends. As had been predicted among the 221 community members surveyed, those with an ''Anglo'' identification had greater objective access to opportunity than did Spanish [$t = 10.63$, $p < .001$] and Indian [$t = 8.59$, $p < .001$] persons. When the three groups were compared with regard to scores on a modified form of Rotter's I–E scale, Anglos were found to be the most internal in contrast to the Spanish and Indians. The Spanish were more external than both Anglos [$t = 5.39$, $p < .001$] and Indians [$t = 3.78$, $p < .001$]. Indians, on the other hand, did not differ significantly from Anglos [$t = 1.39$, n.s.]. Of primary interest, however, is the fact that objective access and perceived control correlated strongly [$r = .50$, $p < .001$, $N = 221$]. The more a person had objective access to opportunity, the more he acknowledged potential control of his own fate. Although ethnic group membership was also linked to perceived control, the access to opportunity was more decidedly associated with it.

Finally there have been a number of studies in which the effects of familial instability have been examined especially with regard to children's locus of control orientations. Duke and Lancaster (1976) hypothesized that father absence was equivalent to a ''massive dose of fate'' or, in other terms, a lesson in helplessness, and should result in a more fatalistic outlook. Using the PPNSIE, these authors found that children from father absent homes were significantly more external than those from intact homes. These findings were similar to Hetherington's (1972). In her study, Hetherington found girls from father-absent homes, especially when death or divorce had occurred early in the girls' lives, scored more external on the personal control factor of Rotter's scale than did girls from intact homes. A further set of studies have indicated that a high incidence of stressful life events, which could include the breaking up of the primary family, occurring in the early years of a child's life, are associated with locus of control scores in adolescence and young adulthood. Bryant and Trockel (1976) found that affectively significant life changes during the preschool years were correlated with statements of external control as measured by Rotter's scale. Similar findings have been reported by Nowicki (1978). Lefcourt, Von Baeyer, Ware, and Cox (1979) found that negative life events occurring in the preschool years were most highly related to externality for affiliative experiences on their Multidimensional Multiattributional Causality Scale (MMCS), which will be described in a later chapter.

Each of these studies concerned with father absence or life stressors in general would obviously have some bearing upon the opportunities available to the developing child. The objective access to opportunity that Jessor et al. (1968) found to be associated with locus of control scores would seem to be reflected in these relationships between early stressors and their assumed handicaps and later locus of control scores.

CONCLUSIONS

In general, it may be concluded that perceived control is positively associated with access to opportunity. Those who are able, through position and group membership, to attain more readily the valued outcomes that allow a person to feel personal satisfaction, are more likely to hold internal control expectancies. Blacks, Spanish-Americans, Indians, and other minority groups who do not enjoy as much access to opportunity as do the predominant Caucasian groups in North American society, are often found to hold fatalistic, external control beliefs.

The anecdotes at the beginning of this chapter are supported by empirical data reported by various investigators using different measurement devices. Consequently, we may now speak of perceived control in more characterological terms than was the case in the first chapter. There, we addressed the question of whether having a sense of control would make a difference to an organism encountering an aversive event. In this chapter, we have found that deprived social position and severely punishing environments create a sense of fatalism along with infantile and regressive behavior. In the following chapter we will introduce a theoretical orientation that has helped to generate much of the interest in perceived control. In subsequent chapters, we use this theoretical orientation to examine the consequences of maintaining a sense of control as opposed to a fatalistic attitude.

3
Social Learning Theory: A Systematic Approach to the Study of Perceived Control

INTRODUCTION AND BACKGROUND

A quick perusal of the previous chapters makes it evident that the perception of control is not a provincial concern. Learning theorists with interests in the investigation of fear and stress, social psychologists who experiment with attribution processes, and clinical psychologists attempting to cope with their patients' helplessness and lack of confidence have all contributed to the growing literature dealing with the perception of control. The largest body of empirical data about perceived control, however, derives from Julian Rotter's social learning theory. It is in Rotter's theory that perceived control occupies a central place within a systematic formulation. Although only a brief description of Rotter's views will be presented here, several books and articles contain detailed discussions of his theory (Rotter, 1954, 1955, 1960, 1971; Rotter, Chance & Phares, 1972).

According to Rotter's theory, a person's actions are predicted on the basis of his values, his expectations, and the situations in which he finds himself. The formulation for predicting behavior at a specific time and place is as follows:

$$BP_{x,s_1,R_a} = f(E_{x,R_a,s_1} \& RV_{a,s_1})$$

This formula reads: the potential for behavior x to occur in situation 1, in relation to reinforcement a, is a function of the expectancy of the occurrence of reinforcement a following behavior x, in situation 1, and the value of reinforcement a in situation 1.

This complicated formulation loses some of its obscure overtones when translated into a concrete example: The behavior of a young male collegian approaching an attractive female of the species and engaging in a series of appropriate

32

courting behaviors, including eye contact, smiles, and mellifluous and witty conversation, is predictable with knowledge of the student's expectancy that his particular manner of approach will elicit reciprocal affective responses from this particular woman who he no doubt has been observing previously, at this place (cocktail party), and with the additional knowledge regarding the degree to which the woman's positive response is desired by him at this particular time.

In this formulation, the importance of expectancies is not secondary to values. It is this equal emphasis upon value, expectancy of reinforcement, and situational specificity that makes Rotter's theory unique among learning theories that more commonly accentuate only the value or motive end of predictive formulae. For our present purpose of explicating the place of perceived control within social learning theory, we will shift our attention to Rotter's more general formula which reads as follows:

$$NP = f(FM \ \& \ NV)$$

The potentiality of occurrence of a set of behaviors that lead to the satisfaction of some need (need potential) is a function of: a) the expectancy that these behaviors will lead to these reinforcements (freedom of movement); and b) the strength or value of these reinforcements (need value). It is with the term "freedom of movement" that we approach the location of the locus of control construct in social learning theory.

Rotter (1954) defines freedom of movement as "the mean expectancy of obtaining positive satisfactions as a result of a set of related behaviors directed toward the accomplishment of a group of functionally related reinforcements. A person's freedom of movement is low if he has a high expectancy of failure or punishment as a result of the behaviors with which he tries to obtain the reinforcements that constitute a particular need [p. 194]."

In essence, freedom of movement is a generalized expectancy of success resulting from man's ability to remember and reflect upon a lifetime of specific expectancy-behavior-outcome sequences. Reverting back to our example of premating behavior, the male undergraduate, after a few years of commingling with the opposite sex, should establish a fairly stable estimate of success probability for eliciting feminine interest. This "stable estimate" would constitute his freedom of movement.

Perceived control is defined as a generalized expectancy for internal as opposed to external control of reinforcements. Like freedom of movement, it is an abstraction deriving from a series of specific expectancy-behavior-outcome cycles. However, where freedom of movement concerns the likelihood of success, the generalized expectancy of internal versus external control of reinforcement involves a causal analysis of success and failure.

Let us return now to our student in his frozen state of approach toward an attractive female undergraduate. We may assume that he has accumulated a fund of information, deriving from similar past encounters, from which he has developed a generalized expectancy of success (freedom of movement). We may also assume that he understands why he arrives at the outcomes that he does. The student may have experienced many rebuffs in the past and developed a low freedom of movement regarding his ability to engineer satisfactory interactions with women. At the same time, he no doubt acquired beliefs regarding the causes of his failures. He could attribute his failures to his own personal characteristics—homeliness, stupidity, lack of assertiveness, wit or conversational ease; or he may be in the habit of berating women for their perverse blindness in not recognizing his superlative qualities. "Women are all sluts," he may feel, "unable to appreciate the less than smooth, sensitive male."

Two such opposing interpretations of failure are examples of the internal and external poles of the locus of control dimension. Granted the generality of these expectancies for individuals holding such opposing views, we might conjecture that some individuals who attribute their failures to their own internal characteristics will become depressed following their failures, whereas others might busy themselves in improving their social manners in the hope of altering the outcomes of future encounters. The person who more readily attributed his social failures to the perversity of females, on the other hand, could perhaps become the perpetrator of sadistic acts upon women.

Habitual interpretations of failure may differ from one person to another. and success will not necessarily be interpreted in a similar way by different persons. Let us recreate our student, this time in the guise of a friendly, outgoing person who has had little difficulty in approaching women for whatever purposes he has had in mind. He has a high freedom of movement for social encounters so that he engages in each new interaction with enthusiasm. While such an individual will, in all probability, describe himself as a socially successful person, there is no certainty that he will attribute his success to internal characteristics. Instead, he may actually feel puzzled about why women are attracted to him and blithely regard himself as being very lucky to be surrounded by such warm and generous women. Concepts such as "love at first sight" and the like may be part of his explanatory language.

These examples illustrate the fact that it is not the simple registering of success and failure experiences that is pertinent to the generalized expectancy of internal versus external control, but rather it is the interpretation of the cause of those experiences. It differs from the expectancy of success or failure in that it is concerned with our beliefs about how reinforcements are determined and should, therefore, provide an independent contribution along with freedom of movement and need value to the prediction of goal-directed activity.

In order to account more fully for our student's manner of approach to women, we should like to know how much he values female company in contrast to other activities, how successful he believes he would be if he were to approach women in his characteristic ways, and, whether he believes that the outcomes of his attempts are a function largely of his own behaviors or are dependent on external circumstances such as "the nature of women." Thus we can see that the internal processes that are often described by "self-oriented" theorists are implicit in social learning theory. With the locus of control construct, we are dealing with a person as he views himself in conjunction with the things that befall him, and the meaning that he makes of those interactions between his self and his experiences.

In social learning terms the construct, perceived control, is referred to as a generalized expectancy of internal or external control of reinforcement. The formal terms, the generalized expectancy of internal control, refers to the perception of events, whether positive or negative, as being a consequence of one's own actions and thereby potentially under personal control. The generalized expectancy of external control, on the other hand, refers to the perception of positive or negative events as being unrelated to one's own behavior and therefore beyond personal control.

The source of interest in this construct did not begin simply with theoretical concerns but with problems encountered in psychotherapy. Rotter's social learning theory, unlike other similar approaches, has developed with a conjoint commitment to psychological research and clinical practice. As Rotter (1966) describes it: "The stimulus for studying such a variable has come from analysis of patients in psychotherapy. . . . Clinical analysis of patients suggested that while some patients appear to gain from new experiences or to change their behavior as a result of new experiences, others seem to discount new experiences by attributing them to chance or to others and not to their own behavior or characteristics [p. 2]."

There is an apocryphal story about a patient engaged in psychotherapy that illustrates how an external control orientation can militate against improvement in therapy. A therapist trainee was said to be in despair about the progress of therapy with his patient. As a social-learning oriented clinician, the therapist had actively sought out significant persons in the patient's life who could deliver valued reinforcements to the patient. The passive, depressed, inadequate-feeling patient had often complained that no one cared about him or his achievements. The therapist subsequently instructed the patient's wife and employer, who were willing collaborators, in the "how and when" to reinforce the patient for his efforts. As a consequence, the wife and employer later reported that they were becoming rather pleased with the patient, and the patient himself reported that he had begun to feel more appreciated for his efforts. Nevertheless, he continued to appear depressed and suffered with feelings of inadequacy. When, in exasperation, the therapist confronted the patient with *the facts,* as he saw them, challenging the patient's perceptions, the patient countered with his tour de force: "True, things are improving—my wife and boss do attend to me more than they used to. They appreciate me more. *But, that's only because of you—you instructed them to be more appreciative of me.*"

In other words, no matter what the experiences one has, if they are not perceived as the results of one's own actions, they are not effective for altering the ways in which one sees things and consequently the way one functions.

Analogous therapy experiences have been reported by other therapists with differing theoretical orientations and have been explained by such constructs as ego strength, self-esteem, inferiority feelings, hopelessness, "can-ness," etc. From no other clinically relevant personality theory, however, has such an accumulation of research pertaining to perceived control developed.

In dealing with the kind of phenomenological data described above, the social learning theorist was almost bound to construct an expectancy variable to explain the patient's self-described inertia. The best theoretical statement introducing the expectancy of control construct was offered by Rotter (1966) in his review of research with the locus of control:

> In social learning theory, a reinforcement acts to strengthen an expectancy that a particular behavior or event will be followed by the reinforcement in the future. Once an expectancy for such a behavior-reinforcement sequence is built up the failure of the reinforcement to occur will reduce or extinguish the expectancy. As an infant develops and acquires more experience he differentiates events which are causally related to preceding events and those which are not. It follows as a general hypothesis that when the reinforcement is seen as not contingent upon the subject's own behavior that its occurrence will not increase an expectancy as much as when it is seen as contingent. Conversely, its nonoccurrence will not reduce any expectancy so much as when it is seen as contingent. It seems likely that, depending upon the individual's history of reinforcement, individuals would differ in the degree to which they attributed reinforcement to their own actions.
>
> Expectancies generalize from a specific situation to a series of situations which are perceived as related or similar. Consequently, a generalized expectancy for a class of related events has functional properties and makes up one of the important classes of variables in personality descriptions.... A generalized attitude, belief, or expectancy regarding the nature of the causal relationship between one's own behavior and its consequences might affect a variety of behavioral choices in a broad band of life situations. Such generalized expectancies act to determine choice behavior along with the value of potential reinforcements. These generalized expectancies will result in characteristic differences in behavior in a situation culturally categorized as chance versus skill determined, and they may act to produce individual differences within a specific condition. [p. 2].

In this discussion Rotter explores the manner in which internal cognitive processes interact. The child is described as not assimilating new learnings if action-outcome sequences are perceived as being noncontingent. That is, he will not learn from his experiences unless he believes that these experiences are lawfully related to his own actions. If events are only randomly paired, there would seem to be little reason for attending to them with an intent to learn. In fact, the term parataxic distortion was coined by Harry Sullivan (1954) to connote just such an immature readiness to learn from what are only randomly connected events. It is evident, then, that the readiness to perceive contingency between one's actions and outcomes is an essential element in understanding how man comes to terms with his daily experience.

Some individuals, as was noted in Chapter 2, develop unshakeable beliefs that valued reinforcements occur only by chance, and that men are not the masters of their fates. In contrast, others may strongly believe that humans get their due desserts, that man is responsible for his own fate. As suggested above, persons with such contrasting perspectives should differ considerably in the degree to which they are able to assimilate and learn from their experiences. The fatalists perceive no contingency between action and outcome, whereas those espousing internal control beliefs readily perceive such contingencies.

In later chapters, we will focus upon research on locus of control conducted within a social learning framework. In order to provide important background information, we will first examine the earliest social learning studies that helped to produce confidence in the belief that locus of control was indeed an important variable in behavior predictions.

EARLY EMPIRICAL INVESTIGATIONS

To test the assumption that the expectancy of control influences the way individuals behave, an obvious starting place is in the manipulation of specific task expectancies. In the first of several studies in which the expectancy of control was manipulated through task directions, Phares (1957) found evidence to support the contention that perceived control did matter. Phares developed two novel judgment tasks. In one, subjects were required to match sample paint patches of varying shades of gray: in the other, they matched lines of slightly varying length. In both tasks, subjects had to judge whether a particular color or line was identical to a standard color or line that stood on a board some distance from them. To make these discriminations even more difficult, the standard color was presented against varying backgrounds, and the standard lines were presented at different angles from true vertical. Consequently, the judging was so difficult that it was nearly impossible for subjects to know with any certainty whether they were correct, or whether the tasks were skill or chance determined. In light of such ambiguity, Phares instructed half of his subjects that the tasks were so difficult that success on them was more a matter of luck than skill. The other half were informed that the tasks were a matter of skill and that some subjects were able to perform well at them.

Except for these different instructions, all subjects received the same series of experiences in the task. After each judgment, the subject was informed as to whether he was correct or not. This feedback was prearranged so that all subjects received the same sequence of "successes" and "failures." After each feedback, the subjects were asked to wager a number of poker chips to indicate their expectancy of being correct on the succeeding trial. Of primary interest in research employing this "level of aspiration" paradigm, is the manner in which subjects set their expectancies as a function of prior successes and failures. In the Phares experiment the interest centered on expectancy setting as a function of successes and failures when those reinforcements were perceived as controllable (skill) or random (chance).

As hypothesized, Phares found that reinforcement or feedback under "skill conditions" had a greater effect upon the manner in which subjects set their subsequent expectancies. Changes in the amount of chips wagered were significantly greater when subjects received skill than when they received chance instructions. Subjects receiving chance instructions more often "stood pat," which is a fair strategy in a gambling game. There was more shifting of expectancies among skill-instructed subjects, but chance-instructed subjects tended to make more "unusual shifts," i.e., shifts that do not conform with one's previous experience. For example, chance-instructed subjects were more likely to increase their expectancies of success subsequent to failure, and to decrease their expectancies of success following success. More subjects who had received chance directions bet a lower number of chips after a "correct" and more chips after an "incorrect" judgment than did subjects in the skill condition. In other words, subjects given chance directions responded as if each success reduced a finite supply of luck, or as if, after failure, the likelihood of success increased.

Phares' investigation provided an early indication that knowledge of a subject's perception of control was useful for predicting the type of judgments he would make in response to success and failure in a given task. If a task is perceived as being solvable through the exercise of skill, then subjects will seriously use their experience with that task as a basis for making estimates as to their future likelihood of success or failure. On the other hand, if the results of performance are perceived as random occurrences, then subjects are more likely to ignore feedback and will begin behaving in a manner similar to that of a gambler.

Some attribution researchers (Weiner, Nierenberg, & Goldstein, 1976) have contended that the results from studies such as Phares' have been misinterpreted. Weiner et al. suggest that expectancy changes are more a function of the attribute's stability than its source. Thus, if a person regarded himself as not having the ability to succeed at the task (a stable internal attribute), he would not readily change his expectancies as a result of some brief experiences with the task. If, however, he believed that effort (an unstable internal attribute) were responsible for the outcome, he would be more likely to change his expectations in tandem with his expected efforts. In other words, the stability of the cause (luck is less stable than task difficulty, effort is less stable than ability) would account for experience-expectancy relationship more than would the source (internal vs. external) of the cause.

On the other hand, Gregory (1981) has taken to task those investigations in which stability and locus have been studied separately. In brief, Gregory finds that fair comparisons have not been drawn and he is able to conclude that "in both the success and failure conditions, internal components contribute as much to success expectancies as do stable components [p. 92]."

A study by James and Rotter (1958) confirmed Phares' findings that perception of control predicted the manner in which people would respond to their performance outcomes. These investigators devised an experiment in which they were able to examine the effects of perceived control on the resistance to extinction after learning trials administered with partial versus 100% reinforcement. A time-honored research finding in psychology has been that persons who are partially reinforced in learning experiments (e.g., 50% reinforcement) will persist for a longer period of time after the occurrence of reinforcement than those reinforced 100% of the time. Indeed, such findings have often been raised as an argument for the use of patial reinforcement in educational settings to generate prolonged efforts at learning without the teacher's close attention.

James and Rotter interpreted this partial reinforcement phenomenon in social learning terms, asserting that subjects who perceived the task as experimenter-controlled, which is typically the case in learning experiments, would readily perceive a shift from 100% to 0% reinforcement as a change in the experiment. Subjects who had received partial reinforcement, on the other hand, would not discern the change in reinforcement rate as quickly, largely because the shift from partial to nonreinforcement was not as obvious.

In contrast, however, it was reasoned that if subjects believed that the reinforcements gained from their efforts were skill determined (Internal), then different results would obtain. A shift from a 100% to a 0% reinforcement schedule might be interpreted more in terms of a sudden loss of the "touch," or some such internal attribute that could be compensated for with concerted effort. Such a phenomenon is familiar to sportsmen such as bowlers, where 'set' and fluidity of body movement are required, and without which skilled performance deteriorates. Largely because quick extinction would not be obtained after subjects had received 100% reinforcement during early trials in a skill-determined task, James and Rotter hypothesized that perceived control would prove to be a mediating variable for determining subjects' responses to partial versus 100% reinforcement schedules.

Subjects were presented with a card-guessing game in which they were to predict whether each subsequent card bore an X or an O. The cards were presented in a manually operated tachistoscope-like apparatus. From the subject's viewpoint, each card dropped behind a closed shutter. After the subject stated his guess, the shutter opened and the card was revealed; the shutter then closed and another card dropped into place. From the experimenter's position there was a double-faced card with either an X or an O on it. When the subject stated his guess, the experimenter slid the card in the desired direction. In this way, the experimenter was able to control the outcome or reinforcement for each guess.

Before each trial, consisting of seven presentations and guesses, subjects registered their success prediction on a scale from 1 (failure) to 10 (success). The subjects were divided into four groups: 100%-skill, 100%-chance, 50%-skill, and 50%-chance. Skill and chance conditions were created through instructions, e.g., "Before each trial I would also like you to estimate how well (skill) you feel you will do,'' or, ''how lucky (chance) you feel you will be.'' The subjects in the 100% reinforcement group were given 7 guesses on each of 10 trials. They were told that they were correct in 5 or 6 out of their 7 guesses on each trial. The 50% reinforcement group was given the same 10 trials, half of which were successes. After the 10th trial, extinction began, and subjects were told that they were correct on 3, 2, or 1 out of the 7 guesses they had made within each trial. The instructions had previously defined such a low rate of correct guessing as due to chance; only trials in which 5 or more correct guesses were made out of 7 were credited as better than chance. In addition, subjects were penalized for inaccurate estimations and rewarded for accuracy in their total scores.

The results obtained were consistent with the researchers' expectations. With chance instructions, the usual resistance to extinction differences were obtained between partial (29.05 trials) and 100% reinforcement conditions (15.55 trials), showing that partial reinforcement generated greater resistance to extinction [$t = 4.43$, $p < .001$]. With skill instructions, however, the results were in the opposite direction, though failing to reach statistical significance (100%-skill: 22.90 trials; 50%-skill: 19.75 trials; $t = 1.61$, n.s.). The 100%-chance group extinguished more quickly (15.55 trials) than the 100%-skill group (22.90 trials), producing a $t = 2.99$, $p < .01$; and the 50%-skill group extinguished more quickly (19.75 trials) than the 50%-chance group [29.05 trials, $t = 3.50$, $p < .001$].

Thus, James and Rotter were able to demonstrate that expectancies regarding the controllability of outcomes make a considerable difference in the way subjects will construe changes in their experience. Extinction trials in a learning experiment may be perceived as failures by a subject, necessitating an increase in effort. On the other hand, the onset of extinction trials may be taken as evidence regarding the experimenter's behavior, signalling that the task has been changed. In the latter circumstance, subjects may even assume that it is their ''awareness'' that is under investigation so that it is the ''right'' or more intelligent choice to cease their efforts. These conflicting interpretations would seem to derive from the subject's perception of the task as one that does or does not test competence, and therefore is or is not controllable through one's own efforts.

The greatest impetus for interest in locus of control derived from the creation of an assessment device, as is often the case in personality research. In Phares' (1957) investigation, a short Likert-type scale was used as a measure of locus of control. Phares' scale contained 13 items stated as external-control-oriented attitudes and 13 as internal-control-oriented attitudes. In Phares' study, in which skill and chance sets were created by the use of instructions, he found that the 13 items stated as external-control-oriented attitudes produced low level correlations, bordering on statistical significance: Individuals with external attitudes behaved in a fashion similar to subjects who had received chance instructions. That is, subjects who espoused external control attitudes made more unusual shifts of expectancies, and yet made less and smaller shifts in expectancies that were congruent with their experiences than did subjects who had scored low on the 13 external control items.

Subsequently, James (1957) developed a larger scale, referred to as the James-Phares scale, which contained 26 items based on those that seemed to be the most useful from Phares' study. James also found low but significant correlations between his measure of locus of control and his subjects' responses to success and failure. Subjects characterized as holding an external control orientation exhibited smaller increments and decrements in expectancy statements following success and failure, and produced more unusual shifts than did internal control oriented persons.

These early studies demonstrated that specific expectancies of control were manipulable experimentally, and that generalized expectancies of internal-external control were assessable with paper and pencil devices. In subsequent chapters, it will become evident to the reader that these results opened up a research area that has rapidly mushroomed beyond its originator's most vivid expectations. Since the first introductory review of locus of control research (Rotter, Seeman, & Liverant, 1962), enough new and varied studies have appeared to stimulate several long review articles (Gilmor, 1978; Joe, 1971; Lefcourt, 1966, 1972, 1976, 1980; Phares, 1973, 1976; Rotter, 1966, 1975; Strickland, 1977) and these reviews were in need of updating almost before the print had dried. The remaining chapters are devoted to the attempt to catch up to this rapidly expanding research literature.

4 Locus of Control and the Resistance to Influence

INTRODUCTION AND BACKGROUND

In the wake of World War II, Western man found himself in a state of dumbfoundedness. As the gates of concentration camps opened and the vestiges of a ruined humanity emerged, the fantasy of basic innocence and honor in human nature was shattered. People asked how a "civilized" nation could descend into such bestiality and barbarism. Some of the aggrieved and self-righteous awaited revenge and judgment to occur at the Nuremburg trials. There, the victors expected confirmation of their beliefs, that each Nazi officer would be found to be corrupt, guilty, and personally evil. However, the trials failed to satisfy the prosecution's desire for simple justice and elucidated some sinister implications for man. Arendt (1963) cites an example. When asked, "How was it possible that all you honorable generals could continue to serve a murderer with such unquestioning loyalty?", one general replied that it was "not the task of a soldier to act as Judge over his supreme commander. Let history do that or God in heaven [p. 101]."

Since those times, we have seen the question of responsibility for atrocities recur in many forms and in different circumstances. Hannah Arendt's *Eichmann in Jerusalem: A report on the banality of evil* (1963) exposed to us at length a man who clearly demonstrated the fact that the most horrendous acts derive more from obedience or compliance to social order than from sadistic impulse; hence the subtitle of Arendt's volume.

During his recollection of a meeting of SS and Nazi elite convened to deliberate about the "Final Solution," the mass murder of millions of Jews, Eichmann reflected upon the waning of his sense of repulsion at the thought of such

violence. Arendt (1963) notes that, seeing that other civil servants were enthusiastic about the espoused plans, Eichmann recalled: "At that moment, I
sensed a kind of Pontius Pilate feeling, for I felt free of all guilt. Who was he to
judge? Who was he to have his own thoughts in this matter? [p. 101]."

> As Eichmann told it, the most potent factor in the soothing of his own conscience
> was the simple fact that he could see no one, no one at all, who actually was against
> the Final Solution. He did encounter one exception, however, which he mentioned
> several times, and which must have made a deep impression on him. This happened
> in Hungary when he was negotiating with Dr. Kastner over Himmler's offer to
> release one million Jews in exchange for ten thousand trucks. Kastner, apparently
> emboldened by the new turn of affairs, had asked Eichmann to stop 'the death mills
> at Auschwitz' and Eichmann had answered that he would do it 'with the greatest
> pleasure' but that, also, it was outside his competence and outside the competence
> of his superiors-as indeed it was [p. 103].

In an attempt to describe the atmosphere of those times, Eichmann and several
witnesses spoke of the legal web within which victims and captors alike were
trapped.

> Eichmann . . . at least dimly realized it was not an order but a law which had turned
> them all into criminals. The distinction between an order and the Fuhrer's word was
> that the latter's validity was not limited in time and space, which is the out-standing
> characteristic of the former. This is also the true reason why the Fuhrer's order for
> the Final Solution was followed by a huge shower of regulations and directives, all
> drafted by expert lawyers and legal advisers, not by mere administrators; this order,
> in contrast to ordinary orders, was treated as a law. [p. 133].

In other words, the horrors perpetrated by the Nazi officials were legitimate,
conforming to acceptable standards, and men like Eichmann felt that it was not
for them to question, since what they were asked to do was legitimate. Evil in
Nazi Germany had lost the aura by which most people recognize it, a unique
quality of temptation to violate standards; and the common man, such as
Eichmann, no longer felt able to judge what was right on some transcendent scale
of values.

Confusion regarding legitimacy, moral judgment, and abnegation of a sense
of moral integrity is no longer viewed as an aberrant phenomenon. With today's
rapid shifting of perspectives it is difficult for individuals to retain an abiding
sense of morality. All too many examples of man's capricious nature abound.

Stanley Milgram (1963, 1965) conducted a series of experiments in the early
1960s that indicate what history makes obvious, that harmful behavior can occur
on demand and that such a happenstance is not uniquely characteristic of but a
few odd social groups. Milgram, in the name of science, required subjects to
administer a series of increasingly severe electric shocks to the hand of a respect-

able looking middle-aged man. Although no actual shocks were delivered, to the naive subject it appeared as if he were administering painful shocks to the victim. Milgram varied several elements in the experimental situation in the hope of deterring subjects from a too easy compliance. Although some variability in subject's behavior was obtained, the overall results were such as to cause Milgram (1965) to conclude:

> With numbing regularity, good people were seen to knuckle under the demands of authority and perform actions that were callous and severe. Men who are in everyday life responsible and decent were reduced by the trappings of authority, by the control of their perceptions, and by the uncritical acceptance of the experimenter's definition of the situation into performing harsh acts.
>
> What is the limit of such obedience? At many points we attempted to establish a boundary. Cries from the victim were inserted; they were not effective enough. The victim claimed heart trouble; subjects still shocked him on command. The victim pleaded to be let free and his answers no longer registered on the signal box: subjects continued to shock him. At the outset, we had not conceived that such drastic procedures would be needed to generate disobedience, and each step was added only as the ineffectiveness of the earlier techniques became clear. The final effort to establish a limit was the Touch-Proximity condition. But the very first subject in this condition subdued the victim on command, and proceeded to the highest shock level. A quarter of the subjects in this condition performed similarly.
>
> The results, as seen and felt in the laboratory, are to this author disturbing. They raise the possibility that human nature, or more specifically the kind of character produced in American society, cannot be counted on to insulate its citizens from brutality and inhumane treatment at the direction of malevolent authority. A substantial proportion of people do what they are told to do, irrespective of the content of the act and without limitations of conscience, so long as they perceive that the command comes from a legitimate authority. If, in this study, an anonymous experimenter could successfully command adults to subdue a 50 -year old man and force on him painful electric shocks against his protests, one can only wonder what government, with its vastly greater authority and prestige, can command of its citizenry [pp. 261-2].

Lest Milgram's research be considered idiosyncratic to a laboratory investigation, recent events deriving from the American experience in Vietnam bolster the cause of Milgram's concerns. The trial of Lieutenant Calley caused extended debate regarding the responsibility for horrendous acts committed in the service of legitimate authority. Calley, the officer in charge of an advancing platoon, had given orders for his men to kill each and every person in the village of My Lai, including infants, the elderly, and men and women alike.

Details of atrocities in Vietnam were common enough that the My Lai slaughter might never have gained much attention. However, the very 'atmosphere surrounding the massacre' with the resulting questions pertaining to personal responsibility generated a groundswell of public indignation. Some were outraged at the barbarism per se and of the denial of responsibility by different military officials. Others expressed indignation that a comparatively low-ranking officer should have been assigned the blame that in their view should have been shared by the entire leadership that created such a callous atmosphere. Still others resented the fact that a man in the service be held accountable at all since they did not see him as acting on his own volition.

Kelman and Lawrence (1972) conducted a survey in which a sample of Americans were questioned about the Calley trial and other similar instances in which responsibility for personal actions had been raised in the past; of 989 respondents only 34% approved of Calley's having been brought to trial. Most pertinent to the thesis to be presented in this chapter is the finding that those who believed that an individual soldier bears responsibility for his actions showed marked and consistent differences in their general beliefs about responsibility from those who believed that a soldier should not be accountable for his actions.

Kelman and Lawrence (1972) interpreted responsibility attribution differences in terms of the manner in which individuals feel integrated into their national group. Those who denied responsibility were described as normatively integrated persons:

> An individual who is normatively integrated is bound to the system by virtue of the fact that he accepts the system's right to set the behavior of its members within a prescribed domain. Here we are dealing, one might say, with legitimacy in its pure form, in which the question of personal values and roles has become irrelevant. Acceptance of the system's right to unquestioning obedience may be based on a commitment to the state as a sacred object in its own right, or on a commitment to the necessity of law and order as a guarantor of equitable procedures. The normatively integrated member regards compliance with the system as a highly proper and valued orientation. When he is faced with demands to support the system he is likely to comply without question, since he regards it as his obligation to do so [pp. 204-5].

Kelman and Lawrence note the similarity of the normatively integrated individual with deCharm's characterization of the "pawn" (deCharms, 1968). The pawn is said to perceive his actions as under the control of authorities, and in relinquishing control to these authorities, the pawn is said to disavow responsibility for his nation's policies.

In contrast, Kelman and Lawrence (1972) argue, the person who views Calley and others like him as responsible for their actions, is said to be characterized by ideological or role integration. Ideological integration occurs when the person "is bound to the system by virtue of the fact that he shares—at an internalized level—some of the basic values on which the system is established [p. 20]." Such a person is said to comply with system demands when he sees those demands as consistent with the underlying values of the system to which he is committed. Role integration occurs when an individual is bound to the system through the roles he is engaged in and compliance depends on the extent to which the relevant role has been made salient by the situation at hand. As Kelman and Lawrence (1972) state:

> In any event, whether their integration into the national system is primarily at the level of values or at the level of roles, most responsibility accepting respondents are probably socialized and integrated in a way that gives them a greater sense of ownership of the system. Their demographic characteristics, i.e., their generally higher levels of socio-economic status and education, are consistent with this orientation. Realistically, their educational background and the occupations to which it admits them provide them greater opportunity to become active agents in the society and a greater sense of participation in shaping its policies and running its affairs. Even when they do not feel quite free to question national policies in terms of underlying values and to give or withhold their support on that basis, they are less inclined to the view held by most responsibility denying respondents that these policies are beyond question and that their personal values are entirely irrelevant to them [pp. 207–208].

In their discussion concerning the perception of responsibility, Kelman and Lawrence accentuate one element that would seem to be a primary difference between those who accept and those who deny responsibility, i.e., a skeptical or questioning attitude.

> In the Milgram experiments not all of the subjects remained submissive to the experimenter; at My Lai not all of the men followed Calley's orders to shoot the captured civilians. Those who resist in these situations have somehow managed to maintain the framework of personal causation that applies in "normal" situations. Perhaps they have never made the radical shift in perception of the situation described by Milgram, or perhaps they are better able to differentiate between legitimate and illegitimate demands and feel freer to make choices on that basis [p. 181].

Thus, resistance to orders and the acceptance of responsibility when one is compliant to them is said to derive from the person's maintenance of a framework of personal causation, and the ability to differentiate or assess the quality of demands made upon him. As Kelman and Lawrence have suggested, the dimension of actor-pawn may well define those who can resist orders and accept responsibility from those who are more compliant but responsibility-eschewing individuals. Likewise, the locus of control dimension describes the manner in which one commonly ascribes responsibility for one's experiences. Persons who perceive themselves as the active determiners of their fates should more readily accept responsibility for their outcomes and, therefore, should be more discriminating about what they will and will not do in obeisance to others.

We will propose in this and the following chapter that the maintenance of an internal control orientation is a bulwark against unquestioning submission to authority. The data in support of this contention can be viewed as inconclusive, and perhaps inadequate. Nevertheless, the consistency of results, even when not anticipated, allow us to step out on a limb in addressing one of today's major problems: the maintenance of a moral order among men.

EMPIRICAL RESEARCH

Conformity and Compliance Research

The first investigation linking locus of control to influence resistance was conducted by Odell (1959), who found a significant relationship $[r = .33, p < .05]$ between a prototype of Rotter's I–E scale and Barron's Independence of Judgment scale. Externals showed greater tendencies to conform on Barron's scale. (This latter test had originally been developed as a correlate of conformity in Asch-type situations.)

A second study utilizing an Asch-like conformity situation was conducted by Crowne and Liverant (1963). These investigators assessed the confidence statements of students made during two conformity tasks. In one, the subjects were asked to rate how certain they felt about their own judgment, from 0 (no confidence) to 10 (very high confidence), immediately after making each judgment. The task required subjects to distinguish on each of 20 trials, the larger of two groups of dots that had been presented tachistoscopically for a 1-sec interval.

As is customary in Asch conformity tasks, the subject stated most of his decisions after his supposed peers had publicly stated their judgments. However, the peers were collaborators of the experimenter whose judgments were prearranged in such a manner that they often were in complete agreement about many choices that were obviously wrong. The subject, therefore, had to be willing to deviate from a consensus if he was to be true to his own senses.

The second manner of presenting this task substituted the betting of money for the simple statements of confidence. Subjects were given $10 in quarters. On each of 20 trials, the subject could bet nothing, $.25 or $.50 on each of his judgments. Subjects had been instructed that they could keep a portion of their winnings so that there was some value in making accurate assessments.

Differences between statements of confidence by internal- and external-control-oriented subjects, as measured on the 60-item prototype of Rotter's I–E Scale, were in the expected direction but not pronounced. When betting was substituted for the verbal expression of confidence, however, externals were found to conform more than internals $[t = 2.35, p < .05]$. Of even greater interest, externals bet less when their judgments were independent of their peers than they did on trials on which they had yielded to the consensus $[t = 2.68, p < .02]$. That is, when externals conformed to their peers' decision they were willing to bet larger amounts of money on the correctness of those decisions than they were when they made less conforming or independent judgments. The greatest differences between internals and externals in amounts bet occurred on those trials during which subjects made independent judgments, i.e., on those trials when they responded before their peers had expressed their judgments.

The Crowne and Liverant study indicates that when the stakes of success are of some value to the individual, persons characterized as internals are more trusting of their own judgments than are externals. The difference between the groups was apparently due to the fact that externals have more confidence in the consensual judgments of others than they do in their own independent judgments.

At about the same time that Crowne and Liverant were examining the correlates of conformity, Pearl Gore (1962) was investigating personal characteristics that contributed to compliance with the experimenter's bias during psychological experimentation. Gore administered a set of Thematic Apperception Test pictures with the stated purpose of learning which cards provoked longer stories from subjects. During the test administration, through smiles and vocal intonations, she attempted to manipulate subjects into producing longer stories to selected pictures. In one condition, in which Gore offered no hints or suggestions as to what was expected, no differences were obtained between internals and externals. Likewise, when the experimenter explicitly indicated which pictures she thought were most likely to elicit longer stories, no differences were obtained. However, when the experimenter smiled and dropped such choice comments as, "Now let's see what you can do with *this* one," internals produced significantly shorter stories than did externals.

Gore's investigation suggests that internals are not more resistant to the experimenter's bias in general than are externals, but that they resist a certain kind of influence technique. Some writers have termed this technique subtle manipulation, as opposed to explicit suggestion. However, it is also possible to construe the technique difference in the language of interpersonal intentions.

If an experimenter conveys his expectations to a subject he may, in effect, be perceived as sharing his hypothesis with the subject, thus inviting the subject to join him in a curious objective attitude toward the criterion behaviors. This shared attitude would be one that expresses respect for the subject as a person rather than as an object to be manipulated and influenced. In contrast, the "subtle coercion" described above pits experimenter against subject and suggests that the subject will be affected, as if a passive pawn, by the characteristics of the TAT card. The experimenter is, in effect, saying, "You won't be able to resist this one—I know," suggesting that the experimenter knows something that the subject does not and is therefore in a position to more easily predict the subject's behavior than is the subject.

It will be our contention as we review other relevant investigations that the internal resists being placed in positions where he is the pawn who is 'put down,' so to speak, by the assumed knowledge of others. If the expert or experimenter, on the other hand, offers a more collegial atmosphere, the internal should not then be as resistant to influence as when he perceives himself as the *target* of manipulation.

Two studies are immediately relevant to this conjecture. Strickland (1970) found that internals were more likely than externals to deny having been influenced during a verbal conditioning experiment. In this task, subjects were reinforced: that is, the experimenter nodded her head and murmured "umm-humm" after the subject answered with verb responses. The subject's job was to select a word from a group of four words that went best with some common noun. The effect of reinforcement was expected to increase the choice of a verb as the proper response *unbeknownst* to the subject. That is, the subject was to be 'fooled' by the experimenter into doing the latter's bidding without his conscious consent. At the end of the task, subjects were interviewed to ascertain whether they had become aware of the reinforcement contingency. Internals and externals did not differ with regard to their being aware of the experimenter's behavior. However, among those subjects who had become 'aware' of the contingencies, externality was associated with acceptance of the experimenter's influence. Strickland (1970) states: "Subjects characterized as internal tended to deny the influence of the experimenter and appeared to follow their own inclinations in regard to giving the correct response [p. 376]." Similar findings have been reported by Jolley and Spielberger (1973) and Alegre and Murray (1974), who have also found that among "aware" subjects externals condition more easily than internals.

In other words, among those subjects in Strickland's experiment who recognized that the experimenter was doing something deliberate to manipulate them, and who also denied being influenced, the more internal individuals proved to be less conditionable. On the other hand, toward the end of the extinction trials, after the experimenter had ceased her cajoling, manipulative responses, the internal-aware subjects showed a significant increase in verb responses. In essence, this small group of subjects seemed to say: "I know what you're trying to do to me and I'll show you you can't make a fool out of me;" in essence a reassertion of "I, the actor," and a denial of "me—the object of manipulation."

Strickland's findings are mirrored fairly closely in another verbal conditioning experiment conducted by Getter (1966). This investigator found that the most responsive "conditioners" were his most external subjects. The more internal subjects, as in Strickland's experiment, behaved in a seemingly paradoxical fashion, producing the conditioned response (words ending in *ion*) largely during extinction trials, after the experimenter had ceased emitting reinforcements.

In these three studies, then, internals are found to behave in a somewhat oppositional manner, doing the reverse of what the experimenter would trick them into doing. Only when Gore explicitly instructed her subjects as to what she anticipated did the difference in compliance between internals and externals diminish.

Other researchers have reported findings that help us avoid falling into the trap of assuming that internality is simply a euphemism for stubbornness. As in Gore's study, Ritchie and Phares (1969) did not find that internals were consistent resistants to influence, whereas externals were always likely to succumb. Internals shifted their opinions in the direction of an influence message as did externals in this experiment. However, externals were found to shift their views most when the influential arguments were attributed to a prestigious government official. Internals did not differ in their response as a function of the status of the source. When the arguments regarding government budgets were attributed to a college sophomore they were not less effective with internals than they were when attributed to the then U.S. Secretary of the Treasury, Douglas Dillion. By contrast, as can be seen in Figure 1, externals exhibited more attitude shift with the prestigious attribution and less with the low status attribution than internals, who seemed responsive to the arguments regardless of the assumed source. These findings have been replicated by McGinnies and Ward (1974), though only with American subjects. Subjects drawn from four other cultures did not show similar effects.

As further evidence that internals are not always more resistant to influence than externals, James, Woodruff, and Werner (1965) found that more internal males quit smoking for a specified length of time than did external males after hearing the United States Public Health Service Surgeon General's report con-

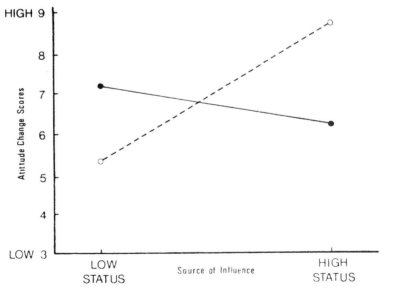

FIGURE 1   Mean attitude change scores as a function of locus of control and status of influence source. (●) Internal; (○) external. (Adapted from Ritchie & Phares, 1969, page 438.)

cerning the link between cancer with cigarette smoking. Likewise, E. S. Platt (Mausner & Platt, 1971; Platt, 1969) reported more success at influencing the smoking behavior of internals than of externals. Platt used role-playing procedures in which subjects acted out the roles of physician and patient during a medical examination. This examination concluded with a diagnosis of cancer and patients had to actively think about the arrangements necessitated by hospitalization and imminent death. Platt found that the greatest changes in smoking behavior occurred among individuals who were both internal and believers in the link between smoking and illness.

These investigations suggest that internals are not simply resistant to any influence but are discriminating about what influences they will accept. Authority per se has little direct effect upon their readiness to accept a point of view. However, when internals accept the information, as in the Ritchie and Phare's investigation, and in the smoking studies discussed above, they do change behaviorally in response to influence. In each of these studies, where internals do shift in their attitudes or behaviors, there is less likelihood that subjects view themselves as manipulated objects. The prestige condition in the Ritchie and Phares study is the only instance in which "oughts" or pressures for conformity are evident, and in that condition internals were less influenced than were externals. The smoking studies had as vehicles of influence nonpersonally directed public information, and role-playing, in which subjects took an active part in creating their responses. In neither case was external pressure brought to bear in a way as to curtail the decision-making process. The subject had to arrive at his own conclusions, and it is this opportunity, perhaps, that is the essential precondition if internals are to be influenced.

Two other investigations expressly concerned with locus of control and responsiveness to influence underscore the reliability of the previously reported findings (Biondo & MacDonald, 1971; Doctor, 1971). Biondo and MacDonald attempted to manipulate the 'level of subtlety' in their study so as to examine previous contentions that internals are more markedly resistant to subtle than to obvious influence attempts. The curves in Figure 2 suggest that, regardless of the style of influence, externals were more compliant than internals. In addition, the latter appeared to be even more oppositional in the presence of obvious coercion than they were with subtle influence. These findings, which have been replicated elsewhere (Cravens & Worchel, 1977), seem to refute the conjectures offered previously. If one examines the methodology employed in Biondo and MacDonald's study, however, one can as easily conclude that subjects perceived themselves as objects of manipulation in both the "low" and "high" influence conditions.

Three different groups of subjects were asked to express on paper their evaluation of the marking system at their university. Immediately after completing their evaluations and passing them forward, another person, introduced as a graduate student in education, addressed the class and explained that he was conducting

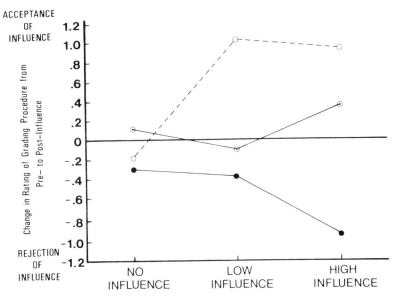

FIGURE 2   Attitude change as a function of locus of control and level of influence manipulation. (●) Internal; (○) external; (◉) middle. (Adapted from Biondo & MacDonald, 1971, page 414; © 1971 Duke University Press.)

research upon grading systems. The experimenter then passed out mimeographed sheets containing information about the grading procedure that had just been rated. One group received no additional information from that which had been provided earlier. The low influence communication ended with the statement that "This grading procedure has been widely accepted at other universities and appears to be one of the best ever used." The high influence communication ended with, "Taking everything into consideration, it is obvious that this is a very good procedure. I don't see how you have any choice but to rate this procedure highly."

Following these influence attempts subjects were asked to rerate the grading procedure. Though Biondo and MacDonald report that there were no expressions of suspicion obtained, the very procedures described here, which involved a sequence of rating-information-rerating, seems to be an obvious attempt to assess influenceability without admitting as much. In essence, subjects are given no chance to debate or defend their position, little time to actively rethink their reasons for previous judgments, and are placed in a position in which if they do shift their judgments they must view themselves as easily manipulable, deferrent to 'expert opinion,' and perhaps unstable. To so rapidly alter one's opinion must be perceivable by subjects as the experience of being influenced. As such the internal, if our thesis regarding aversion to passive manipulation is correct,

should resist such attempts at influence whether the statements are short (low influence) or long and somewhat embellished (high influence).

The other study by Doctor (1971) essentially replicated the verbal conditioning results obtained by Strickland and Getter. The one difference was that awareness of contingencies was not associated with a negative response on the part of internals. Rather, externals who were aware of the contingencies exhibited the greatest degree of conditioning, which accounted for most of the differences obtained between internal and external subjects. In other words, external subjects on becoming aware of the experimenter's purpose, willingly submitted to his machinations, whereas internals showed no clear disposition to cooperate or resist.

There have been a number of other studies examining compliance and influenceability as a function of locus of control. Ryckman, Rodda, and Sherman (1972) found that externals were more conforming to the opinions of a higher status other person regardless of whether that person's expertise was relevant or not to the issues at hand. Sherman (1973) also conducted an attitude change study contrasting the effects of persuasive messages from without and of self-originated counter attitudinal essay writing upon subjects grouped according to their scores on Rotter's I-E scale. In accord with our own conclusions regarding self-generated versus externally induced arguments for change, internals were found to have changed more following their writing of counter attitudinal statements than in response to others' persuasive arguments, whereas the reverse obtained for the external sample.

In addition to Sherman's study, at least two other groups of investigators have reported data relevant to influence resistance. Snyder and Larson (1972) found that externals were more accepting of extensive personality descriptions derived from minimal test data than were internals. Since this was the very procedure used by Phares, Ritchie, and Davis (1968) that had led those researchers to posit a greater defensiveness regarding failure among internals, the strong possibility exists that the lesser recall by internals of the "personality" interpretations may have derived more from original disbelief than from repressive tendencies. Secondly, Felton (1971) found that the "Rosenthal effect," the impact of an experimenter's expectancies upon a subject's performance, was maximal when the subject was external and the experimenter internal with regard to locus of control.

Other investigators, although not focusing upon social influence per se, have found, with some reliability, that externals are facilitated and internals distracted and impeded by the presence of social stimuli during various task performances (Baron, Cowan, Ganz, & McDonald, 1974; Baron & Ganz, 1972; Fitz, 1971; Pines, 1973; Pines & Julian, 1972). In an extrapolation from these data, this writer and his colleagues, (Lefcourt, Hogg, & Sordoni, 1975) found that internals were more comfortable, as indicated by the frequency of fidgets, when working in isolation than when "feeling observed" by a video camera operating behind a mirror. In direct reverse, externals were found to fidget considerably more often when alone than when observation was made salient.

The overall evidence, then, consistently suggests that externals are more attentive, positively responsive, and facilitated in their task performances by the presence of social cues. Internals, on the other hand, seem to be more resistant to social influences and are, at the least, distracted by social cues as they attempt to cope with various tasks.

Resistance to Experimenter's Influence

In addition to those investigations that have been specifically designed to assess compliance, a series of studies conducted by this author and his colleagues (Lefcourt, 1967; Lefcourt, Lewis, & Silverman, 1968; Lefcourt & Siegel, 1970; Lefcourt & Wine, 1969) revealed that internals were unresponsive to the experimenter's instructions, suggestions, and manipulations, whereas externals readily capitulated, behaving, almost to a man, in accord with task directions. In one study, (Lefcourt, 1967) the achievement-oriented behaviors of internals and externals were compared when instructions varied the degree to which achievement was stressed. Achievement-oriented patterns of performance were obtained from 91% of the external subjects when task directions emphasized the challenging nature of the task. When the task, Rotter's Level of Aspiration Board (Rotter, 1954) was administered without such instructions, only 18% of external subjects responded in an achievement-oriented fashion. In contrast, samples of internal subjects exhibited little change in behavior as a function of the different instructions.

In another study using the level of aspiration technique, Lefcourt, Lewis, and Silverman (1968) initially found no performance differences between internals and externals in response to skill versus chance directions that were given before the task. However, at the end of the experiment, when subjects were asked how they had actually perceived the task, externals were found to have been more accepting than internals of instructions, which suggested that this truly skill-demanding task was chance determined. On the other hand, externals had been somewhat less likely than internals to have accepted the more veridical skill instructions. It was concluded, therefore, that internals were less compliant than externals in response to directions that challenged their own more probable interpretations.

A similar finding in regard to the way in which externals respond to experimenter's directions was reported by Lefcourt and Wine (1969). Part of this experiment had concerned the effect of the experimenter's stated purposes on subjects' attentiveness. The number of observations of things unique to an experiment room were recalled by internals and externals in two conditions: One in which the purpose of the experiment was not defined for the subjects, and another in which the experiment was described as focusing upon attention. All subjects completed a series of unrelated tasks while in the experiment room. The number of observations made of items in that room was obtained after subjects had been seated in a second room. Unique to the experimental room were several "planted items": an erotic Shakespearian sonnet on the blackboard, signs advertising various events, etc. The number of unique stimuli recalled was much greater overall when the experiment was described as pertaining to attention. Moreover, the external group exhibited the greatest shift in the number of observations made. Internals had observed somewhat more of the unique items than externals in the noninstructed condition, though this difference was not statistically different. With instructions focusing upon attention, however, externals recalled significantly more unique items than did internals, and more than their external counterparts in the uninstructed condition. Internals, on the other hand, barely changed at all with the different instructions.

In this experiment, then, the directions that simply alerted subjects as to what processes the experimenter was interested in had the effect of altering externals' perceptual behavior. Since subjects hadn't been aware that the immediate room was to be the target of their attentions, it was as if externals began to use their eyes when they knew that the experiment was concerned with attention. In contrast, internals seemed unresponsive to the experimenter's interests.

In these and other studies, then, evidence has been found that indicates that persons holding an internal locus of control withstand pressures directing them to behave in certain circumscribed manners. This is not true in all instances, although the exceptions to this generalization are revealing. Internals do yield to pressures, but not to the same pressures as externals. When acted upon as an object of experimentation, internals become almost playfully negativistic, as in the verbal conditioning investigations. However, internals do respond positively to reasoned arguments, regardless of the status of the source, readily respond to directives that seem congruent with their own perceptions, and shift in attitudes and behavior when engaged in role-playing that allows more active participation and self-direction. Externals appear to be responsive to the status of the influencer and more ready to accept the suggestions and directions of an experimenter.

Morally Relevant Behavior

At this point we may now return to the reason for our initial interest in the resistance to influence. It would seem from the studies reported above that an internal locus of control is associated with a tendency to be circumspect in the face of pressure to yield to influence. However, as of yet there have been few investigations linking locus of control with the kinds of influence resistance that have been investigated by Milgram. Nor has locus of control been implicated in studies of real complicity in evil or immoral acts. Internals are more likely to resist some forms of social pressure than are externals. Whether such resistance would persist against heightened pressure or increased inducements to acquiesce are questions requiring further empirical test.

There are some investigations, however, which do approach the issue of moral responsibility and locus of control. R. C. Johnson, Ackerman, Frank, and Fionda (1968) have investigated the relationship between locus of control and the resistance to temptation as part of a project concerned with moral development and personal adjustment. These authors used a ''complete-a-story'' device in which the hero of an incomplete story experienced social pressure directing him toward the violation of some social norm (drug use, illicit sex, etc.). Subjects completed stories in which the hero was either at the point of decision or when he had to face the consequences of his acts. Among male undergraduates, Johnson et al. (1968) found that the more internal the subject, as measured by the I–E scale, the more likely he was to complete stories in which the hero resisted pressure. And, in those stories in which transgression had already occurred, internals were more likely than externals to have the hero acknowledge guilt about his having yielded to pressure.

Although the reliability and validity of these data can be subjected to question, taken together with the research noted above, the findings are intriguing. Johnson's results indicate that the relationship between locus of control and resistance to influence can be extended to moral decision making. A study by C. D. Johnson and Gormly (1972) provides further support for the link between locus of control and resistance to temptation. When fifth-grade boys and girls were classified as cheaters and noncheaters on the basis of a behavioral test, a significant difference in scores on Crandall's IAR scale was obtained. Female pupils who had cheated were more external than their noncheating peers. Male pupils had results in the same direction, though the differences between cheaters and noncheaters were decidedly less extreme than among the females.

However, findings that link locus of control with cheating behavior are not free of complexity. In two studies (Karabenick & Srull, 1978; Srull & Karabenick, 1975), locus of control has been used to successfully predict cheating behavior during the solution of the unsolvable puzzles that Glass and Singer (1972) had used in their research. In both of these studies, subjects were asked to report the number of line-tracing puzzles they had solved correctly. Since only 3 out of 25 puzzles were solvable, any claims to correct solutions beyond the 3 solvable puzzles indicated cheating. In both studies, half the subjects had received directions stressing the skill required for succeeding at the task; the other half had been instructed that luck was the major determinant of outcomes.

The results from both studies were similar: Internals were found to cheat more in the 'skill' condition; externals cheated more in the 'chance' condition. These findings were reflected in the correlations between I–E scale and cheating in each condition: $r = .70$ with chance, $r = -.73$ with skill directions.

Karabenick and Srull (1978) conjectured, albeit with interview information to bolster their arguments, that internals and externals were more apt to cheat when success at the task was related to the ways in which these persons liked to perceive themselves—as skilled or as lucky. Regardless of the interpretation, however, it is evident that cheating per se is not a simple correlate of locus of control, and as Karabenick and Srull contend, interactions with task descriptions are to be expected.

In another study with pertinence to morality, Midlarski (1971) found that internals were more likely to help another individual that were externals despite the fact that they were penalized for doing so. In this investigation, subjects found themselves in a position where it was possible to help a fellow subject (actually a confederate of the experimenter) to finish a task of sorting small objects into separate groups. As each item was lifted from a grid a moderate level electric shock was received by the subject. The confederate performed at a slower rate than the subject such that the latter had the option of helping the confederate after finishing his part of the task. A fairly strong correlation [$r = .54$, $p < .001$] was obtained between helping and Midlarski's shortened form of the I–E scale. These findings linking locus of control with altruism and helping behavior have been replicated elsewhere (Midlarski & Midlarski, 1973; Ubbink & Sadava, 1974).

These studies indicate that internals are more tolerant of discomfort in doing what they consider to be correct than are externals. This finding matches that of Johnson et al. (1968), whose subjects had to make the choice between resisting pressures to commit immoral acts and suffering ostracism, loneliness etc. In the one case internals tolerated pain for actively doing what they considered correct; in the other, they expressed a willingness to risk social rejection for maintaining what they construed as proper behavior.

Another indication of the relevance of locus of control to morality derives from a low magnitude, but significant correlation [$r = .16$, $p < .05$, N = 227] between the I–E scale and the Mach V scale (Miller & Minton, 1969). The latter scale assesses the espousal of Machiavellian attitudes including the readiness to be opportunistic and to be guided by indiscriminate cynicism and suspicion. As the correlation indicates, the more external persons tend to agree with Machiavellian positions more than do internal individuals.

Several investigators have attempted to explore the relationship between locus of control and moral judgment maturity. Though there has been some conflicting evidence, persons classified as internal have been found to score more highly on devices assessing moral judgment maturity. Alker and Poppen (1973), for example, found internals more likely to use principled reasoning in Kohlberg's moral judgment interview than were externals. Bloomberg (1974) examined the relationship between locus of control and moral judgment as assessed by Rest's Defining Issues Test (Rest, 1976). Little evidence was found for a relationship between locus of control and moral judgment. However, internals did choose a significantly greater average percentage of items characterized as principled and differentiated moral reasoning.

Finally, Connolly and McCarrey (1978) have found that moral judgment orientation, assessed by Rest's test, was related to various factors of Rotter's scale differently for males and females. For males, internality with regard to social system control was associated with judgment maturity. For females, the reverse was the case: The higher the social system control, the lower were the moral judgment scores. On the other hand, the more internal females were with regard to the personal control factor of the I-E scale, the more they were represented in the moderate and high moral judgment categories. For males, the personal control factor was unrelated to moral judgment. Connolly and McCarrey (1978) attempted to interpret these differences in accord with sex-role formulations. Nevertheless, it is obvious that ambiguities exist in the literature that attempt to draw relationships between locus of control and moral judgments though there is obviously some meaningful overlap between these constructs.

Finally, in a study that bears the closest similarity to Milgram's study of obedience, evidence has been presented that externals are more apt to do harm to another when socially pressured to do so. Propst (1979), in a study designed to evaluate the effects of deindividualization upon the readiness to harm another person with electric shocks, found that externals were the most likely to shock another person, especially when participating in an individuated condition. That is, when subjects felt more visible or known to the investigator, having given word association test responses to him, those who were more external were the most likely to shock another person in accord with the investigator's directions. As Propst noted, subjects were more careful to conform to the experimenter's demands when they were individuated and external—a condition perhaps, not unlike that which characterized Eichmann at his meetings with Nazi officials.

CONCLUSION

Though most of the research discussed in the previous sections lacks the dramatic quality so obvious in Milgram's research, it lends support to the contention advanced earlier that internal locus of control can operate as a bulwark against the unquestioning submission to authority. Insofar as the researcher is a legitimate authority, and defiance against his often demeaning requirements can be taken as the readiness to resist authoritarian dictates, there is some encouragement for discussing locus of control as pertinent to the Eichmann and Calley cases. If these individuals had remained able to question the commands and legitimacy of their superior officers, they might not have been the infamous "collaborators" that they did in fact become; and, if they had perceived themselves as responsible actors rather than as externally controlled pawns, they might have been more questioning and consequently more resistant to the dictates and persuasions of others.

If our hypothesis is correct, then when a person believes he is the responsible agent or source of his own life's fortunes, he will resist influence attempts that aim to bypass his own sense of moral justice, and will only respond to those appeals that address themselves to his own beliefs and values. In effect, the internal will not, like Eichmann, experience the "Pontius Pilate feeling," a surrender of a sense of responsibility when one succumbs along with others to manipulation.

5 Locus of Control and Cognitive Activity

INTRODUCTION

In the previous chapter, Kelman and Lawrence (1972) explained the differences between persons who indiscriminately capitulate and those who selectively respond to the demands of authority as follows: "Those who resist . . . have somehow managed to maintain the framework of personal causation that applies in normal situations. Perhaps they have never made the radical shift in perception of the situation . . . or perhaps they are better able to differentiate between legitimate and illegitimate demands [p. 181]." Inherent in this explanation is the assumption of cognitive activity that facilitates making fine discriminations. Individuals must maintain their sense of personal causation, according to Kelman and Lawrence, despite the onslaught of bewildering situations that tempt them to surrender their sense of personal control and responsibility.

Writers throughout the ages have depicted man's struggle to maintain his sense of personal responsibility in the face of pressures that threaten to destroy his very individuality. The *Book of Job,* Kafka's *Trial,* Koestler's *Darkness at Noon,* and Heller's *Catch 22* present man as he is twisted by God, fate, the Devil, and relentless, omnipotent social systems. With such forces arrayed against him, it is perplexing that man attempts to, and often succeeds in, remaining stable in his "framework of personal causation."

The degree to which man is capable of questioning his own assumptions, the degree to which he is in the habit of deliberating over his options and is attentive to information relevant to his decision-making—to that degree will he be less assailable by forces directed against his integrity. If Eichmann had been more able to ponder the ramifications of Nazi requests for complicity, perhaps he would have looked more askance at the enthusiasm exhibited by his fellow bureaucrats for participating in the execution of the "Final Solution." In other words, a man can be led more easily to surrender his moral precepts when he has, through lack of thought, failed to discern the portents inherent in his decisions.

The investigations that are reviewed in this chapter indicate that locus of control is a correlate of the kinds of cognitive activity, that should facilitate the maintenance of personal causation. If an individual wishes to know about himself, his capabilities, his limits, and his potentialities, then he should seek out situations in which it is possible to test his mettle. Persons who customarily do so are referred to as "open to experience," "nondefensive" and "self-actualizing" in various theoretical frameworks. For the present purposes, such individuals who readily assimilate information about themselves will be described as having an internal locus of control.

The idea that locus of control is related to cognitive activity appeals to common sense. Persons holding internal control expectancies should be more cautious and calculating about their choices, involvements, and personal entanglements than are individuals with external control orientations. Otherwise, the probability of internals being able to regulate their experiences would be lessened. This loss, in turn, would diminish the degree to which they are able to remain actors rather than pawns of fate. Such self-direction should entail more active cognitive processing of information relevant to the attainment of valued ends, and should be reflected in the types of strategies that characterize an individual.

INFORMATION ASSIMILATION

The first study linking locus of control and cognitive activity was conducted by Seeman and Evans (1962). They used a 12-item measure of powerlessness, derived from Rotter's I–E scale, to predict knowledge about a disease among sufferers of that disease. External-oriented tubercular patients were found to have less knowledge about tuberculosis than internal tubercular patients, the correlation between powerlessness and knowledge being $r = .31$, $p < .01$. In addition, when the staff of the sanitorium were asked to estimate their patients' knowledge about tuberculosis, internals were rated as more knowledgeable than externals.

The results of this study support the assertion that internals avail themselves of information, even if it has negative connotations for themselves, more than do externals. It has been assumed that this difference derives from the fact that internals believe that they can act in their own behalf and therefore require more information, whereas externals more readily accept dependency on more competent others and thus have less need of information.

Seeman (1963) tested these assertions in another institutional setting with a measure of active information gathering that had definite functional utility. He presented reformatory inmates with three types of information varying in utility, and six weeks later assessed the subjects' retention of that information. Of the three types of information, only one type, related to parole attainment, was of instrumental relevance to the reformatory inmates. Examples of parole information were as follows:

1. About 85% of successful parolees have taken part in some kind of voluntary education program during their prison term.
2. In 60% of the cases where parole is delayed beyond the date set by the board, difficulty in arranging employment is the main reason for the delay.

The second type of information was "incidental knowledge about the reformatory," examples of which are:

1. It costs about $5 per day to keep an inmate at this reformatory.
2. A survey at the reformatory showed that 65% of the men had no disciplinary actions on their record.

The third type of information was "knowledge of long range, distant opportunities," examples of which are:

1. It has been estimated that the demand for unskilled workers will continue to decline in the 1960s, with the loss of about 2500 such jobs per year.
2. A sizable increase in federal funds for vocational training of young adults who have a prison record is predicted by 1965.

Seeman predicted that powerlessness would be related to more accurate recall of parole information, but not to the recall of less goal relevant types of knowledge. The results supported Seeman's hypothesis. Internals recalled more parole relevant information than externals $[r = -.23, p < .05]$ whereas incidental reformatory information $[r = -.16, n.s.]$ and long range opportunity information $[r = -.09, n.s.]$ were not significantly related to the powerlessness measure. Furthermore, when Seeman differentiated among inmates on the basis of conduct reports, for those who were more or less likely to be hoping for parole, the relationship between powerlessness and parole knowledge increased considerably $[r = -.40, p < .05]$.

Seeman's results led him to conclude that an individual's sense of powerlessness governs his attention and acquisition processes. Since Seeman reported his results, several investigators have published research findings that bear further upon the hypothesized relationship between locus of control and cognitive activity. In one such study, Davis and Phares (1967) gave subjects the task of influencing another person regarding his attitudes toward the Vietnam war. The subjects were led to believe that the experimenters had a file of data available about each individual who was to be the target of influence. The primary measure was the number of questions that each subject asked about the specific individual whom they were to influence.

The investigators anticipated that internals would generally seek more information than would externals, in order to improve their likelihood of being effective. In addition, they examined the effects of instructions given to the subjects: One group received "skill directions," which stressed ability as the major determinant of success; a second group received "luck directions," which emphasized the fortuitous combination of the personality characteristics of influencer and influencee as primary causal factors of influence success; a third group was given no specific instruction regarding the causes of success or failure at influence.

Internals asked more questions than externals when skill and no instructions were given, as may be noted in Figure 3. When the directions stressed luck as the causal factor, internals and externals did not differ from each other. However, it is notable that externals asked more and internals asked fewer questions in the chance condition than the equivalent groups in the skill and no instruction conditions.

These results would seem to indicate that internals are more likely to engage in the preliminary steps of data gathering than are externals, when information

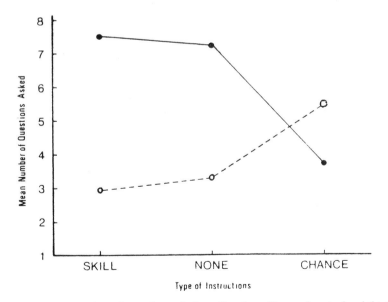

FIGURE 3   Mean number of questions asked as a function of locus of control and the type of instructions. (●) Internal; (o) external. (Adapted from Davis & Phares, 1967.)

seeking seems pertinent to outcome determination. In turn, such information seeking should increase the probability that internals will more often succeed in skill-demanding tasks than their external counterparts.

In another study reported by Phares (1968), internals and externals were compared in their use of information for decision making. All subjects learned 10 bits of information about each of four men until they were able to recall that information without error. A week later, the subjects were asked to guess which of eight girls, and which of ten occupations, were best suited to each of the four men. Financial rewards were offered for correct matchings, and subjects were asked to list their reasons for their matches. The criterion measure was the number of reasons provided for each match. Internals were found to give more reasons, more than 50% more, than externals. When only correct reasons were counted the difference increased dramatically: Internals gave more than three times as many correct reasons as externals for justifying their social and occupational matchings. These differences led Phares to conclude that internals make better use of information than externals despite the fact that both might have equivalent funds of information.

In the Seeman (1963) investigation, the information gathering superiority of internals was only found when the information in question was relevant to important goals such as the earning of parole. It is possible, then, that internals may recognize the relevance of information for goal attainment more quickly than do externals. In addition, it is possible that internals have a clearer sense of their own purposes and values than do externals, and are therefore more responsive to opportunities for fulfillment of those purposes. Parole, for example, is not always totally desired by reformatory inmates, especially if they foresee little chance to improve their fates outside the institution. Because externals can be assumed to be more doubtful than internals about their abilities to cope with daily life demands, it is more likely that externals would regard parole with some ambivalence and would therefore be less responsive to opportunities likely to facilitate parole.

McKinney (1975) has explored the relationship between locus of control and what he refers to as "value clarity" and "value relevance." Using the semantic differential, McKinney had his subjects evaluate positive and negative attitudes toward each of three realms—academic achievements, interpersonal morality, and general competence. The distance between a subject's positive evaluation of the positive attitude and his negative evaluation of the paired negative attitude was used as a measure of value clarity. Thus if the difference between the ratings of "making a good grade" and "flunking a test" were very great indicating that the good grade was rated as very good and flunking a test as very bad, it could be said that the subject clearly values achievement. In brief, McKinney found that internals had higher value clarity scores than externals across all three values realms $[F = 18.49, p < .01, 1/47]$. In a second study, McKinney found these data replicated $[F = 7.24, p < .01, 1/54]$ and with ratings for relevance also found internals to be more decisive than externals concerning the relevance of each attitude for themselves [$F = 5.69$, $p < .025$, 1/54].

It is possible, then, that the better assimilation and use of information by internals may reflect the fact that internals are more apt to recognize the pertinence of information for their purposes. In turn, this may be due to the fact that they are more certain of their purposes and values than are externals and are consequently more ready to perceive the opportunities that will facilitate value realization.

ATTENTION

Another cognitive function that has been examined in locus of control research is that of attention; that is, the ways in which individuals focus upon cues of relevance for goal attainments. Lefcourt and Wine (1969) observed subjects as they attended to another person with whom they were trying to become familiar. The subject's task was to interview two of the experimenter's assistants, with the object of finding out as much as possible about each of them. Ultimately they were to write personality descriptions of the assistants as part of a final examination for a personality course. One assistant behaved in an appropriately pleasant manner, engaged in eye contact and often smiled and exchanged pleasantries with the subject. The second assistant studiously avoided eye contact with the subject and behaved in a restrained aloof manner. It was hypothesized that the uncertainty caused by the behavior of the second assistant would arouse more curiosity and attentiveness among internal than among external subjects.

In Figure 4, the frequency of looking at the facial area of the students is plotted as a function of the assistant's behavior and the subject's locus of control. The curves illustrate that internals attended to the assistant's face more often than externals when the assistant behaved in the more puzzling avoidant fashion. Externals, on the other hand, looked somewhat more at the conventionally behaving assistant. These differences produced a significant interaction [$F = 6.13$, $p < .02$, 1/16], indicating that locus of control and the assistant's actions jointly affected the subject's looking behavior.

When the number of behavioral observations reported in final papers was counted, internals had made more observations than externals about both the conventional and puzzling assistants [$F = 4.33$, $p < .05$, 1/20]. Internals had recorded more observations [$M = 6.09$] of the quizzical than of the conventional [$M = 5.00$] assistants, though the differences were not significant. In addition, attention to the face of the quizzical assistant was positively related to the number of observations reported [$r = .68$, $p < .01$].

Lefcourt and Wine concluded that internal subjects were more likely to attend to cues that help resolve uncertainties. The more conventional assistant offered less challenge to subjects because he was predictable. The aloof assistant, by

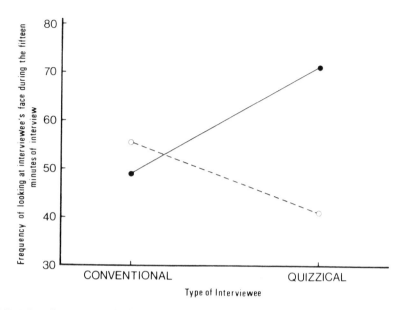

FIGURE 4 Frequency of looking at the interviewee's face as a function of locus of control and interviewee behavior. (●) Internal; (○) external. (Adapted from Lefcourt & Wine, 1969.)

contrast, behaved less predictably and thus created an interpretation challenge for the subject: Was the assistant inordinately shy? Was the subject repulsive to the assistant? Or, was this a contrived situation and a test of his own ability to draw out the assistant? Since the task at hand was to make sense of the assistant's verbal and nonverbal actions, the subject had to be vigilant if he was to be able to resolve the uncertainties that the aloof assistant aroused.

Three different studies beginning with one by Rotter and Mulry (1965) have indicated that internals devote more attention to decisions about skill-related matters than do externals. Rotter and Mulry used a very difficult matching task similar to those described in Chapter 3 (James, 1957; Phares, 1957). Half of the subjects were instructed that the perceptual acuity required of them for successful matching was a special skill; the other half were instructed that success was more a matter of chance. In the actual matching task, all subjects received the same sequence of 'rights' and 'wrongs.' The major findings from this study are illustrated in Figure 5, which makes it clear that internals spent more time deliberating about their decisions than did externals when the task was thought to be skill demanding.

Externals were somewhat more deliberate with chance directions, though this difference was not statistically significant. The major factor that produced the interaction [$F = 6.67$, $p < .025$, 1/116] was the increased length of time taken by internals to make decisions in the skill condition.

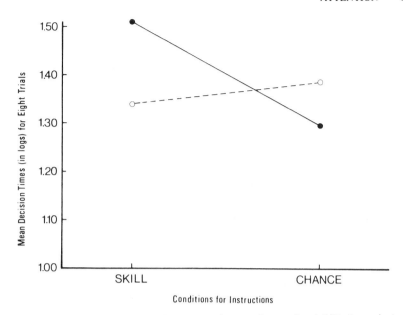

FIGURE 5   Mean decision times as a function of locus of control and skill–chance instructions. (●) Internal; (○) external. (Adapted from Rotter & Mulry, 1965.)

These results reflecting upon the different approaches by internal and external individuals to skill versus chance tasks has been replicated with some variation in other studies. Julian and Katz (1968) reported that internals required more time to make decisions as the difficulty of decision making increased. Externals did not vary as much with the difficulty level of the tasks, behaving as if there were no differences between simple and difficult choices. Another similar experiment (Lefcourt, Lewis & Silverman, 1968) essentially replicated the Rotter and Mulry study with some embellishments. These investigators used the Level of Aspiration Board, described previously, and tried to alter subjects' expectancies regarding the skill-chance nature of the task through instructions. Initially, no differences between internal and external subjects were obtained with respect to decision times. In retrospect, these investigators suspected that some of their subjects might have regarded the chance instructions as specious since the Level of Aspiration task obviously requires some skill. Therefore, subjects' written reports were examined to see whether they believed the instructions they had received. It was found that externals had accepted the experimenter's instructions more readily than had internals, especially when those directions had emphasized chance determination. Decision time data were then reanalyzed using the subjects' own judgments as to the skill and chance determination of the task outcomes. With subjects' perceptions used to form groupings the results obtained were as illustrated in Figure 6. On each observed characteristic, internals were

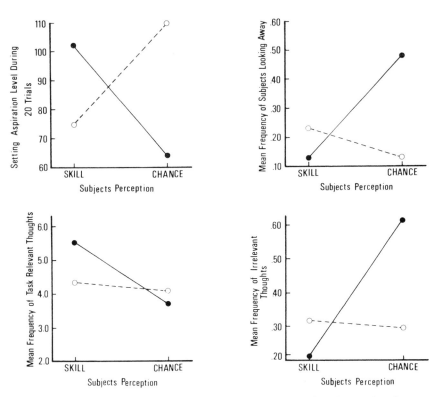

FIGURE 6   Decision times, inattentiveness, task relevant, and task irrelevant thoughts as a function of locus of control and skill versus chance perception of task. (●) Internal; (○) external. (Adapted from Lefcourt, Lewis, & Silverman, 1968.)

found to be more cognitively engaged when they perceived the Level of Aspiration Board as a skill-demanding task. Internals who perceived the task as skill determined spent more time in decision making, were less likely to allow their attention to wander from the task, and recalled having had more task relevant and less task irrelevant thoughts than did internals who believed that the task was chance-determined. The reverse tended to be true of externals, though it was only with regard to decision-making times that the magnitude of their change was sufficient to generate statistical significance.

In another study concerned with decision making, Wheeler and Davis (1978) asked students to help evaluate the acceptability of a potential new faculty member. When the candidate was seen as having many options, there were no differences in the decisiveness of judgments between internals and externals. However, when the candidate was seen as being in more "desperate straits," internals were more apt to report feeling uncertain and in need of more information than were externals. As an interesting footnote, though internals appear to be more cautious and uncertain in their decision making when choices are challenging or of some importance, Johnson and Kilmann (1975) report that, among male subjects at least, internals express greater confidence in their problem-solving abilities than do externals. Thus, the cautiousness exhibited by internals should not be used to infer insecurity or general hesitance. Rather, it may be due to their deliberate approach to decision making that internals come to feel more confident of their decisions.

In the aforementioned studies, then, internals were found to show considerably more variability than externals. Their attentiveness, concern, and interest changed with the types of situations in which they were engaged. If the task offered a challenge to competence or seemed to be important, then internals became more deliberate in their decision making during that task. Less skill-demanding tasks or less important decisions, on the other hand, elicited some carelessness and impulsivity from internals. Externals did not seem to draw such sharp distinctions about tasks as internals were wont to do. When task instructions did affect them, however, it was the more chance-determined tasks that elicited their greater attention and deliberation.

PSYCHOLOGICAL DIFFERENTIATION

Pursuing the concern with attention differences, Lefcourt and Siegel (1970a) examined the reaction time performances of internal and external subjects. Although no differences were obtained in reaction time performance as a function of locus of control, these investigators (Lefcourt & Siegel, 1970b) did find some success in predicting performance with a measure of field dependence: Field-independent subjects had shorter reaction times (greater attentiveness) with self as opposed to experimenter-controlled stimulus onset during the reaction time procedure. More important for the present purposes, however, was the reasoning for the use of the field dependence variable in this experiment. Witkin and his colleagues (Witkin, Dyk, Faterson, Goodenough, & Karp, 1962) have expanded upon their earlier research with perceptual field dependence, describing a concept referred to as psychological differentiation. They speak of differentiation and identity in such terms that the overlap with the locus of control construct is apparent:

> With respect to relations with the surrounding field, a high level of differentiation implies clear separation of what is identified as external to the self. The self is experienced as having definite limits or boundaries. Segregation of the self helps make possible greater determination of functioning from within, as opposed to a more or less enforced reliance on external nurturance and support for maintenance typical of the relatively undifferential state. [p. 10].

A relationship between I-E and differentiation, or at least a similar pattern of relationships for these variables with different criterion behaviors, could be anticipated on the basis of the apparent similarities between the locus of control and differentiation constructs.

Rotter (1966) had previously reported that no empirical relationship had been found between the I-E scale and the Gottschalk Figures Test (one measure of differentiation). Chance and Goldstein (1971), likewise, found a nonsignificant relationship between I-E and performance on the Embedded Figures Test. However, in the latter investigation, internals improved steadily from trial to trial as they progressed through the Embedded Figures Test.

Other investigators have also failed to find a relationship between locus of control and various measures of differentiation. Strahan and Huth (1975) found no relationships between factors in the I-E scale and the Group Embedded Figures Test. Likewise, Roodin, Broughton, and Vaught (1974), O'Leary, Donovan and Hague (1974), McIntire and Dryer (1973), and Nisbett and Temoshok (1976) found no relationships between embedded figures tests and I-E scores.

On the other hand, some positive relationships have been reported. Massari (1975) found a relationship [$r = .40$, $p < .05$] in one group out of four (third-grade girls) between interview measures of locus of control and differentiation. More decisive results have been reported by Crandall and Lacey (1972). Using the Intellectual Achievement Responsibility scale (IAR), these investigators found internality to be associated with embedded figures test performances for both sexes [$r = .51$ for males and .55 for females]. With Age and IQ partialled out, however, the magnitude of the relationship for males diminished to insignificance, though the correlation obtained with females remained robust [$r = .52$]. These authors argue that since performance on the embedded figures test requires close attention to stimulus cues, the sorting of relevant from irrelevant information, and the efficient use of information, the task can easily be seen as relevant to achievement. Therefore, they reasoned that the IAR may be the more appropriate locus of control measure for exploring relationships between locus of control and differentiation.

Since locus of control and differentiation measures have only occasionally been found to be related to one another and yet seem to be related to other criteria in similar ways, some investigators have attempted to use the variables conjointly. Deever (1968), and Lefcourt and Telegdi (1971) have each reported data suggesting that the two variables can produce interesting and complementary data. Although these investigators found no relationships between measures of differentiation and locus of control, they both reported evidence to the effect that the constructs are similar in predicting assertiveness, the experiencing of oneself as a distinct source of causation, and the tendency to be self-reliant rather than acquiescent and conforming. That these variables might prove complementary to each other in predicting such criteria received its first support in an honor's thesis supervised by this author. Bax (1966) found significant correlations between I–E and a TAT measure of differentiation [$r = .37$, $p < .001$, $N = 96$] and lack of assertiveness [$r = .35$, $p < .001$, $n = 96$] in the expected directions.

Deever (1968), found that high differentiation and internal control were related to a greater reliance upon one's own reinforcement history than on group norms for the prediction of performance. In this experiment, subjects had to state how sure they were of success for each trial in which they were to compare the length of two similar lines. The procedure was a typical level of aspiration task with two additional elements: Correctness feedback was rigged beforehand; and subjects were provided with norms of peer performance for each trial.

Both differentiation, as measured by the Embedded Figures Test, and locus of control, generated significant main effects. Internals and highly differentiated subjects expressed greater confidence of success and differed more from the provided norms than externals and less differentiated subjects. Despite similar relationships with the criterion measures, locus of control and differentiation were unrelated [$r = .02$].

Lefcourt and Telegdi (1971) used both locus of control and the rod and frame measurement of differentiation in an attempt to predict scores on measures reflecting cognitive activity. The dependent measures consisted of performance on Mednick's Remote Associates Test, Barron's Human Movement Threshold Inkblot Test, and an incomplete sentences test. As predicted, internal-highly differentiated subjects surpassed all other subjects on each measure. However, external-low differentiated subjects proved to be second, and the incongruent groups (internal-low differentiated, external-high differentiated) were the poorest on each measure. In this study, neither locus of control nor differentiation alone produced a significant main effect in the prediction of cognitive activity. Only in combination were significant results obtained.

More recently, Tobacyk, Broughton, and Vaught (1975) found support for the congruence findings of Lefcourt and Telegdi (1971). These investigators found that the more congruent subjects (Internal-field independent; external-field dependent) showed less discrepancy between ideal and real self Q sorts than did incongruent subjects (internal-field dependent, external-field independent). The greatest differences were obtained between field independent internals and field independent externals. These results were replicated in a study of the autokinetic effect. External-field independent subjects proved to be the most susceptible to the autokinetic effect, whereas internal-field independent subjects were the least apt to display the effect.

Bloomberg and Soneson (1976), also using the variables together, found that internal-field independent subjects had disproportionately higher scores on Kohlberg's moral judgment interview than subjects classified in each of the other three combinations. In the one other study that made use of both locus of control and differentiation, Erickson, Smyth, Donovan, and O'Leary (1976) found no "congruence effect" in the prediction of defensive styles and MMPI indices of psychopathology among a sample of alcoholics. However, as is often the case with alcoholics, the distribution obtained with I-E scores was markedly skewed [$M = 6.91$, $SD = 3.88$], a point that will be discussed in a later chapter. With scores so skewed toward the internal end of the dimension, it is quite likely that there were many false-internals in this study, leading one to question the representativeness of the results.

From the data that has been made available thus far, it is possible to conclude that locus of control and differentiation can be used conjointly to afford better predictions than either variable might do alone in certain circumstances. Although relatively independent, there may be more convergence when the locus of control scales used focus more upon achievement outcomes, a point that should be explored in future research.

SENSITIVITY

Throughout most of the research described above, evidence has been presented that supports the assumed relationship between locus of control and cognitive activity. Whether the focus has been on attention, deliberation, inquisitiveness, or utilization of information, internals have more often been found to be active and alert individuals than have externals. Sometimes the differences between internals and externals have varied with the ostensible qualities of the task or have occurred only in combination with other measures. Nevertheless, an internal locus of control seems to be a sine qua non of being able to steer oneself more clearly and appropriately through the vagaries and confusions of different situations.

One characteristic of internals that may contribute to this "self-steering" process is their assumed greater sensitivity to the meanings or reinforcement opportunities inherent in different tasks and situations. In the first of a series of studies, Lefcourt (1967) demonstrated that externals could behave like internals in achievement tasks if the experimenter made explicit reference to the meaning of the task in which the subjects were to be engaged. In this way, externals were directed toward the significance of their task performance, or in other words, were instructed as to what realm of reinforcements were to be experienced. Given such direction, externals performed in a more achievement-oriented fashion than their equivalents in uninstructed conditions. In contrast, the behavior of internals did not change with varying degrees of "cue explication." The tentative conclusion drawn from these results was that internals were more ready to perceive the challenges inherent in different situations and consequently had little need of directions that emphasized the meaning of those situations.

Subsequent studies have supported this contention. Lefcourt, Gronnerud, and McDonald (1973), for example, enlisted a sample of subjects for an experiment ostensibly concerned with verbal facility. The subjects were tested on a battery of

TABLE 1
Stimulus Words in the Double Entendre Word
Association List[a]

1 fly	11 light	21 sugar	31 measure	41 *HUMP*
2 face	12 work	22 *NUTS*	32 *BLOW*	42 *PET*
3 plant	13 *RUBBER*	23 cross	33 garden	43 *TOOL*
4 voice	14 health	24 *MAKE*	34 *COCK*	44 *SUCK*
5 earth	15 ocean	25 carpet	35 stove	45 *BANG*
6 miss	16 *BUST*	26 *CRACK*	36 *MOUNT*	46 *ASS*
7 door	17 fire	27 lamp	37 city	47 *BALLS*
8 alone	18 watch	28 *SCREW*	38 *QUEER*	48 *PUSSY*
9 good	19 *SNATCH*	29 paper	39 water	49 *BOX*
10 ride	20 drink	30 *PRICK*	40 *PIECE*	50 *LAY*

[a]Derived from Lefcourt, Gronnerud, & McDonald, 1973.

measures requiring different verbal skills. Last among these devices was an orally administered word association test during which subjects had to respond to a series of verbal stimuli with the first word that entered their minds. The list of stimulus words, however, was no ordinary list, but contained a gradually increasing number of sexual double entendres. As can be seen in Table 1, the list began innocently enough until Number 13, "rubber." Subsequently, every third stimulus word was another double entendre until Number 24. Afterward the number of double entendres increased until, at the end of the list, all words were sexual double entendres.

On completion of the previous verbal tests subjects were, no doubt, expecting more of the same—more predictable, almost-boring tests on the way to fulfilling their required stint as subjects. Beginning with the first double entendre, however, the seeds of doubt were planted. With the word "rubber," subjects were often bemused at their own private associations. Only rarely, however, were they apt to redefine the task at this point. But, after "bust," and then "snatch," the alert subject should have become suspicious, slowly concluding that the test was something other than what the experimenter had purported it to be. In short, where the initial covert associations were likely to be attributed to one's own predilections to think "dirty thoughts," the subjects should gradually have shifted their attribution of responsibility to the experimenter—"It's not me, but him. He's doing this deliberately for some undisclosed purpose."

While the test was being administered, the time that was required for the subject to respond was closely monitored. The latency of a response given to a stimulus word in word association tests has classically been used as a measure of conflict. If a subject entertains two competing responses and must choose between them, then the time taken to respond will be substantially longer than when he has only one potential response to give to a particular stimulus. In this experiment, the delay in response time was used to indicate that subjects were choosing between the responses relevant to each of the two meanings of the stimulus words.

Second, Lefcourt et al. (1973) had videotaped the facial and bodily movements made by subjects as they responded to the word list. These recorded data allowed for the observation of visible changes that indicated subjects were becoming aware of the "odd" nature of the stimulus list. These data were like the "light bulb effect" used in cartoons to show that a cartoon character has "seen the light."

In Figure 7, it is apparent that internal subjects were the first to show the predicted delay in response time. Internals exhibited excessive delays (greater than the 80th percentile of response times given to all nondouble entendre stimuli) between the second and third double entendres, on the average. On the other hand, the average external did not exhibit his first excessive delay until the fourth or fifth double entendre. As a further point of interest, it can be seen that external-field-dependent subjects, the hypothetically most external individuals, were the very last to exhibit an excessive delay. These results indicate that external-field-dependent subjects were the last to become aware of the response choice afforded by the double entendres, or required more instances to become as cognizant of the double meanings as the more internal subjects.

Most significant of the facial expressions recorded were those of smiles and laughter. As illustrated in Figure 8, internals smiled and laughed decidedly more often than did externals as the sexual content of the list increased. As the list progressed, then, internal subjects noticed the dissonant elements in the word list

FIGURE 7   The number of first double entendre to elicit excessive response time (> 80th percentile). (Adapted from Lefcourt, Gronnerud, & Mcdonald, 1973.)

FIGURE 8 Frequency of smiles and laughs during the presentation of first sixteen words. Adapted from Lefcourt, Gronnerud, & Mcdonald, 1973.)

more quickly than externals and were bemused at their discovery. Other evidence from this experiment included sex content of responses, startled looks, visible changes in attitude toward the experimenter, etc. Generally, the results supported the contention that internals would be quicker at noting changes in the conditions about them, and would be quicker to respond to their perceptions. In essence, internals were not as easily duped for as long a period as were externals, due to a greater readiness to recognize and cognitively come to terms with change.

Another investigation concerning perceptual sensitivity was reported by Wolk and DuCette (1974). Subjects were given the task of reading a story in which they were to search for typographical errors. After five minutes' exposure to the reading material, subjects were given a test that asked for recall of names, dates, incidents, and other salient aspects of the story. The subjects, then, were assessed for the intentionally perceived (typographical errors) as well as for incidentally perceived material (story content). When this test was completed, the subjects were given the original story again and told to memorize the dates contained in it. This provided a second measure of intentional learning. After five minutes, subjects were asked to recall the dates, and were also asked to remember the names contained in the story, a second measure of incidental learning.

Wolk and DuCette found that internals did consistently better than externals on both intentional and incidental learning measures. Internals found more typographical errors, recalled more story content, recalled more dates when instructed to and recalled more names when not directed to do so than did externals. In each case the differences were statistically significant.

Wolk and DuCette (1974) replicated these results in a second experiment in which they varied several aspects of the task directions. The results from both experiments allowed the investigators to conclude that internals are more "perceptually sensitive."

> Because the intentional task required a quick, efficient scanning strategy, it is suggested that basic, pre-attentive processes differentiate the internal from the external. . . . The more interesting aspect of these studies, of course, was the fact that internals demonstrated higher levels of incidental learning. Incidental learning is a phenomenon dependent on the acquisition of less prominent aspects of a stimulus array, and since such acquisition has been interpreted as the product of a more attentive and organizing system, it follows that the internal differs from the external in the manner in which he organizes and uses information [p. 98].

Another point of interest was made by Wolk and DuCette. When scores on intentional and incidental learning were correlated within the internal and external samples, the differences between groups were marked. Intentional and incidental learning were strongly related for internals [$r = .80$ and $.58$] but were weakly related for externals [$r = .09$ and $.06$] in the first study. In the second experiment, these findings were repeated, with internals exhibiting high magnitude correlations between the two types of learning [$r = .52$ and $.58$], whereas externals exhibited the same low magnitude relationships as previously [$r = -.11$ and $.20$].

When these researchers clearly instructed subjects that they should be attentive to the story content as well as to search for typographical errors, externals showed a positive relationship between intentional and incidental learning [$r = .45$ and $.58$]. Internals, on the other hand, showed no changes with the clarifying instructions. Wolk and DuCette (1974) concluded:

> If the external can be characterized as an individual who, relative to the internal, possesses less active perceptual cognitive processes . . . but who also fails to use these processes efficiently, then extremely low correlations between intentional and incidental performance are meaningful. Thus, under a condition of ambiguity (Study I and the low cue explication condition of Study II), the external deals with the components of the task as if they were discrete. This lack of continuity in the task is a function of the external's failure to structure stimuli effectively, as well as an inefficient allocation of attention during the task itself. Because of this lack of continuity, how the external does on one task has no relationship to how he performs on the other. However, when the task is further explicated, that is, when attention is directed toward the significance of the content of the story, making the task more integrated, the relationship between intentional and incidental perfor-

mance becomes extremely strong for the external and nonsignificantly different from that of the internal. Thus, it appears that the external does not make full use of his attentional system until stimuli are made more salient or prominent. For the internal, such an explication is redundant, since his strategy has been to deal with the task in a more organized fashion all along. It is suggested then, that the external, relative to the internal, possesses a less active perceptual-attentive system (there are still significant overall performance differences in incidental learning between internal and external Ss under the high-cue-explication conditions), but that the external also fails to use this system as efficiently as possible, especially under conditions of ambiguity [p. 99].

A number of other investigations have provided support for these earlier findings. Baron and Ganz (1972) and Baron, Cowan, Ganz, and McDonald (1974) found that "self-discovered" feedback during the performing of a task led to better performances by internals and worse by externals. When the experimenter offered verbal feedback during the task, on the other hand, externals improved, whereas internals performed worse than in the self-discovery condition. In both studies, socially mediated feedback seemed to help externals, a finding similar to that of the "cue explication" studies.

Taub and Dollinger (1975) and Dollinger and Taub (1977) explored the effects of providing purpose and/or extrinsic reinforcements in two studies. In both investigations, the description of the study as having relevance to pilots' decision making during flights led to improved coding scores by externals. In the earlier study, the subjects were also offered a small reward. Externals were found to perform better on the coding task with either provided purpose or reward, or the combination of both, than if they had neither. In complete contrast, internals didn't vary at all with each of the conditions. In addition, when subjects were asked to rate the task in the later study externals downgraded the task in the "no purpose" condition whereas internals did not differ between the no purpose and provided purpose conditions.

Gregory and Nelson (1978) likewise used an extrinsic reinforcement to facilitate performance on an angle-matching task. The decision times for this impossible task were the criteria of interest. Whereas internals failed to differ when offered a reward for performance, externals spent more time in deliberation when offered explicit reinforcement.

Gregory, Chartier, and Wright (1979) partially replicated the learned helplessness experiment by Hiroto (1974). In this adaptation of the earlier study, cues were provided that made it explicit whether there was a contingent or noncontingent relationship between subjects' responses and the termination of an aversive tone. When the contingencies were made explicit—that responses could lead to the escape from the aversive tone—externals improved in their performance; in contrast, internals showed no improvement in comparison to internals in the no-cue control groups. On the other hand, when explicit cues were provided that indicated a lack of contingency between response and termination of the tone, internals' subsequent performances deteriorated markedly. The results from these studies led Gregory et al. (1979) to suggest that externals could be helped to behave in more adaptive ways by the provision of explicit cues that inform them of the ramifications of their actions, a point that seems redundant for internals.

Finally, in a study by Stewart and Moore (1978), internals were found to ignore the incorrect cues provided by an experimenter while attempting to estimate the passage of a specific amount of time. Externals were more likely to respond to the experimenter's looking up from his stop watch and consequently made less accurate judgments than internals. The interaction between cue conditions and locus of control produced a very large effect [$F = 147$, $p < .001$, 1/42], suggesting the major impact that cues have for the more external subjects.

Each of these studies serve to reinforce the conclusions drawn from the early discussion of cue explication effects. Externals seem to require that a structure be offered before they are likely to perform in an adroit fashion. Internals, by contrast, seem to be searching for the meaning of the various situations and tasks in which they are engaged without being told to do so. Perhaps it may be fair to speak of perceptual styles when discussing locus of control and various performance criteria. Internals engage in their life tasks with curiosity as to the purposes and meanings of those tasks. Externals, although not bereft of desires for accomplishment, do not seem as likely to question the point of the demands made upon them and as a consequence may find less reason to participate with enthusiasm until they are instructed as to the potential value of a task.

OTHER COGNITIVE CHARACTERISTICS

In addition to alertness and sensitivity that seem to be correlates of locus of control, a number of investigations have been reported that reveal certain other propensities and cognitive skills associated with this dimension. For example, Dinardo and Raymond (1979) found that internals were better able than externals to exclude intrusive thoughts when attempting to meditate. Subjects were asked to focus upon either a real candle flame or an imagined one. Although the real flame was easier for everyone to focus on, avoiding all thought intrusions, it was particularly the more internal subjects who succeeded in avoiding intrusions in both conditions.

Such basic skills as concentration have also been examined in other studies, along with locus of control. Brecher and Denmark (1969) found that internals were more verbally fluent than externals, and Ludwigsen and Rollins (1971) found that internal children were better at recognizing random forms than were external children, particularly when they had invented their own names or labels for each form. With regard to information seeking, Williams and Stack (1972) and DuCette and Wolk (1973) have found further data that reveal that internals are quicker at extracting cues that facilitate the making of accurate judgments than are externals, and that internals are capable of better recall of performances and are more likely to make use of information for drawing estimates of their subsequent performances than are externals.

In addition, externals have been found to be more dogmatic, as measured by the Rokeach scales (Sherman, Pelletier, & Ryckman, 1973) and more likely to believe in supernatural (Randall & Desrosiers, 1980; Scheidt, 1973) and astrological like phenomena (Jorgenson, 1981) than are internals. Between these sorts of beliefs and the differences in skills noted above, externals would seem to be at a disadvantage when it becomes necessary to cope with demands requiring cognitive activity.

Finally, the tendency to use and display humor has been examined opposite locus of control. In one study (Lefcourt, Sordoni, & Sordoni, 1974) the humor responses noted briefly in an earlier report of that study (Lefcourt, Gronnerud, & McDonald, 1973) were explored in greater detail. Internals were found to have more readily come to terms with the uncertainty inherent in that experimental task, recognizing the discrepancies between the experimenter's stated purposes and actions earlier than externals, and then exhibiting that kind of humor (superiority) that implies a laughing down at one's self for having been deceived. This almost relaxed acceptance of shifting purposes was replicated in another experiment (Sordoni, 1979) wherein subjects suddenly encountered material indicating that they had been duped-being shown their own photograph within a group of other pictures of "reputed criminals" about whom subjects were registering impressions. Internals again responded in a more relaxed and mirthful manner when confronted with such dissonance than did externals. Perhaps more germane to the cognitive activity realm are the data in another study by Lefcourt, Antrobus, and Hogg (1974). In this study, internals were found to be more capable of producing humor, or of being witty than were externals, as they engaged in a series of role-playing interactions.

In each of these humor studies, internals were found to more rapidly assimilate the meaning of the ensuing events, and to accept those meanings with less rancor than were externals; and internals were more able to transform a state of uncertainty into one of humor. Externals, on the other hand, seemed to be less quick to come to terms with their experiences and, when grasping the changing demands, exhibited less reactive or productive humor and, at times, appeared dour and irked.

In much of the aforementioned research, then, internals seem to be more cognitively alert than externals. They are more ready to grasp for information that can contribute to the interpretation of and coping with various tasks and situations.

CONCLUSION

Our initial concern was to examine the processes that might allow an individual to resist pressures that could diminish his sense of responsibility. It was noted that internal control expectancies were associated with resistance to coercion, and an assertion was made that cognitive differences between internals and externals might account for differential responses to such pressures.

It would seem that the assumed differences in cognitive activity between internals and externals have been demonstrated. Internals have been found to be more perceptive to and ready to learn about their surroundings. They are more inquisitive; they are more curious and efficient processors of information than are externals.

Granted these differences, it may be asked whether an Eichmann or a Calley might have been more able to resist complying with horrendous requests had they been more able to think about the demands made upon them. Would Eichmann have so easily succumbed to his "Pontius Pilate" feeling had he been able to juxtapose his initial moral revulsion with the enthusiasm spurred on by competition with his fellow bureaucrats?

Our data suggest that a self-acknowledged pawn such as Eichmann lacks the very cognitive processes that would enable him to examine and evaluate his choices and decisions. Unable to scrutinize his own responses and decisions, he may fail to even see that he has choices available to him. Lacking the perception of choice, he will yield easily to external pressures, be they for good or evil.

6 Locus of Control and Achievement-Related Behavior

INTRODUCTION

In the preceding chapter it was concluded that certain cognitive activities were more characteristic of individuals with internal rather than external control orientations. One possible interpretation derivable from these findings is that locus of control is an epiphenomenon, a mere diagnostic indicator of a person's natural capacities for achievement; that is, the more intelligent and achieving a person is, the more likely he will perceive himself to be an active, effective person. The research described in this chapter fails to support a simplistic, one-to-one relationship between locus of control and achievement. As in most instances, when a topic is closely scrutinized, the observed relationships are found to be anything but simple and conclusive. Nevertheless, it will be apparent that locus of control plays a mediating role in determining whether persons become involved in the pursuit of achievement.

The link between locus of control and cognitive activity appeals to common sense. In like fashion, common sense suggests that a disbelief in the contingency between one's efforts and outcomes should preclude achievement striving. Without an expectation of internal control and without persistence despite imminent failure, the postponement of immediate pleasures and the organizing of one's time and efforts would be unlikely. Common sense would dictate that these characteristics, essential to any prolonged achievement effort, will occur only among individuals who believe that they can, through their own efforts, accomplish desired goals. Individuals must entertain some hope that their efforts can be effective before they can make the sacrifices that are prerequisites for achievement.

The most commonly observed achievement activity occurs within school settings. Scholastic achievement requires that a youngster persist at activities such as reading when his immediate inclinations might be to play, daydream, or to socialize with his friends. The promise of future satisfactions to be derived from achievement effort is not always obvious. At the same time, daily activities, which may consist of repetitive practice, are often not very enjoyable and may interfere with a more pleasuresome activity. Schools, then, like other situations that offer the opportunity for achievement, require a degree of self-management, conscious effort, and the sacrifice of immediate pleasures for the possibility of future goal attainments. As noted above, such sacrifice is improbable if a person entertains doubts about his own potential effectiveness.

Until recently, failure in scholastic achievement was most commonly attributed to a low level of intelligence and success to a high level. In the 1950s, however, an interest developed in the motivation for achievement spurred on by the research of David McClelland and his colleagues (McClelland, Atkinson, Clark, & Lowell, 1953). The impact of this research was to alert psychologists to the importance of variables other than those assessed by intelligence tests for the prediction of achievement activity. In addition, it helped define the components of achievement activity itself so that achievement became less singly identified with course grades.

It was not until the 1960s, however, that personality characteristics relevant to scholastic success began to receive extensive attention. With the rise of "Black Power" and other sundry "power groups," the public began to become aware that various ethnic, racial, and cultural groups differed considerably in their perceptions of many social institutions.

For some, schools had always seemed to be a channel to opportunity, and the sacrifices required for schooling were deemed worthwhile. For others, schooling seemed to lead nowhere and served little function other than that of a detention center. For the latter, the self-control and discipline demanded in school seemed oppressive and self-destructive. Among persons holding such views, achievement in school would be unlikely. In fact, slum-dwelling blacks who find the schools to be remote, repressive, middle-class institutions, usually score at least one standard deviation below white averages on tests of intelligence and achievement.

The Coleman report (Coleman, Campbell, Hobson, McPartland, Mood, Weinfeld, & York, 1966) directed further public attention to the personality characteristics among the disadvantaged that limit their potential for achievement. Of immediate importance were the findings concerned with expectancies for control. Coleman and his colleagues found that, among nonwhite children, achievement was best predicted by a measure of the child's belief that academic outcomes were determinable by his own efforts. Pettigrew (1967) summarized the relevant findings from the Coleman report as follows:

Student attitude variables are surprisingly strong independent correlates of performance for all groups of children, though different attitude measures predict white and Negro achievement. An "academic self-concept" variable—measured by such items as "How bright do you think you are in comparison with the other students in your grade?"—proves more significant for white performance. But a measure of "fate control" or "control of the environment"—indicated, for example, by disagreeing that "good luck is more important than hard work for success"—is much more important for Negro performance.   Having experienced an unresponsive environment, the virtues of hard work, or diligent and extended effort toward achievement, appear to such a [minority] child unlikely to be rewarding. As a consequence, he is likely to merely "adjust" to his environment, finding satisfaction in passive pursuits. It may well be, then, that one of the keys toward success for minorities which have experienced disadvantage and a particularly unresponsive environment—either in the home or the larger society—is a change in this conception [pp. 283–284].

In a later volume, Coleman (1971) himself reflected upon his findings with the sense of control:

The importance of attitudes such as this is the effect such an orientation toward the environment can have on other resources, by creating an active, driving stance toward the environment rather than a passive one. Suggestive evidence of its importance is provided by a striking result: those 9th-grade Negroes who gave the "hard work" response scored higher on the verbal achievement test, both in the North and South, than those whites who gave the "good luck" response, even though . . . the average Negro scored from 2.7 to 3.8 years (in different regions) behind northern urban whites and nearly as far behind whites from other regions. Although it is not possible to separate cause and effect by use of these data, this result does suggest an enormous potential impact of such an orientation in the creation of other resources. [p. 28].

These data and theoretical discussions are not without precedent; the problems had previously been diagnosed in similar terms and then ignored. Arnold Rose (1948), in a condensed version of Gunnar Myrdal's *The American Dilemma* (1944), wrote:

The ambition of the Negro Youth is cramped not only by the severe restrictions placed in the way by segregation and discrimination but also by the low expectation from both White and Negro society. He is not expected to make good in the same way as the white youth. And if he is not extraordinary he will not expect it of himself and will not really put his shoulder to the wheel [p. 218].

In a later section of his book, Rose commented upon the sense of futility felt by blacks in regard to their striving for valued goals, and the resultant antisocial or lethargic stance with which they met life's challenges:

Negroes know that all the striving they may do cannot carry them very high anyway. They often feel, "Oh, you might as well make the most of it; what the hell
difference does it make?" In this spirit, life becomes cheap and crime not so bad.
Thus both the lack of a strong cultural tradition and the caste-fostered trait of
cynical bitterness combine to make the Negro less inhibited in a way which may be
dangerous to his fellows. They also make him more lazy, less punctual, less
careful, and generally less efficient as a functioning member of society[p.302].

Rose, Myrdal, and others (see Chapter 2) have initimated that the sense of
personal control is an important determinant of achievement-oriented behavior.
In the next section of this chapter, the empirical relationships between achievement activities and the locus of control will be explored through a review of
relevant investigations.

ACADEMIC PERFORMANCE

The first investigation to implicate locus of control in the literature concerned
with achievement-related behavior was reported by the late Vaughn Crandall and
his colleagues at the Fel's Research Institute (Crandall, Katkovsky, & Preston,
1962). These investigators used a number of personality measures in the hope of
predicting achievement behaviors as they were reflected in free-play activities,
the Stanford-Binet Intelligence Test, and the California Achievement Tests. The
predictor measures included a TAT measure of need for achievement, a scale for
assessing manifest anxiety, the child's own statement regarding concern for intellectual attainment, expectations of intellectual success, intellectual achievement standards (the child's own definition of success), and the first form of the
Intellectual Achievement Responsibility Questionnaire (IAR). The latter (see
Appendix) was comprised of 36 items, half concerned with successes and half
with failures in the realm of achievement. Children had to choose whether the
success or failure experiences described in each item would be primarily the
results of their own behaviors or would more likely be caused by external agents
such as parents or teachers.

Two free-play measures of achievement were based on the child's activity
during a week's day camp at the Fel's Institute. The main playroom was stocked
with miscellaneous play materials and equipment conducive to achievement activity. Each child was free to play with whatever he chose. Examples of intellectual and achievement materials were books pertaining to scientific and other
informational topics, games involving intellectual competition such as checkers,
chess, Chinese checkers, jigsaw puzzles, form-boards, arithmetic and reading
flash cards, and a variety of intellectual quiz games.

Observers time-sampled the children's playroom activity, recording both the
amount of time spent in intellectual activities during 15 observation periods, and

the intensity of striving in these activities. The latter was defined in terms of the degree of concentration that the child exhibited, ranging from "playing around" to strong concentration with the use of observable personal achievement standards.

Of all the measures employed by Crandall et al. (1962), the IAR proved to be the most strongly related to the time spent in intellectual free-play activities [r = .70, p < .05] and to the intensity of striving in those activities [r = .66, p < .05] among the boys. For the girls, on the other hand, the rs were .01 and .00 respectively. In other words, for boys, the attribution of responsibility was of considerable importance for predicting achievement activity, whereas for girls it was totally irrelevant. Personal value for intellectual attainment was the only significant correlate of free-play achievement activity for girls.

When performance on intelligence and achievement tests was correlated with the predictor variables, a similar pattern of results was obtained. The IAR was significantly related to each test for the boys [r = .52, p < .05 with intelligence: r = .51, p < .05 with reading achievement; r = .38, p < .05 with arithmetic achievements], but totally unrelated for girls [r = .00; r = −.13, respectively]. With regard to the achievement test results, these correlations are of signal interest in view of the fact that none of the other achievement-related variables (need-achievement, anxiety, value for intellectual achievement, etc.) were significantly related to achievement tests for the sample of boys.

These findings have been replicated, but with some differing results (Chance, 1965). With the same tests (Stanford-Binet, California Achievement Tests, and the IAR) Chance found a similar pattern of correlations among third-grade boys [r = .34, p < .01 for intelligence; r = .50, p < .01 for reading achievement; r = .46, p < .01 for arithmetic achievement; and r = .56, p < .01 for spelling]. However, where Crandall et al. (1962) had found the IAR questionnaire to be unrelated to achievement among girls, Chance (1965) found rs = .34, .45, .51 and .38 between IAR and each of the respective achievement variables. These correlations were all significant at the p < .01 level except for the first, which was significant at the .05 level.

In a later study conducted by the Fel's group (Crandall, Katkovsky, & Crandall, 1965), further data were presented regarding the IAR-achievement behavior correlations. Among third-, fourth-, and fifth-grade boys and girls, the IAR was found to be significantly related to reading, math, language, and total achievement test scores from the Iowa Tests of Basic Skills. In addition, report card grades for this sample were associated with the IAR.

The IAR, as may be seen in the Appendix, contains two sets of questions. Half pertain to attributions of responsibility for success (I+) and half to attributions for failure (I−). The total IAR score noted above is a composite of internal attributions for both success and failure. When Crandall et al. (1965) evaluated I+ and I− separately with the achievement measures, the results were a bit perplexing and inconsistent. All achievement test measures and report card grades were highly related to I+ [rs ranging between .40 and .60] "indicating that the greater the young girls' [grades three and four] sense of responsibility for her academic success, the more successful she is likely to be [p. 10]." Scores for attributions of responsibility for failure, on the other hand, were significantly correlated with the nine measures for fifth-grade boys with rs ranging from .34 to .53. To make matters more confusing, in grades 6, 8, 10, and 12, scores on the California Achievement Tests were only occasionally related to IAR scores, though significant relationships between report card grades and total IAR scores did obtain in these upper grades. A ninth-grade sample, on the other hand, produced results similar to the first study by Crandall, Katkovsky, and Preston (1962). Achievement test results for reading, language, and arithmetic were related to I+ scores for boys [rs in the .50s] but not for girls.

Thus, what seemed to be a simple set of predicted relationships is obviously beset by unpredictable variability. Girls and boys differ in characteristics that were assumed to be related to achievement. Age or grade level makes a difference, and we are now introduced to the concept of locus of control as a less pervasive or general characteristic—one that may be usefully divided into components such as responsibility attribution for success versus failure experiences.

Other investigations have borne out the fact that achievement activity is associated with locus of control, though not consistently and not without occasional paradox. Franklin (1963) found internality related to the amount of time that high school students spend in doing homework; James (1965) reported that internals were more persistent in their attempts to solve complex logical puzzles, and the Fel's investigators (McGhee & Crandall, 1968) have found replication of their previous findings: Report card grades of both boys and girls were associated with locus of control in samples of children in grades 6 through 12, and scores on the Iowa Achievement test favored internal children in the third through fifth grades with some variability between sexes and the I+ and I− measures.

In a study using large samples of eighth- and eleventh-graders from the Chicago schools, Lessing (1969) found that the Sense of Personal Control, as assessed by Strodtbeck's Personal Control Scale (Strodtbeck, 1958), was correlated with grade point averages even when IQ scores had been statistically partialled out; that is, among both the more and less intelligent pupils, a sense of personal control was related to actual school achievement. Harrison (1968) likewise found that a sense of personal control allowed for some prediction of success in school regardless of the socioeconomic status of the children's homes; that is, an internal orientation as measured by Harrison's own "View of the Environment Test" predicted academic success among both advantaged and disadvantaged children. This result, as well as that reported by Lessing (1969), indicate the strength of the association between the sense of control and achievement behavior. Intelligence test performance and socioeconomic status have a reliable and robust relationship with achievement criteria. That a sense of control, measured by different devices, can add to the already high magnitude relationships between socioeconomic class, IQ, and achievement behavior, attests to the value of locus of control in formulas devised to predict achievement behavior.

Nevertheless as the studies noted above and others reveal (Katz, 1967; Nowicki & Roundtree, 1971; Stephens, 1973), the relationships between various measures of locus of control and achievement behaviors are often riddled with inconsistent, and, as Stephens puts it, "weird" results.

Bar-Tal and Bar-Zohar (1977) have organized a tally sheet revealing the number of studies that have affirmed the locus of control-achievement relationship. Among the 36 investigations that they reviewed, only one study had reported a negative relationship between locus of control and achievement, and four had reported no significant relationships. The one negative finding (Massari & Rosenblum, 1972) was obtained from female college students whose grades in a psychology course were associated with externality on Rotter's I–E scale [$r = .27$, $p < .10$] and externality on the attribution-for-success subscale from the IAR [$r = -.39$, $p < .01$ with I+].

On the other hand, 31 investigators reported finding positive relationships between locus of conrol and achievement. Some investigators such as Messer (1972) have found support for the simple generality that an internal locus of control (IAR scale) is associated with higher grades and achievement test scores even when IQ and cognitive impulsivity are controlled. More interesting was Messer's finding that boys who assumed responsibility for success (I+) and girls who assumed responsibility for failure (I−) were *the* most likely to have obtained higher grades and achievement test scores. A contrary finding, however, was reported by Little and Kendall (1978). With a sample of 45 juvenile delinquents, locus of control (assessed by the Nowicki-Strickland I–E scale—NOSIE) was found to be unrelated to seven measures of academic achievement when IQ was partialled out. However, the very wide range of IQ scores in this sample indicate that it was not the representative sort of sample from which one would wish to draw general inferences about the predictive power of locus of control. Little and Kendall (1978) rightfully contended that locus of control may not be appropriate for predicting achievement among such deviant samples as theirs.

The sex-linked difference noted by Messer (1972) has been reflected in others' work pertaining to locus of control and achievement. Nowicki (1973) and Duke, and Nowicki (1974), for instance, have found that externality, as assessed by the ANSIE (Nowicki-Strickland I–E scale for adults), was associated with achievement for females [$r = .39$, $p < .05$, $N = 26$] as defined by grade point average but internality was related to like achievement for males [$r = -.50$, $p < .02$, $N = 22$]. Subsequently, replication of these data were found in two other samples of college students with rs = .63, $p < .01$, $df = 38$ and .42, $p < .05$, $df = 26$ for females and rs = −.48, $p < .01$, $df = 36$ and −.42, $p < .05$, $df = 24$ males. These findings were interpreted in terms of an assumed fear of success among females.

Consequently, it can be concluded that the verbal expression of perceived causality has different meaning for males and females, at least insofar as scores on current assessment devices are concerned. To further substantiate and add to the confusion regarding sex-related achievement differences, Wolfgang and Potvin (1973) reported that Rotter's I–E scale affords some prediction of classroom participation and academic performance among female elementary school pupils, but not of their male equivalents. However, in this study it was the more *internal* female who had higher average grades and was more likely to be a high classroom participator than was the more external female. In contrast, locus of control was not associated with either achievement criterion for males. These results, although confirming the relevance of sex differences, also reveal the considerable confusion in this area. Different scales used in each study may account for some of the reversals reported. However, the paradoxical findings between sex, locus of control, and achievement behavior seem to be of such perplexity that it will require considerably more theoretical attention toward such issues as socialization of the sexes than it will continued empirical demonstrations to bring some sense of order to this seeming chaos. Nowicki's (1973) own discussion of his results begins this very endeavor with discussions of such concepts as the fear of success among females.

Other investigators have found quizzical sex differences in this realm of research, though not as paradoxical as the above. Gordon (1977), for example, found that among male children, locus of control was related to grade point average but not to achievement test scores. For females, locus of control was associated with achievement test performance but not with grade point average. In both cases, it was the more internal child who outperformed the external child. These results can also be interpreted in terms of female's fear of success in that grade point average is a reflection of much public activity that is relevant to sex role prescriptions. Performance on achievement tests, on the other hand, is private and singular and should therefore be less subject to the strain toward conformity with sex role demands. Consequently, it is possible that for females, grade point average is a more conflict-ridden index of achievement activity than is achievement test performance.

Some support for these conjectures can be derived from studies by Nowicki and Duke (1978) and Nowicki (1981). Using digit symbol performance as an indication of achievement, these investigators encouraged their university student subjects to improve upon their previous performances for different reasons. In one group the reasons given for improving were essentially competitive, with opponents being male or female. In another group, the reasons given were cooperative ones—that is, subjects' scores were to be added to those of their partners to be used in competition against other pairs of subjects; again, half the subjects had female partners, half had male partners. Internal males were found to improve markedly in both cooperative and competitive conditions regardless of the sex of their partner or opponent. Among females, improvement was notable only when they were asked to cooperate with other females and not with males. The most interesting finding, however, which was replicated in a second study, was that only internal females improved when competing with males. External females seemed unwilling or unable to increase their achievement behaviors when asked to compete with male peers. Thus, it would seem that external females, at least, find the demands of sex roles to be inhibiting of assertive, achievant behavior. Because beliefs in internal control may be thought of as stereotypically masculine, many females may be responding to locus of control scales in accord with feminine role expectations. If such were the case then the inhibition of competitive behavior with males might be viewed as a correlated role enactment, one that could be seen as damaging to potential achievement behavior in coed classrooms.

Not all investigators have found marked sex differences in the achievement area. Rupp and Nowicki (1978), with a rather large sample ($N = 469$ Hungarian children between the ages of 10 and 14) found high magnitude relationships between grade point average and grades in selected courses with the children's Nowicki-Strickland I–E Scale (CNSIE). Internal children were the higher achievers and, among females, teachers' ratings of maturity were associated with internality. Likewise, Reimanis (1973) found the IAR to be associated with teacher's ratings of achievement in a series of classrooms though with some variability; and Bar-Tal, Kfir, Bar-Zohar, & Chen (1980) found that internal high school students attained higher academic achievement and had higher levels of aspiration than their external peers. Even with socioeconomic status partialled out, locus of control remained correlated with standardized achievement test scores.

In recent years there has been a growing trend toward the use of interactionist models. Instead of asking whether internals are more apt to perform competently on achievement tasks than externals, questions have been refined somewhat so that investigators are beginning to ask when and under what conditions locus of control is likely to afford valuable predictions. With regard to achievement, one of the first of such studies was presented by Wright and DuCette (1976). These investigators compared the predictive value of locus of control measures in "open" versus "traditional" classrooms. Using the IAR, Wright and DuCette found that locus of control predicted both Scholastic Aptitude Tests scores (SAT) and course grades in the "open" classrooms where self-direction and participation were at a premium. In the more traditional elementary school classrooms, on the other hand, these relationships were found to be negligble. Two other investigations have revealed similar findings. Arlin (1975) found that among 419 upper grade elementary school pupils internals generally reported higher feelings of satisfaction with their schooling than did externals, but that in an "open" school setting this difference was most marked. In the more traditional setting, the differences in rated satisfaction and attitudes toward teachers paled to insignificance. As a side note, all of the teachers in Arlin's study had been rated as excellent by both their principals and supervisors. Thus, the rated satisfaction of pupils in this study can be said to be truly meaningful. Parent, Forward, Canter, & Mohling (1975) have found similar results in a study concerned with the teaching of computer programming. In this study, 54 college students were assigned to high versus low discipline conditions. Discipline in this study indicated external structuring so that in the low discipline condition more self-paced learning was likely to occur. Interactions were found between conditions and Rotter's I–E scale in the prediction of performance and satisfaction. Externals performed and enjoyed the high discipline more than they did the low discipline condition. Internals did not vary as much with conditions but performed slightly better with the low discipline condition.

Most recently, Harpin and Sandler (1979) and Harpin (1980) have explored the interactions between locus of control and teacher control in some detail. In the earlier of the two studies, classrooms were classified as high or low in perceived control via the Classroom Environment Scale (Moos & Trickett, 1974), and subjects were classified via the IAR, in the hope of predicting achievement behavior and adjustment problems. For males, Teacher control and IAR produced significant interactions. External males had more adjustment problems in low than in high control classrooms. In contrast, the results for females were not interactive. Female internals were seen by their teachers as having fewer behavior problems in all classrooms, though external females received higher grades in both high and low control classrooms than did internals.

In the second study (Harpin, 1980), classrooms were again classified by the Classroom Environment Scale, students by the IAR, and a relevance of control measure. In the latter, these seventh- to ninth-grade children were asked how much it mattered to them whether teachers exercized control and determined the structure of their classrooms. A large number of dependent measures were collected that assessed competence (grades, behavior ratings of frustration tolerance, compliance with rules, adaptive assertiveness, originality in school work, verbal involvement in class, establishment of a positive relationship with the teacher, etc.) as well as maladjustment in the classroom, school anxiety, and self-esteem.

The results from this rather exhaustive study indicated that for internals who regarded the classroom control as relevant for their behavior, better adjustment, performance, and competence was found in classrooms rated low than in those rated high in control. Among externals, by contrast, the relevance variable did not help to produce significant interaction effects; high relevance externals did not differ with the structure of their classrooms. Most important is the fact that, for subjects who rated the relevance of classroom structure as low, no findings emerged for classroom environment. In essence, subjects were able to forecast whether or not the structure of their classrooms was going to affect their school-related behavior with considerable accuracy.

In two other studies, a variable was used that bears some resemblance to Harpin's "relevance" variable. Batlis and Waters (1973) and Batlis (1978) used locus of control scores as a moderator variable while examining the relationship between perceived instrumentality and performance outcomes. University student subjects were questioned regarding the relationship between getting an A on a course examination and 12 given outcomes. Those who indicated that the grade was related to valued outcomes were said to be high in instrumentality. Subsequently, instrumentality scores were correlated with performance criteria for internals and externals. In the first study (Batlis & Waters, 1973), subjects who scored highest on Resultant Achievement Motivation and were internal exhibited the highest magnitude relationship between instrumentality and course exam grades. In the second study (Batlis, 1978), the relationship between instrumentality and performance produced an $r = .63$, $p < .01$ among internals, and an $r = .18$, ns among externals. The difference between these correlations was significant.

In both the Harpin and Batlis studies, locus of control was used in a more interactive design. These studies included the specific expectancy variable labeled as relevance in one and instrumentality in the other. These variables provided for the subjects' assessment of one specific attribute in the study—the relevance of an independent variable in the Harpin study, and the meaning of the dependent measure in the Batlis studies. The use of locus of control as a moderator of the specific expectancy-outcome relationship suggests that the cognitive assessments of internals may be more veridical or functional than those of externals. The statements of the externals may be more reflective of wishes or normative responses than they are of actual beliefs or values.

The achievement behavior of adults has been observed in a few other studies of note. Most interesting for those concerned with graduate student accomplishment, Otten (1977), in a five-year outcome study, found that a combination of Rotter's I–E Scale and an autobiography measure of locus of control allowed for some prediction of student progress in graduate work. Internals were more likely to have obtained their PhDs in five years, or to have dropped out, than were externals. Externals, on the other hand, were more likely to be still working toward their degrees after five years or had received terminal MA degrees. Six out of 15 internal graduate students had received their PhDs within 5 years, whereas none of the externals had.

In another study with graduate students Nord, Connelly, and Daignault (1974) found that locus of control and aptitude measures allowed for some prediction of grades in courses at a graduate school of business. Even with aptitude partialled out, this relationship remained significant. Finally, Prociuk and Breen (1975) reported being able to predict undergraduates' grade point averages making use of Levenson's three-factor locus of control scale (Levenson, 1973a). These investigators interpreted Levenson's three factors into terms that reflect upon the veridicality of subject's self-descriptions. Subjects whose highest scores were on the ''Internal Control'' factor were regarded as true internals. Those whose highest scores were on the ''Powerful Others'' factor (who attributed outcomes to powerful others) were said to be defensive externals—those who attribute cause to others as a means of avoiding responsibility for failure; and those whose scores were highest on the "chance" factor were referred to as true externals. Prociuk and Breen (1975) hypothesized that true internals would prove to be the most achievant of their student sample but that defensive externals would be considerably more achievant than true externals. Their results supported these contentions and they concluded that the ambiguities and problems in predicting achievement behavior from locus of control measures could be reduced by making use of devices for differentiating between true and defensive externals.

More molecular approaches to the area of achievement have revealed some further support for results reported earlier. Gozali, Cleary, Walster, & Gozali (1973), for example, have replicated the findings of Julian and Katz (1968) that pertain to the tendency for internals to require more time before answering difficult than easy problems. Externals, on the other hand, were found to vary less with item difficulty, thus showing lesser adaptability to task demands than internals. Gozali et al. (1973) suggest, then, that such differences in the appropriateness of responding may be the kind of mediating link that can help to account for relationships between locus of control and achievement.

One other study (Karabenick, 1972) has immediate relevance for the achievement area. Karabenick plotted out curves for the valence of failures and successes against varying probabilities of success among subjects classified according to their locus of control scores. Each subject was asked, in effect, how much satisfaction he attained from success and how much dissatisfaction resulted from failures on given tasks (anagrams and substitution tests) with designated difficulty levels. These data revealed some interesting results with regard to locus of control. When the tasks were construed as being very difficult, internals were found to value success more than did externals, whereas the reverse was the case for assumedly easy tasks. Similarly, the dissatisfaction resulting from failure was greater for internals than for externals when the task was thought to be easy, whereas externals seemed to be more discontent with failure experiences than internals when the task was perceived as being difficult. The affective responses of internals, then, were more in accord with what might be expected from realistic, goal-directed, achievement-oriented individuals. On the other hand, the affective responses of externals betray a lesser confidence in their goal pursuits reminiscent of what were referred to as avoidant or irreal responses in the level of aspiration literature. To strongly regret failure at difficult tasks and to be too joyous in response to success at simple tasks suggests an individual with little awareness of or faith in his own potentialities.

DEFERRED GRATIFICATION

As in the case of achievement tasks, locus of control is often relevant to the willingness to defer gratification, though not always in a consistent and comprehensible way. It is plausible to assume that internals are more accustomed than externals to engaging in the execution of long-range plans. The very process of planning and working for distant goals would only seem to be sufferable if the individual believed that he was able to determine the results of his efforts. Externals, by definition, find the paths from initiation to completion fraught with uncertainty. Why should externals postpone immediately available pleasures for distant goals when daily events occur by some nonpredictable design?

Distant goals require the sacrifice of immediate pleasures. As a writer struggles to express his ideas on paper, the warm sunshine of an Indian summer day can act as a seducer, pulling him away from a long and possibly fruitless enterprise. Throughout a morning's work he may find himself beleaguered with ambivalence—angered at his self-inflicted deprivation and yet pleased at being able to control himself during the continuation of long-range activity. On other days, the weather and scenery might not be as tempting and competitive. Throughout any long-range endeavors, however, such as research activity or book writing, temptations inevitably recur. To maintain the pursuit of distant goals despite temptation seems to require a faith in the reliability of one's perceived world. A disbelief in the predictability of daily events should hinder one in long-range activities and, most clearly, if a person were an unpredictable commodity to himself he would never embark on lengthy drawn out enterprises. In short, to keep himself pressing on to the completion of a long-range project, a person must feel relatively secure in his world. He can not feel as if uncertainty stalks his every move. He must know with some level of assuredness that he is reliable and capable of bringing off his project. Otherwise, the tempting sirens of daily pleasure would be all too compelling. If tomorrow brings us possible calamity, why deny oneself today's small offerings of pleasure. Long-range efforts become absurd if we know that we will be encountering daily uncertainty.

Empirically, the first support for this assumed connection between locus of control and the ability to defer gratification was reported by Bialer (1961). This investigator offered a series of choices to a sample of children. The first involved a choice among improbable wishes—"Which would you rather have, the best kind of automobile right now—and you'd have a driver's license and know how to drive it too—or have the automobile and a million dollars a year from now?" The choice of the "automobile now" resulted in a score of 0, the delayed choice, a score of 1. The second choice was between a single piece of candy now, or four pieces on the following day. The former choice resulted in a 0 score, the latter, a score of 2. Third, the subjects were offered a choice between a penny now, and ten pennies on the following day. If the child opted for the single penny he received a 0. If the child selected the 10 pennies delayed choice, he was then given a further option of 5 pennies now or 10 tomorrow. If the child initially chose the 10 pennies versus the one, he received an additional 2 points. If he subsequently elected to take the 5 pennies, he was given no further credit. If, on the other hand, he chose to delay again, selecting the 10 pennies, he received an additional 2 points. In total then, the child could receive scores between 0 and 7.

With his own locus of control scale (see Appendix), Bialer found that deferred gratification was associated with an internal locus of control [$r = .47$, $p < .001$, $N = 89$]. As Bialer had suggested when offering his hypothesis, internals seemed to be better able to maintain the tension associated with delays than externals. "The more mature child, aware that his own efforts can forestall failure, and being able to maintain the tension generated by the postponement of immediate need satisfaction, should therefore choose to defer his gratification [p.306]."

Although this investigation offers some support regarding locus of control and the ability to defer gratification, it differs sufficiently from the previous discussion to warrant attention. In the Bialer study, the delay was just between "now" and "tomorrow." No effort or persistence at a difficult and frustrating task was required. The choices presented to the children were certain and were not contingent upon specific efforts. On the other hand, Bialer's procedures and those circumstances confronting a person engaged in long-range pursuits offer similar challenge to one's ability to overcome the tensions experienced in rejecting seductive diversions. The immediate small pleasure is tempting, a hurdle over which one must pass if he is to achieve larger goals. To ignore an immediate prize for more enticing prizes later involves the ability to resist temptations, and to not feel excessive arousal at being denied immediate pleasures. It is this resistance to temptation that is common to the simple task of tolerating a delay of pleasure and the more complex persistence in the service of long-range goals.

The commonly employed technique of offering youngsters either a small prize immediately or a larger gift to be delivered at a later date was developed by Alvin Mahrer (1956) and used in an extensive set of investigations by Walter Mischel (1966). Although much of the research with delay of reinforcements has involved simple waiting, as in Bialer's study, some of Mischel's research has examined delayed reinforcement choices when effort and work are required.

Mischel, Zeiss, & Zeiss (1974) presented findings from a series of investigations in which they made rather precise predictions of persistence with their own Stanford Preschool Internal-External Scale (SPIES—see Appendix). The SPIES, like the IAR, is composed of two measures: the perception of negative outcomes and the perception of control over positive outcomes. In this study, Mischel et al. (1974) predicted that internality for success experiences would be associated with persistence at activities that are instrumental to the achievement of valued goals, whereas internality for failure would be associated with behavior aimed at avoiding aversive circumstances.

In each of the studies described by Mischel et al. (1974), children were offered the options of accepting small rewards early in the task or working for some period of time for larger prizes. The children could quit at any time and accept a less valuable prize. Although the results in several studies varied in magnitude, Mischel et al. (1974) found that internality for success was positively related to persistence in the effort to obtain the larger, delayed prizes. Correlations ranged from .32, $p < .05$ to .66, $p < .01$ in different experiments with varying conditions.

In contrast, internality for failure was not related to the children's choices. However, when the children anticipated losing previously earned prizes depending on their performance on selected tasks, internality for failure proved to be more valuable than internality for success in predicting practicing behavior; that is, children who perceived themselves as responsible for failure practiced more than those who felt external with regard to failure on a task in which they anticipated punishment for failure. These findings occurred, however, only when the children were led to believe that they could avoid punishment by their performance. On the other hand, when performance and outcome (whether or not the child would lose his prizes) were made to seem unrelated, the correlations were significant but negative—that is, the more internal the children felt regarding failure, the less likely they were to practice. Thus, Mischel and his colleagues were able to demonstrate the value of considering causal attributions of success and failure independently—and of differentiating between work aimed at securing delayed rewards and work aimed at averting delayed punishments.

Persistence at a difficult task has been found to be related to locus of control in two other studies (Karabenick & Srull, 1978; Srull & Karabenick, 1975). Subjects in these experiments were allowed to attempt a maximum of 13 puzzles beyond an inital set, all of which were unsolvable. The effect for locus of control was highly significant in the first study [$F = 135.06$, $p < .001$, 1/64] and was replicated in the second study [$F = 82.92$, $p < .001$, 1/56]. In both cases internals persisted at this impossible task whereas externals were more likely to quit after experiencing their initial failures.

Other researchers have reported interesting if mixed findings with regard to locus of control and deferred gratification. Zytkoskee, Strickland, and Watson (1971), for instance, found that both an internal locus of control and self-imposed delay of gratification were common to certain groups. Poor Southern black children were decidedly more external than poor white children on Bialer's locus of control scale and were more likely to choose immediate small reinforcements than to wait three weeks for larger reinforcements. However, despite the coincidence of locus of control and a preference for delayed larger reinforcements, the two variables were unrelated for the total sample [$r = .09$, *n.s.*]. In a subsequent study, Strickland (1972) contrasted the results of black and white children as they chose between immediate and delayed reinforcements that were offered by white or black experimenters. Three hundred sixth-graders completed the locus of control scale and were then offered one 45–rpm record immediately or three records if they could wait for three weeks. Strickland found again that blacks were more likely to choose the immediate, smaller reinforcement and were more external than whites as assessed by the Nowicki-Strickland locus of control measure. However, Strickland found that the choice of immediate reinforcement was most prevalent among blacks when the experimenter was white. With a black experimenter, delayed reinforcement preference increased considerably. For the black children, the race of the experimenter was more important than locus of control for predicting their willingness to delay. However, for white children, locus of control was significantly related to choice behavior. Those white children who chose the delayed reinforcement were more internal than were those who preferred the immediate reward. In further contrast to black children, the experimenter's race was irrelevant to white children's choices.

Strickland's research indicates that the willingness to defer gratification is predictable, though often on the basis of rather different variables. If security or predictability of one's phenomenological life is of the essence for choosing the delayed reinforcement option, as suggested earlier, then the differences between black and white children are worthy of comment. For the white child, the major source of unpredictability may be thought of as personal; that is, he is sufficiently differentiated from others so that his experiences are viewed as personal-what happens to him is, relatively speaking, a function of his unique identity. Thus, when offered a choice of immediate versus delayed reinforcement, his self-perceptions predict his responses. For black children, however, *race* is a major source of uncertainty. When interacting with white persons, variation in responses is great enough that prediction of the white person's behavior becomes problematic. An optimal strategy to adopt when predictions approach a 50–50 level of accuracy is to stick with one bet. Then one will be correct at least half the time. In this case, a black child might conclude that he should never trust a white person to follow up on his word. If a 50–50 choice level may be considered generous in describing the actual probability with which whites have fulfilled promises to blacks in the South, it is possible to imagine how black children could have developed a pervasive cynicism regarding promises from whites. When offered a choice of immediate versus delayed reinforcement then, the black child looks outward—the source of unpredictability and insecurity is to be read in the social milieu, and not within oneself. If the source of the promise is a white person, one set of expectancies is evoked; if a black person, then it is another set. In either case, the elements in the external world bear considerably more importance for determining stability than would the personal characteristics of the black child.

Strickland's data then, contain some support for the predicted locus of control-deferred gratification relationship. If our conjectures should prove accurate with further empirical tests, the limits of this relationship may also be evident.

Other investigators have reported varying results as they have compared locus of control and deferred gratification. Walls and Smith (1970) found locus of control related to delay among second- and third-grade children, with internals choosing to wait for a 7¢ as opposed to an immediate 5¢ prize. However, Walls and Miller (1970) found no relationship between the same variables with a small sample of welfare and vocational rehabilitation clients, though both variables were related to education. The more educated the clients, the more internal they were and the more likely they were to prefer delayed reinforcement.

In the earlier study by Walls (1970), a relationship between locus of control and accurate judgment of time was also noted. Internals were more accurate in judging the lapse of a minute. This finding is of interest in view of the fact that correctness of time judgments is, in turn, related to the preference of delayed reinforcement (Mischel, 1961).

In addition to time judgment, locus of control has been found to be correlated with other time-related measures such as future time perspective (Platt & Eisenmann, 1968; Shybut, 1968). Internals are found to have a longer future time perspective than externals; in addition, measures of "delaying capacity" (Kagan's Matching Familiar Figures Test and the Porteus Mazes) have been found to be related to locus of control (Shipe, 1971), though the device of immediate versus delayed reinforcement was not related to either the delaying capacity or locus of control measures in Shipe's investigation.

A more convincing test of the linkage between I–E and deferred gratification has been reported by Erikson and Roberts (1971). Institutionalized adolescent delinquents were offered the opportunity of attending public school away from the grounds of a reformatory. Although this is often an exciting diversion for reformatory inmates, this opportunity was granted with the proviso that the inmates' release from the institution would therefore be delayed. Subsequently those who decided to accept this "real" delay choice were compared with those who did not. One question served as the dependent measure of locus of control. The inmates were asked: "Why is a boy transferred to 'ZB' (the name of the delayers' cottage)?" The responses were then classified as internal, external, or neutral. Only one internal attribution was made among nondelayers (5%) in comparison to 8 internal responses (40%) among delayers. In this very real delay choice, then, internal attributions were more common among those selecting the delayed choice. Although this measure of locus of control consists of only a single answer, the veridicality of the choices lends credence to the obtained findings.

Overall, the studies reported support the hypothsized relationship between I–E and the ability to defer gratification in the pursuit of long-range goals. As with achievement, the findings are often variable and at times inconsistent. Various measures such as time judgments and time perspective are linked with locus of control, and it is evident that the perception of time is of some importance in man's perception of himself as an active determiner of his life's directions. A most apt reference, then, may be made to a study by Melges and Weisz (1971) of suicide.

These investigators enlisted the aid of 15 patients who had recently made a serious attempt at suicide. The subjects were asked to reconstruct, as vividly as possible, their state of mind immediately prior to their suicide attempt. Subjects were left alone with a tape recorder into which they delivered a soliloquy, imagining aloud the events and feelings that were going through their minds at the time of the suicide attempt. Both before and after the soliloquy, subjects were asked to complete a number of tests, including one concerned with the perception of one's future, and another, a modified version of the I–E scale.

Melges and Weisz were interested in examining the effects of increased suicide ideation on each of the measures administered. Their findings indicated that increases in suicidal ideation were associated with changes toward a more negative evaluation of the personal future, changes toward less internal control, and changes toward less extension of a span of awareness into the future. In turn, changes in personal future were correlated in the same direction with changes in the locus of control [$r = .61$, $p < .05$]. A negative outlook for the future and external control expectancies were associated with each other and, in turn, with suicidal ideation. Likewise, changes in locus of control correlated with changes in temporal extension into the future [$r = .63$, $p < .05$], suggesting that as one feels increasingly helpless, one's span of awareness of the future diminishes.

The image of an individual at the brink of suicide, being trapped within the immediate moment, for whom the future has ceased to exist as a meaningful and positive force, and who experiences himself as helpless to effect his fate toward positive ends, spells out for us the potential mutual relevance of the perceptions of time and personal control, as have few of the previous studies.

CONCLUSIONS

Research has indicated that achievement effort and the willingness or ability to tolerate delays in the attainment of reinforcements are related to the perception of causation. Confirmatory evidence exists in support of the hypotheses and observations of researchers who have attempted to explain the high rates of failure at achievement activities among members of particular groups. Individuals who develop with little expectation that life's satisfactions and misfortunes can be determined by personal efforts have been less apt to exert themselves or to persist over lengthy time intervals in the pursuit of distant goals; and, as it oftentimes has been contended, such exertion and persistence are the sine qua non of achievement activity. Congruent with the more personal material discussed in earlier chapters, research findings indicate that the engagement in achievement activity or long-range skill-demanding tasks is unlikely if one views himself as being at the mercy of capricious external forces. However, as noted above, the empirical data are not often without paradoxical inconsistencies or failures at replication.

In recent years, attribution theorists have explored causal attributions in a manner that has helped to improve upon previous attempts to predict achievement-related behavior. Most notable among these investigators is Bernard Weiner (Weiner, 1979; Weiner, Heckhausen, Meyer, & Cook, 1972) Weiner, Russel, & Lerman, 1979), who has with some success added the dimensions of "stability" and "controllability," which interact with locus of control in predicting achievement behaviors. Figure 9 contains a diagrammatic presentation of Weiner's early model that combined locus of control and stability of cause. As

LOCUS OF CONTROL

	Internal	External
Fixed	ability	task difficulty
Variable	effort	luck

STABILITY

FIGURE 9 The perceived determinants of success and failure. (From Weiner, Heckhausen, Meyer, & Cook, 1972.)

can be seen in this figure, internal causes are divided into those that will remain fairly constant, such as ability, and those that can vary for different reasons, such as effort. External factors may also be variable, such as luck, or stable, such as in the difficulty of a given task.

On the basis of experimentation with this paradigm, Weiner has concluded that the choice to engage in achievement activity is mediated by internal-variable factors, such as effort, that generate positive feelings; that is, persons who perceive that outcomes in achievement activities are determined by variations of their own effort, as opposed to their more constant ability, will find more pleasure engaging in their pursuits. Second, persistence despite failure is said to be more likely if the causes of failure are seen as variable. If bad luck or lack of effort have been responsible for failure, then hope for improvement is still plausible. If one's effort or luck has been failing then change is possible and perhaps imminent.

It is premature to speculate at this point on all the yet to be reported data that such a discriminating use of perceived control measures may offer. Let it suffice to say that the uncertainties generated by inconsistent findings noted in this chapter may be resolvable as the more differentiated conceptions of locus of control offered by Weiner and Mischel, and the more complex interactive designs described by Batlis (1978) and Harpin (1980), are employed in the attempt to predict achievement related activities.

7 Locus of Control and Coping Behavior

INTRODUCTION

In Chapter 1 , evidence was presented suggesting that perceived control can moderate the impact of potentially stressful experiences. However, most of the studies discussed in that chapter consisted of laboratory analogues, and those reports that focused on real life events consisted for the most part of anecdotes or uncontrolled observational data. In this chapter we will explore the relatively recent literature that concerns the manner in which people cope with their real life stresses. While there has been an upsurge in empirical studies linking locus of control and stress management, there have also been a number of books published in the 1970s concerned with survival in the face of extreme stress.

The book *Alive* (Read, 1974) describes in detail how plane crash survivors in the Andes mountains coped with incredible hardships and imminent threats to their survival. The differences between various survivors were marked: Some passively awaited death; others battled against seemingly insurmountable odds. Those who remained impassive appeared to disbelieve in the value of effort and quite often were given to expressions of hopelessness. Those who struggled actively to survive and ultimately escape from their mountain prison exhibited consistent resourcefulness in helping to maintain the remaining survivors—even to the point of engaging in cannibalism of the deceased.

It isn't clear whether these differences in the response to duress reflected longstanding beliefs regarding control or even temperamental differences among the victims. However, intuition, as well as other similar stories about survivors, encourage us to believe that the perception of control did play a vital role in determining the ways in which these people coped with their circumstances.

In another personal account of the ways in which an individual came to terms with stress, *Alexander Dolgun's Story* (Dolgun & Watson, 1975) recounts the grim life of a young American who was abducted by the Soviet secret police from a street in Moscow in 1948 and lived his next 24 years in various prisons and labor camps throughout the Soviet Gulag. Dolgun's story contains all of the horrors and tortures that Solzhenitzyn has described. What makes his story unique and relevant for our purposes is the resourcefulness that Dolgun displayed in the face of unrelenting savagery, along with his recall of the thoughts and fantasies that occupied his mind during captivity. Though many of Dolgun's reminiscences implicate perceived control as a tool for his survival, there is one point in his story that does so with a heightened sense of drama.

Dolgun was being interrogated nightly by a particularly savage official who took pleasure in kicking him, hitting him with a truncheon, and otherwise mutilating him. He was not permitted to fall asleep at all, though a bed was lowered from the ceiling each night. The bed was subsequently returned to its position in the ceiling at daybreak so that he would not have the opportunity to rest comfortably during the daytime. Sensing that this could be the beginning of the end for him, Dolgun began to save the tiny scraps of coarse paper that were issued to him daily to be used as toilet paper. He hid these bits of paper and chewed them carefully to create a papier-mâché wad with which he could fill up the striker plate into which the bed latched when it was placed in the ceiling. He reasoned he could then replace the bed so that it appeared to be firmly locked in place. These machinations were employed so that if he felt that his agony was increasing beyond endurance, he would be able to use the bed as a quasi-guillotine and end his life. As the author noted: "It was not pleasant . . . to make such a plan . . . yet it gave me a small but psychologically necessary handhold on some elements of control over my future, and it gave me access to an escape route if what was happening got beyond the point where I could bear it. [p. 121]."

Similar to the control mechanism in the Glass and Singer (1972) investigations (see Chapter 1), Dolgun had provided himself with a "button," an "out" if the situation became intolerable. Having the button, so to speak, Dolgun became more capable of enduring the unendurable.

A third survival book entitled *Lost* (Thompson, 1975) provides the clearest case for assuming that stable beliefs about control are pertinent to how people cope with hardships. The book describes the ordeal of three persons who were shipwrecked in the Pacific Ocean for 73 days, living in a foot and a half of trapped air space in the hull of an overturned trimaran. The victims were the ship's owner, his brother-in-law, and his brother-in-law's wife. The woman died; the two men were eventually rescued. One of the men, the owner of the boat, was a devout Seventh Day Adventist who insisted that their survival and rescue was up to God. Given this self-abnegation, he did little to actively help their survival possibilities other than to "challenge" God to deliver them. When that ploy failed, he easily succumbed to hopelessness and despair. His brother-in-law, on the other hand, was an ardent believer that "God helps those who help themselves." From the moment they had become imperiled he organized their available resources and went so far as to arrange "intellectual" and "social activities" for the three of them so as to counteract the panic, numbness, and depression that threatened to overwhelm the others. This believer in self-responsibility mused at the end of his story about the differences between himself and his brother-in-law, who died shortly after their rescue: "I proved that if a man husbands his energy and uses his powers resourcefully, then that man can pass—marked, but basically unharmed—through the most excruciating of ordeals. [p. 238]."

What makes *Lost* so pertinent to this discussion is that the predispositions of the two brothers-in-law were so divergent with respect to beliefs about responsibility and were of a long-standing nature. Their behavior while suffering duress reflected these predispositions faithfully; the polar opposite behaviors they displayed were analogous to those of the survivors described in *Alive*. Therefore, it becomes increasingly plausible to suggest that stable beliefs about control offer some prognosis for the ways in which different people are likely to cope with stressful situations.

Finally, this author (Lefcourt, 1980) has described the case of a man who managed to survive a near fatal plane crash with aplomb. The physical condition of the victim was critical for a long period of time and he was required to undergo countless operations to be pieced together again. The important point that the victim made to me throughout our discussions was that he never relinquished his responsibility for himself in the recovery process. Consequently, he endured much pain as he surreptitiously engaged in rehabilitative exercises that the medical staff discouraged, and actively engaged in the decisions that had to be made along his route to recovery. In my encounter with this victim, it was difficult not to admire the way in which the man had survived. His espoused beliefs regarding his responsiblity were evident at each stage of his recovery, and his appearance at the time I met him revealed little of the pain and bodily damage that could have been expected. Moreover, he did not simply dwell upon his recovery but was already engaged in the pursuit of new plans and adventures, including the purchase of a new plane to replace the one that had been destroyed in the crash.

In each of these cases some evidence has been found that resourcefulness and resilience in the encounters with stressful experience reflect the beliefs held by individuals that they are responsible agents who are at least partially responsible for what befalls them. In the remainder of this chapter we will review empirical studies that explore these assumed connections between beliefs regarding control and the ways in which people come to terms with stress.

EMPIRICAL FINDINGS

In an extensive review of the literature concerning experimental studies of the effects of stress on task performances and social behavior, Cohen (1980) concluded that there is a clear demonstration that increased control over a stressor decreases the deficits in poststimulation performance. The findings were so pervasive that Cohen was forced to wonder if perceived control may simply lead to better performance in general rather than just in response to stress.

Beyond the experimental literature there have been a number of investigations concerned with the ways in which an internal locus of control modifies the experiencing of various "real life" stressors. Among those studies there is one that has some bearing upon the last example that was noted above concerning the process of recovery from physical disability.

Cromwell, Butterfield, Brayfield, and Curry (1977) examined the ways in which cardiac patients responded to a range of procedures administered in the intensive cardiac units to which they had been admitted. The specifics of treatment, whether the patient was an active participant, a passive patient, with or without distractions, had differential impact upon patients varying in locus of control. These findings will be discussed in the chapter concerned with change and therapeutic implications. For the present chapter, the data of interest are those that reflected the manner in which different persons coped with the life-threatening experience of a myocardial infarction.

The patients classified as internal via Rotter's I–E scale were rated as being more cooperative and less depressed during their stay in the intensive care unit than were externals. On three highly intercorrelated physiological measures (sedimentation rates, serum glutamic oxaloacetic transaminase levels, and lactate dehydrogenase levels), externals were found to have worse prognostic ratings than internals. Additionally, externals had higher peak temperatures during intensive care and remained longer in the intensive unit and in the hospital itself than did internals.

Although it is possible to raise many questions about the inferences to be drawn from data such as these, one hypothesis is that internals behave in ways that do not exacerbate their conditions. Their greater cooperativeness and absence of depression suggests that they more actively joined in the struggle for survival than did externals, whose prognosis seemed worse for the way in which they responded to their infarction. It is arguable, of course, that the lesser cooperation and depression among externals reflected their poorer states of health or that locus of control scores themselves may have been affected by present health status that was indicated by the physiological indexes. Though these latter possibilities cannot be ruled out with finality, the likelihood that relatively stable beliefs and styles of responding to nursing care would vary so largely as a function of momentary health status would seem to be low. Consequently, these data, at the least, are suggestive that the responses to life-endangering threats such as myocardial infarctions may be moderated by personality characteristics such as locus of control, and that an external locus of control may be associated with behavioral responses that bode ill for persons suffering with particular physical maladies.

A number of other investigators have attempted to examine the manner in which locus of control can moderate the effects of different stressors. The strains involved in medical education (Kilpatrick, Dubin, and Marcotte, 1974), in re-covering from hurricane-caused flooding (Anderson, 1977), in commuting to work (Novaco, Stokols, Campbell & Stokols, 1979) and in adapting to Marine Corps training (Cook, Novaco, & Sarason, 1980) have each been explored with some success with reference to the locus of control construct.

Kilpatrick, Dubin, and Marcotte (1974) obtained mood ratings from medical students in each of the four classes that were on campus at one time—freshman, sophomore, juniors, and seniors. The students were classified as internal or external from scores on Rotter's I-E scale, and moods were assessed by the Profile of Mood States (POMS-McNair, Lorr, & Droppleman, 1971). The POMS consists primarily of negative moods (tension, depression, anger, fatigue, and confusion) and one positive mood (vigor). Across all four groups, externals reported experiencing more negative moods than internals. For vigor, on the other hand, an interaction was found. Internals scored reliably high on the vigor scale across all four groups. Externals in the sophmore and junior classes, on the other hand, exhibited a drop in vigor scores in comparision to the freshman and senior classes. These data are limited by their cross-sectional nature. That is, we are not able to determine if the differences observed were a natural sequence over time or reflected cohort differences peculiar to each group. However, given the well-known phenomenon of sophmore slump, it seems reasonable to surmise that after students have bypassed the excitement of orientation and introduction into their new career-focused programs, they must come to terms with the knowledge that they are engaged in a long, arduous, and often tedious pursuit. At this point the distant goals must be kept salient if one is to weather the everyday hardships that seem so enervating. Given the fact that internals have been found to be more ready to defer gratification and to prefer delayed larger reinforcements to im-mediate smaller ones, it would seem likely that internals would be more apt than externals to persist in their efforts after long-range goals. The second and third years, which can seem to be so far from the final goal of graduation, may therefore be more difficult for externals to endure, and their lowered vigor scores in those years may therefore be comprehensible.

Despite the limitations of these data, they are intriguing for what they may reveal about the stresses involved in long-term pursuits. The well-known sophmore slump may be the natural loss of vigor than can occur when students lose the sense of direction that derives from their involvement with distant goals. For the self-described external it may prove to be far more difficult to entertain visions and plans concerning remote goals; as a consequence, mood disturbances may be common, along with an absence of the enthusiasm that may facilitate internals in their long-range, goal-directed activities.

There has been one other study reported that has focused upon the stressful effects of a training program, though the duration of training was for a much shorter period than that involved in medical education. Cook, Novaco, and Sarason (1980) have explored the effects of expectancies upon the adaptation to

Marine Corp recruitment training. With a sample of 254 subjects, the attrition rate during training was relatively low. Nevertheless, with recruits classified as external, midrange, and internal via the Nowicki-Strickland I-E scale (NOSIE), the respective attrition rates were 17%, 13%, and 7%. The recruits who quit for psychological and/or behavioral reasons were significantly overrepresented in the external group.

In addition to attrition rate figures, Cook et al. examined the impact of particular groups, comparing those in which attrition was high with those where it was a rare occurrence. In the low attrition groups, that were assumed to be units with better morale, those recruits whose origins were most unfavorable (broken home, lower socioeconomic class etc.) exhibited the greatest shift toward internality, whereas internal recruits in high attrition groups (low morale units) were found to become more external upon completion of training.

In this study we find some analogy to the Kilpatrick et al. (1974) investigation. Where externals exhibit dysphoria during their medical training that could result in their withdrawal, marine recruits holding external control beliefs are more apt to drop out of their stressful training programs, a probable indication of their dysphoric states.

Two other field studies have examined the role of locus of control in predicting responses to more singular events than were true of the above studies. Anderson (1977) examined the performances of 90 businessmen in a Pennsylvania community for a three-and-a-half-year period following flooding that had been created by Hurricane Agnes in 1972. Anderson assessed these businessmen, whose businesses had been disrupted and damaged, for locus of control, perceived stress, coping behaviors, and organizational performance. With coping behavior classified as problem-solving vs. being concerned with emotional reactions from the categorizations suggested by Kahn, Wolfe, Quinn, Snoek, and Rosenthal (1964), externals were found to have used, fewer problem-solving coping methods $[r = -.54, p < .001]$ and more emotion-directed coping devices (withdrawal, hostility etc. $[r = .80, p < .001]$) than internals. In addition, externals were more likely to have perceived their circumstances as being highly stressful $[r = .61, p < .001]$ than were internals. Organizational performance was cleverly assessed by credit ratings made by an independent national organization. Although this article is not entirely clear with regard to this last measure, Anderson was able to conclude that "the task-oriented coping behaviors of internals are apparently associated with a more successful solution of the problems created by the stressful event, since the performance of the internals' organizations is higher [p. 450]."

Finally, Novaco, Stokols, Campbell, and Stokols (1979) examined the effects of commuting to work on 100 employees of two companies. The employees were classified by the length of time and distance spent commuting. When the employees reached their places of work they were asked to perform two tasks, one the unsolvable puzzles that Glass and Singer (1972) had used as a measure of persistence and frustration tolerance, and a digit symbol task that requires both speed and attentiveness. Those who commuted the longer distances were found to be more emotionally upset than those whose travel distances and times were shorter. Locus of cotrol was found to interact with distance travelled in predicting task performances. When commuting distances were short, externals were found to perform better than internals persisting longer on unsolvable puzzles and completing more digit symbols. However, when the subjects examined were those who had travelled a medium distance, internals were found to outperform externals. Among those who travelled the furthest distances—those who were most distraught—internals outperformed externals on the digit symbol test. The groups were similar with respect to the unsolvable puzzles.

In this study of commuting as a stressor, internals were found to perform better than externals only when facing greater stress. Of the field studies described above, this was the only investigation where the impact of the degree of stress was examined. If the data in this study are reliable then an answer is available to Cohen's query regarding the pervasivenes of internals' superiority over externals on most performance tasks (Cohen, 1980). It would seem that the differences between those holding internal from those holding external control expectancies become most stark when stresses become greater.

Whether in response to cardiac difficulties, commuting, business disruptions, or the stressful training in medical school or Marine Corps recruitment camps, internals seem better equipped to survive their ordeals. They do not as readily succumb to dysphoric feelings and cease in their efforts to succeed at their various tasks as do those who hold external control expectancies.

If the above studies were the only ones from which such sweeping generalizations derived, the evidence in support of such statements would seem to be relatively thin. However, a number of other investigators have provided supporting data using different methodologies. In contrast to the above studies that have explored the ways in which individuals cope with specific stressful situations, these latter investigators have made use of different life event scales so as to use life stress incidence as an individual difference measure.

Some investigators have simply asked their subjects if the life events they have experienced were controllable, aversive, or anticipated, and then have attempted to predict their emotional reactions to those events. Although some investigators such as Dohrenwend and Martin (1979) and Fontana, Hughes, Marcus, and Dowds (1979) have found that normative judgments of desirablilty and controllability offer better prediction of adjustment than individual assessments of same, other investigators such as Husaini and Neff (1980) and McFarlane, Norman, Streiner, Roy, and Scott (1980) have found individually assessed judgments of the controllability of events predictive of psychiatric symptomotology and subjective strain.

Husaini and Neff (1980) have reported that in addition to the total number of life events, ratings of the undesirability and unpreventability of those events helped to predict depression and general well-being. The greater were the reported number of undesirable and unpreventable events relative to the total number of life events, the higher was the individual's levels of psychiatric symptomotology. McFarlane et al. (1980) similarly found ratings of controllability to be a major factor in the predictions of a scale of subjective strain. Undesirable events over which subjects claimed to have total control did not correlate with strain [rs ranging between .06 and .10]. When the life events were rated as being subject only to "some control," the correlations betwen those events and strain ranged between .09 and .35, the latter being significant at the .001 level. When the events were rated as being uncontrollable, the correlations ranged between .28 and .40, which are significant at the .001 level, given the rather large sample size [$N = 500$].

Another set of studies is distinguished by the assessment of life events used in conjunction with independent measurements of locus of control. The earliest reported studies in which life events and locus of control were used conjointly in the prediction of adjustment measures were those by Manuck, Hinrichsen, and Ross (1975a, b). In the first of two studies Manuck et al. found that all subjects who reported a high number of life changes also scored highly on state and trait anxiety measures. However, among those who acknowledged having few life changes, externals reported much higher state anxiety than their internal counterparts. In essence, externals reported feeling more anxious than internals in the absence of stressful life events. Given a high incidence of stressors, on the other hand, locus of control ceased to be a predictor of anxiety. These findings were mirrored in a second study by these authors with helpseeking for physical complaints as the criterion data. Again, internals who acknowledged having experienced highly stressful life events were equivalent to externals in their seeking of help. Among the low stress groups, however, externals sought help more often than did internals.

Although Manuck et al. (1975a,b) did not find evidence suggesting that locus of control moderates the impact of stressful events, they did interpret their findings as revealing ways in which individuals come to make sense of their experiences. Their contentions, in brief, were that internals may come to feel anxious about failures and dissappointments (reflected in their life event scores) because they more readily attribute causes for those failures to themselves. But among low stressed subjects, who are assumed to have had more positive experiences, externals may be less certain about the causes of their successes and thus derive less pleasure from them than do internals, who may more readily make internal attributions for those successes. In other words, internals may live easier with success whereas externals suffer anxiety regardless of the quality of their life experiences.

More recently, there have been several studies reported in which locus of control has been found to moderate the impact of potential stressors. Johnson and Sarason (1978) evaluated the impact of life stressors as assessed by their own

Life Events Scale (LES—Sarason, Johnson, & Siegel, 1978). In a sample of 121 undergraduates, they found the incidence of negative life events to be more highly associated with depression [$r = .32$, $p < .005$] and trait anxiety [$r = .31$, $p < .005$] among externals than among internals [$rs = .10$ ns, and .15 ns, respectively].

Similar evidence for the moderator effect of locus of control has been reported by researchers at the University of Chicago (Kobasa, 1979a,b; Kobasa, Maddi & Kahn, 1982). These investigators have examined what they refer to as "hardiness," an ability to resist illness despite stress. In these studies, the investigators have attempted to define the characteristics that differentiate people who succumb to illness following life stresses from those who are better able to resist becoming ill. Using the Holmes and Rahe (1967) measure of stressful life events, Kobasa (1979a,b) found that high stress-low illness business executives rated themselves as less stressed than high stress-high illness executives. To describe the differences between these groups of executives, Kobasa assessed what she refers to as the "three Cs": commitment, control, and challenge. To assess the control variable she used measures of locus of control, nihilism, and powerlessness, each of which statistically differentiated the groups. Control, along with a measure of "alienation from self" (commitment) and measures of vegetativeness and adventurousness (challenge) were found to account for hardiness to some degree. Anticipating the criticism that the simultaneous assessments of hardiness, illness, and life stress confuse the issue of causality, since illness itself is a stressor and may help to produce less hardiness, Kobasa, Maddi, and Kahn (in press) conducted a subsequent study in which illness measures that were contemporaneous with the assessment of stressful life events and hardiness were partialled out from the correlations with illnesses occurring one and two years from the time of the original assessment. The three "Cs" were summed into one index of hardiness to be used as a predictor of the responses to stress occurring over that year-long period. Again, Kobasa et al. (in press) found interactions between hardiness and life stress in the prediction of illness. Those who lacked hardiness (external control, low degree of commitment, and less responsiveness to challenge) were the most likely to exhibit the expected linkage between the incidence of stress and illness.

In a similar program of research, Sandler and Lakey (in press) have begun a series of investigations to evaluate the manner in which different moderators can effect the impact of stressful events. Using a life event measure designed specifically for university students, these investigators predicted the relationships between negative life events and trait anxiety and depression with locus of control (Mirel's personal control factor—Mirels, 1970) and social support as moderator variables. For internals the correlations between negative life events and depression [$r = .33$, $p < .05$] and anxiety [$r = .28$, $p < .05$] were of lesser magnitude than the same for externals [$rs = .44$, $p < .01$, and .57, $p < .01$ respectively]. Most importantly, in a multiple regression analysis, significant interactions were found between negative life events and social support in the prediction of depression and anxiety [$Fs = 7.61$ and 7.27 respectively] among internals. Among externals, on the other hand, these interactions were nonsignificant [$Fs = 1.41$ and $.07$ respectively]. Internals who enjoyed high social support showed lesser correlations between negative life events and depression and anxiety. For externals who in general had higher social support scores, there was no ostensible interaction, meaning that social support did not have a moderating effect for that group. These data are intriguing for they suggest that internals make better or more discriminating use of their resources than do externals. That the latter report even higher social support availability than internals make these findings more marked. It would seem as if externals do not use their social contacts effectively to diminish the impact of stressors whereas internals are better able to do so even when those contacts are less pervasive and frequent.

With the exception of the studies by Manuck et al. (1975a,b) then, locus of control has been found to act as a moderator of the stress—emotional upset—illness relationships. Recent research by this author and his colleagues (Lefcourt, Miller, Ware, & Sherk, 1981) may help to clarify or confuse some of the disparities in this research area. In a series of studies we have occasionally found that locus of control operates as a moderator between stressful life events and mood disturbance, whereas at other times we have found results similar to those of Manuck et al. (1975a,b). In a retrospective analysis undertaken to unravel the inconsistencies in our data, it was found that the moderator effect was greatest when the life events we measured had occurred a few years prior to the measurement of mood disturbance. That is, when life events were assessed by the Coddington measure (Coddington, 1972), specifically the life events occurring during the high school years, mood disturbance was highly moderated by locus of control measures; externals exhibited the expected relationships between stress and mood disturbance. However, when the life events assessed were measured by the LES (Sarason, Johnson, & Siegel, 1978) which focuses upon the previous year, our results were similar to those of Manuck et al. (1975a,b). With high stress both groups were equally distraught. In the absence of stress, however, externals remained high in their self-assessed mood disturbance whereas internals were markedly lower in these scores. Finally, when subjects were asked to rate their life satisfaction some five years previous to the present, the moderator effects were found once again. That is, externals, who rated their lives as being low in satisfaction five years earlier, proved to be high in measures of mood disturbance, whereas internals exhibited no significant relationships between life satisfaction (a surrogate for absence of stress) and current mood disturbance. Consequently, we have tentatively concluded that stress has an immediate impact upon nearly everyone irrespective of their locus of control. However, given the passage of time, internals succeed in leaving their disappointments behind them whereas externals seem to continue to carry the weight of those events into their future.

These findings and conclusions require replication and further study before they can be taken seriously. It is obvious, nevertheless, that locus of control does play some role in affecting the ways in which people cope with their experiences. However, that role is complex, interacting as it does with other variables such as time of life stress, social support, and no doubt other variables as well. An honor's thesis supervised by this researcher helps to reveal the confusions and complexities in these studies while at the same time exposing the evident value of using locus of control in the prediction of the response to stress.

Hunsley (1981) used locus of control as well as coping styles in an attempt to predict the relationship between the LES and mood levels and mood reactivity. The former contrasts happy and sad moods so that level goes from low to high; the latter reflects the intensity and frequency of mood changes. For females [$N = 39$], locus of control failed to produce either main effects or interactions, whereas for males [$N = 18$], both achievement locus of control [$F = 5.94$, $p < .05$] and affiliation locus of control [$F = 18.95$, $p < .001$] produced main effects upon mood reactivity. The more external with respect to either goal, the higher was the mood reactivity. With mood level as the dependent measure, interactions were found with locus of control for affiliation; external males had an $r = -.62$ between negative life events and mood level whereas internals had an $r = .10$. In essence, Hunsley (1981) has replicated the moderating effect for locus of control but only with a male sample; females showed no such trends. Consequently, the complexity and potential sources of interaction increase. Nevertheless, these empirical data do allow for some support of the anecdotal and biographical material presented at the beginning of this chapter. Locus of control does play an important role in moderating stress but the questions are evident—for whom, when, and in what circumstances do these effects occur?

CONCLUSION

Between the biographical, experimental, field study, and personality-focused data that have been discussed above a strong argument can be made that an individual's perception of control has much to do with the ways in which that person will encounter his life's stresses. Although there is considerable room for more research to help answer the questions noted at the end of the section dealing with empirical findings, the research to date solidly confirms the expectations suggested in the Chapter 1. Control, perceived and actual, matter in the way that persons wrestle with their life's adversities.

8 Fatalism and Psychopathology

INTRODUCTION

In a book entitled *A Season in Hell,* Percy Knauth (1975) described the way in which helplessness led to even deeper despair during a prolonged depression through which he had suffered. ''As the lack of sleep wore me down, a sense of hopelessness enveloped me. I know that nothing I did could change this situation. There was nothing I could do. I was convinced that I was laboring under some kind of curse so that any efforts of my own to fight this situation were foredoomed to failure [p. 35].''

Knauth's description of his depression is quite revealing. Helplessness and his shame over being so helpless seemed to have compounded the experience of depression, leaving him with an even greater despair and sense of futility than he'd had at the outset of his depressive episode.

When theoreticians attempt to discuss phenomena such as that described by Knauth, readers are often left with a strong feeling of disappointment. Words in general fail to convey the reality of terror experienced by a person undergoing an acute psychotic reaction and the abstruse terminology of systematic theories seems far removed from such immediate experience. Nevertheless, in this chapter we will try to discuss abnormal phenomena using social learning terminology with the hope that the utility of our terms will compensate for their lack of dramatic appeal.

In previous chapters, several attempts to link locus of control with various abnormal phenomena were described. Conversion reaction hysteria, ulcers, depression, and attempted suicide were each discussed as possible concomitants of an external locus of control. The temptation to link locus of control to a wide range of clinical phenomena derives less from a wish to reduce such variety to simplicity than it does from a desire to respond to the compelling symptoms presented by psychiatric patients.

Paranoid individuals speak of their omnipotence, if given to grandiosity, or of abject helplessness before powerful external forces if suffering with delusions of persecution. Manic patients openly dismiss suggestions that they are subject to limitations as are other human beings; depressives insist on their helplessness through inaction if not words; antisocially-inclined individuals may explain their deviations as necessary and beyond personal choice. Despite these differences among clinical groups as diverse as depressives and delinquents, there is often commonality in the tendency to eschew personal responsibility and to espouse an external control orientation.

An immediate connection between psychopathology and locus of control can be established if we return to the topic of deferred gratification discussed with regard to achievement in a preceding chapter. Freud and Mowrer each developed constructs pertaining to the ability to defer gratification—impulse control, time binding, and temporal integration—that, in turn, have been used to explain certain pathological phenomena. Mowrer (1950) has explained the persistence of self-punitive behavior common among persons suffering with neuroses in terms of a failure of temporal integration. Neurotic behavior, characterized by expedient actions designed to avoid immediate challenges at the cost of later suffering, is said to occur among persons who are ignorant about the contingencies between immediate behaviors and later consequences. Mowrer described his position in the following manner:

> If an immediate consequence is slightly rewarding, it may outweigh a greater but more remote punishing consequence. And equally, if an immediate consequence is slightly punishing, it may outweigh a greater but more remote rewarding consequence. Living organisms which are not skilled in the use of symbols are severely limited in their capacity to resolve behavioral dilemmas of this kind and may, as a result, continue indefinitely to manifest so-called nonintegrative behavior. But by introducing the time element . . . it is possible for us to escape from the dilemma which such behavior presents from a theoretical standpoint.
>
> The prodigious capacity found in normal adult human beings for using symbols, i.e., for "reasoning" seems to have what is perhaps its greatest utility in enabling the individual to bring the remote as well as immediate consequences of a contemplated action into the psychological present and thereby compare and balance the probable (anticipated) rewards and punishments in a manner which enormously increases the chances that resulting behavior will be integrative. Such behavior is properly termed rational, in contradistinction to the prerational behavior seen in lower animals. [pp. 453–4].

Deviations other than neuroses have also been interpreted in terms of temporal integration. The psychopathic person, Buss (1966) explains, is said to be unable to delay gratifications:

He cannot surrender a smaller present pleasure for a greater distant goal. He cannot abide routine for long and takes no comfort in a stable, recurrent regime of daily living. He has no sense of time, especially of the future; he senses only the here and now. This makes him prey to almost any momentary temptation or escape from tension, regardless of subsequent consequences. He simply cannot bridge the gap between present pleasure and future punishments. In this respect he is similar to the neurotic who buys a temporary respite from anxiety now at the cost of greater punishment later [p. 435].

The schizophrenic, too, is said to be lacking in a sense of time. When asked to estimate the passing of a second, for instance, schizophrenics commonly make gross overestimates (Maher, 1966). Correctness of time judgments has, in turn, been found to be related to the ability to defer gratification (Mischel, 1961).

Different forms of personality malfunctioning, then, are associated with the inability to defer gratification; and as previously indicated, this inability is more common among persons who hold external control expectancies than among those who perceive themselves to be active determiners of their own fate. Therefore an indirect link, at least, may be assumed between locus of control and the incidence of psychopathology.

Other research reviewed in previous chapters offers support for this hypothesized association. That internals are more cognitively efficient, more alert to the potential meanings of their experiences, and less easily coerced by environmental forces, attests to the importance that an internal locus of control has for effective coping behavior. If a person is able to quickly assess the options available to him in a challenging situation, he should be able to cope more effectively than if he were less astute about his choices; and, if he believed that he was able to effectively act in his own behalf, even aversive consequences would have a less debilitating effect upon him.

What is being suggested in this introduction, then, is that locus of control is pertinent to the development of personality malfunctioning if only in an indirect manner. That one tries to cope with challenges to his sense of well being, or simply persists in the belief that he can cope with adversities bodes well for an individual. Avoidant, defensive mannerisms associated with deviance and malfunctioning should be less evident among those persons who continue to strive after valued goals in the belief that their efforts are meaningful and effective.

DEFENSIVENESS

On the basis of our previous discussion it would seem unlikely that internals are more defensive or avoidant of challenges than externals. Nevertheless, the results from a number of studies have led certain investigators to conclude exactly that, and the reasoning used to draw this conclusion does not lack plausibility.

If one commonly attributes cause for outcomes to one's personal characteristics, then outcomes are self-relevant; that is, one's successes and failures are meaningful for learning about oneself. If one customarily attributes causality to external events, successes and failures should be of little matter as far as one's self-regard is concerned. Failures can be "explained away" in terms of "others," "circumstances," or fate. For the external, outcomes should be of little relevance to self-evaluation since oneself is not held responsible for those outcomes. Consequently, it is reasonable to assume that externals will have little need to defend themselves against failure, but that internals may resort to various subterfuges if they are to retain self-respect subsequent to failure experiences. Empirically, this position received some support in a dissertation by Efran (1963) in which internal high school students were more likely to have forgotten their failures than were external students.

A second study (Lipp, Kolstoe, James, & Randall, 1968) likewise suggested that internals might be more defensive than externals. Physically handicapped internals and externals were compared in terms of perception thresholds for stimuli relevant to physical handicaps. Subjects were shown micromomentary exposures of a series of slides, some of which portrayed physically handicapped persons. These investigators predicted that internals would have lower thresholds (would recognize handicap-relevant stimuli more quickly) than externals. However, their data offered anything but a straightforward confirmation of this hypothesis. With subjects divided into three groups on the basis of James' I–E scale, handicapped externals were found to be the quickest, handicapped internals second, and a sample of midrange I–E-handicapped subjects were the slowest to recognize the stimuli in pictures of disabled persons.

These data do not lend themselves to easy interpretation. If nonrecognition of disabled figures by disabled persons is construed as an instance of defensiveness, then externals can be said to have been the least defensive, though internals were not the most defensive. However, if we do not equate defensiveness with slow recognition of crippled figures but rather we speak of "selective attention to relevant stimuli," these findings can be reinterpreted in a very different fashion. If a handicapped person comes to terms with his disability, managing through compensatory mechanisms to circumvent many of the difficulties resulting from the particular handicap, the sense of being handicapped may diminish in salience; that is, when individuals suffer an infliction, their attention may readily focus upon the resulting disability for some period of time such that fellow sufferers may be sought for comparison and commiseration. However, as one comes to terms with his disability, the salience of the handicap should decrease, and previous interests and pursuits of the individual should reemerge. The amount of time expended upon thinking and speaking about the disability should then become negligible in contrast to the active interests in one's life. In fact, the term hypochondriasis is often used as a term of opprobrium to depict the state when a reemergence of nonhealth-related interests fails to occur. Thus, the handicapped individual who has learned to cope with his disability may become less attentive to handicap-related stimuli in himself or in others than he had formerly been.

In view of this reformulation, we may reinterpret the findings of Lipp et al. (1968) in terms of relevance instead of defensiveness. It would seem that for the external, the handicap still exists as a salient factor in his life. Disability-related stimuli are consequently perceived more quickly by externals perhaps because they have not been as able as internals to cope with the resulting impediments and, consequently, are still overly concerned with their disability.

Evidence from a survey conducted among a large group of nonhandicapped college students (MacDonald & Hall, 1971) lends some credence to the above interpretation. Students were questioned as to how debilitating various physical impairments would be with regard to their social relationships and feelings about themselves. Externals were found to anticipate more severe effects from physical disability than internals. The less pessimistic stance among internals may reflect the belief in their ability to cope with adversity. Armed with such a belief, internals can then be expected to try to cope more adaptively with impairments than externals if mishaps were to befall them. Likewise, internals should not dwell upon their handicaps for as long a time as externals. If these assumptions are correct, then internals should not be as perceptually vigilant for handicap-related stimuli as externals. Be that as it may, however, the conclusion to be derived from the study by Lip et al. is that externals are not more avoidant than internals of the handicap-related material, as had been predicted.

That internals are not always more ''perceptually defensive'' than externals is evident in a study reported by Sauber (1971). In this investigation, the more typical ''dirty word'' stimuli used in perceptual defense research were presented by tachistoscope. Externals were found to have significantly higher thresholds for the recognition of the ''dirty words'' than did internals, especially among the females of the sample.

The first investigation designed specifically to evaluate defensiveness as a correlate of locus of control was reported by Phares, Ritchie, and Davis (1968). These investigators provided their subjects with interpretations from previously administered personality tests. The feedback was prearranged, however, each subject receiving the same eight positive interpretations, for example, ''She is warm and is able to maintain very positive interpersonal relationships,'' and eleven negative interpretations, for example, ''At times, sexual thoughts become a problem and make her doubt her maturity.'' Although internals and externals did not differ in the discomfort that they reported when receiving the interpretations, externals were found to recall more of the 19 interpretations at the end of the experiment than were internals. Phares et al. (1968) had predicted that externals would particularly recall more negative interpretations than internals, because the externalization tendencies of the former should have eliminated possible anxiety responses to the negative interpretations. The results did not actually support this contention, however. Externals were found to recall more interpretations, *in general, both positive and negative,* then were internals.

Though the data failed to clearly support the hypothesized sensitivity to failure among internals, Phares, in a subsequent study (Phares, Wilson, and Klyver, 1971) expressed the belief that the previous experiment had demonstrated that "external subjects recalled more of the negative information than internal subjects. Again it appeared almost as if an external orientation provided ready access to a defense and thus relatively less need to invoke forgetting as a response [p. 285]." Though Phares and his colleagues continued to interpret their findings as if they illustrated a greater "need to forget" among internals, the results from the second experiment made this interpretation of defensiveness less tenable. Internals and externals were failed on two tests that had been described as measures of intellectual functioning. The failure experiences were contrived by including insoluble puzzles among a legitimate set of puzzles. Subsequent to their failure experiences, each subject completed a scale of blame attribution. Under "fair" conditions, when the experimenter had remained quiet, allowing subjects to concentrate on the tasks, internals were decidedly less prone to blame the experimenter or testing conditions than were externals. However, when the experimenter engaged in distracting chatter throughout the test period, this difference in blame attribution between internals and externals diminished.

As Figure 10 makes evident, externals were more likely to blame "circumstances" even when there was little justification for doing so. Internals blamed the experimenter for their failure when it was reasonable to do so but were less likely to hold him responsible when there was little justification for such blame.

These findings suggest that internals are more flexible than externals in their assignment of cause for failure. On the other hand, externals seems less able to accept the implications of failure, blaming external circumstances even when justification for doing so was negligible. This ability to remain flexible in the way one interprets failure experiences would not seem a likely characteristic of a person who was uncomfortable enough to "need to forget" those experiences. The inflexible approach of externals, however, does suggest the strain with which they assimilate their failures. Although this study did not contain the opportunity to forget failure-relevant material, the overdetermined behavior commonly associated with repression as a defense mechanism was clearly less evident among internals than it was among externals.

Two other studies (Phares, 1971; Davis & Davis, 1972) lend additional evidence. Externals seem to behave reliably in their readiness to eschew responsibility for failure whereas internals seem to be less driven to deny or avoid the information availed by failure experiences. In the Phares (1971) study, subjects were administered four tasks described as measures of intelligence. Prior to performing on these tasks, subjects were asked to rank the tests in terms of how much they wished to succeed on them. By arbitrarily limiting the time allowed

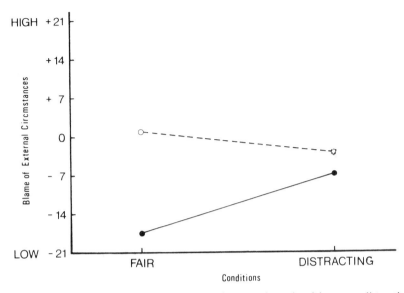

FIGURE 10 Blame attribution for internals and externals under fair versus distracting conditions. (●) Internal; (○) external. (From Phares, Wilson, & Klyver, 1971.)

for task completion, subjects were failed on those tests ranked as either the first or second most preferred. Afterward, subjects were asked to rank the four tests again, this time with the benefit of firsthand experience. Phares found that internals did not shift in their evaluation of the tasks when given the opportunity to rerank their preferences. Externals, however, did shift their preferences away from those on which they had "failed." In two successive studies, Davis and Davis (1972) found that internals readily blamed themselves for their failures more than did externals. Whether failure was incurred on an "intelligence" test comprised of a series of anagrams, or on a test of "social sensitivity" in which subjects had to predict another person's attitudes, externals were less likely to attribute cause for failure to themselves than were internals.

In these experiments, then, externals were found to be more likely to shift about in their judgments and evaluations, and more ready to denigrate tasks or blame other persons for their failures than were internals. Such findings indicate, at least, that failure is more of an irritant to externals, causing them to reorder their constructions of events. The stability of internals, on the other hand, suggests perhaps that there is not the finality in failure that there is for externals. If a person maintains hope or a "wait until next time" approach, failure should not rest as heavy upon him. If he is responsible for his failures, then a bit more effort or familiarity with given tasks may enable him to exercise greater ability in subsequent trials with a task.

In one other study (DuCette & Wolk, 1972) externals were found to make aspiration choices and decisions that could be characterized as providing less feedback and information than the choices of internals. With a homogeneous sample of 173 freshman high school girls, DuCette and Wolk (1972) queried students as to their aspirations for schooling and occupations, their anticipated examination performances, and, as well, provided some puzzles about which subjects made decisions regarding their wish to persist and the levels of difficulty that they would be willing to try. All measures were scored in terms of response extremity; that is, responses were scored as involving no risk at all, moderate risk, or excessively high risk. For example, anticipated test estimates of less than 20% or higher than 80% were considered extreme, as was the willingness to quit after failing one puzzle. Each of the responses was scored for extremity and a $X^2 = 6.09$, $p < .02$ indicated that across dependent measures extreme responses were most common within the external sample. This preference among externals for the very easy or extremely difficult or improbable was said to reflect their lesser desire for feedback relevant to their abilities. The intermediate risk choice preferred by internals, on the other hand, was exactly the sort that would provide more information about one's ability to progress toward goals, and could therefore be characterized as less defensive.

The data within these experiments concerned with response to failure and to performance feedback do not provide us with firm interpretations. However, the ready acceptance of blame for failure and the choosing of options that provide clear self-evaluative feedback by internals provide eloquent refutation of an argument positing a "need" to forget, with all of the connotations of anxiety and defensiveness.

SELF-REPORTS OF PSYCHOPATHOLOGY

Most of the above discussion derives from research conducted in academic settings with contrived challenges for the persons involved. Whatever is lost in the artificiality of this research, however, is gained in the relevance of the content area of that research for such clinical problems as depression. Beck (1967), for instance, has recently written:

> The depressed patient is peculiarly sensitive to any impediments to his goal directed activity. An obstacle is regarded as an impossible barrier. Difficulty in dealing with a problem is interpreted as a total failure. His cognitive response to a problem or difficulty is likely to be an idea such as "I'm licked," "I'll never be able to do this," or "I'm blocked no matter what I do." In achievement-oriented situations depressed patients are particularly prone to react with a sense of failure [pp. 256–257].

Though the investigations discussed above did not deal with clinical problems per se, the pertinence to depression of coping with failure at least is made obvious by Beck. Since internals manifest less perturbance from failure experiences than externals, it might be conjectured that an external locus of control and depressiveness are related. A positive correlation has been reported among college students—the more external the student, the more frequently did he report incidents of depression (Abramowitz, 1969). Similarly, Warehime and Woodson (1971) found externals more apt to acknowledge the experiencing of negative affects, including depressive feelings, than internals, and Goss and Morosko (1970) found a significant correlation between the I–E scale and the Depressiveness subscale of the MMPI among three samples of alcoholic outpatients [r = .24, n.s. with 62 females; r = .31 p < .01 with 100 males; and r = .22, p < .05 with a second group of 100 males].

Several other investigators have more recently found similar results. Calhoun, Cheney, and Dawes (1974) found externality to be associated with relatively enduring symptoms of depression among both males and females, and to transitory depressions as well among males. Naditch, Gargan, and Michael (1975) were able to predict depression scores obtained on the Cornell Medical Index among a large sample [N = 547] of soldiers undergoing basic training. Locus of control and a measure of relative discontent, derived from Cantril's Self-Anchoring Striving Scale, allowed for an interactive prediction of depression. Highly discontented externals had the highest incidence of depressive symptomotology. Haley and Strickland (1977) used the I+ and I− scales from IAR separately to predict depression scores on the Zung depression scale in two samples. It was found to be negatively correlated with depression [r = −.19, p < .03 in Study One and r = −.20, p < .01 in Study Two], whereas I−, the internal attribution for failure, was only weakly related to depression [r = .14, p < .10 in study one and ns. in Study Two]. In this study, the attribution of successes to internal sources seemed to be the obverse of depressive affect. O'Leary, Donovan, Cysewski, & Chaney (1977) were able to predict scores on Beck's Depression Inventory and on the MMPI Depression Scale among a sample of alcoholics with Rotter's I–E scale and Tiffany's Experienced Control Scale (Tiffany, 1967). Externals (I–E scale) with minimal experienced control proved to be the highest on both measures of depression. Finally, Boor (1976) used previously published I–E norms for subjects in several countries and drew comparisons with published suicide rates for those countries. Among those ten countries, New Zealand and Israel had produced the most internal scores and were low in suicide rates. In contrast, Japan and Sweden had the most external scores and the highest rates of suicide. The resulting correlation between locus of control means and suicide rate was r = .68, p < .05, df = 8.

The evidence is sketchy. But what evidences do exist indicate that externals are more likely to admit to depressive feelings than are internals. There is something paradoxical about these data however. Why should one feel depressed about that for which he bears little responsibility? Indeed, why should a person experience anxiety if his world is already perceived as unpredictable and uncontrollable?

If anxiety is defined as the state of anticipation of uncertainty, or of the loss of ability to function adaptively, then it would seem more likely to occur among individuals who believe that they exercise some control over their lives. If the world is already an uncertain and uncontrollable place for an external, then one would not imagine him suffering in anticipation of what he already believes to be the case. Despite this appeal to common sense, empirical data attest to the opposite. As indicated in Table 2, most investigators report a positive relationship between I-E measures and tests of anxiety—persons holding external control expectancies admit to more experience of anxiety than do those who perceive themselves as internals.

The relationships reported between locus of control and anxiety are rarely very large in magnitude. However, the direction of these relationships is consistent and statistically significant. Only facilitative anxiety is more commonly acknowledged by internals than externals and that measure differs radically from other anxiety scales in that its content focuses upon adaptive responses to stress—the subject is queried as to his responses that should facilitate the likelihood of succeeding at stress-provoking tasks. Obviously this measure is not equivalent to other anxiety measures that stress general negative affective responses (Manifest Anxiety Scale) or situation specific anxiety reactions (Test Anxiety-Death Anxiety).

Investigations in addition to those noted in Table 2 have replicated the finding that external control expectancies are related to admissions of anxiety, depression, and general dysphoria (Burnes, Brown, & Keating, 1971; Goss, & Morosko, 1970; Morelli, Krotinger, & Moore, 1979; Platt and Eisenman, 1968; Powell & Vega, 1972). In short, the evidence counterindicates the seemingly sensible assumption that negative affect states such as depression and anxiety should be more common among those who are likely to hold themselves responsible for their successes and failures.

Phares' hypotheses about this apparent paradox seem eminently reasonable. Internals should have greater difficulty coming to terms with failure if such information were taken to be self-relevant. However, the assumption that internals, like classic hysterics, might become repressive and perceptually avoidant of such information is not convincing. Repression and other such avoidance techniques are more often described as primitive defense mechanisms in contrast to intellectualization, isolation, and sublimation. If locus of control can be said to reflect or be related to social competence or social maturity, it would seem unlikely that an internal locus of control would be associated with a set of less mature or more primitive defense mechanisms.

If we allow ourselves to shift our language style, however, a resolution to the paradoxical findings may be possible. Rather than speaking of defenses, as if everyone must repel or protect themselves against daily travails, it may be more

TABLE 2

Correlations between Locus of Control and Various Measures of Anxiety

Anxiety Scale	Correlation with I–E	Reference
Alpert–Haber Debilitating Anxiety	$r = .23$ ns, $N = 47$	Butterfield (1964)
Alpert–Haber Facilitating Anxiety	$r = -.68, p < .01, N = 47$	Butterfield (1964)
Alpert–Haber Debilitating Anxiety	$r = .38, p < .05, N = 31$ (M)*	Feather (1967)
Alpert–Haber Debilitating Anxiety	$r = .07$, ns, $N = 53$ (F)**	Feather (1967)
Alpert–Haber Facilitating Anxiety	$r = .07$, ns, $N = 31$ (M)	Feather (1967)
Alpert–Haber Facilitating Anxiety	$r = -.19$, ns, $N = 53$ (F)	Feather (1967)
Test Anxiety	$r = .36, p < .05, N = 46$ (F)	Feather (1967)
Test Anxiety	$r = .13, p < .10, N = 153$ (M)	Feather (1967)
Test Anxiety	$r = .22, p < .01, N = 323$	Ray and Katahn (1968)
Test Anxiety	$r = .21, p < .01, N = 303$	Ray and Katahn (1968)
Manifest Anxiety	$r = .40, p < .01, N = 323$	Ray and Katahn (1968)
Manifest Anxiety	$r = .30, p < .01, N = 303$	Ray and Katahn (1968)
Death Anxiety	$r = .23, p < .05, N = 77$	Tolor and Reznikoff (1967)
Alpert–Haber Debilitating Anxiety	$r = .25, p < .01, N = 142$ (M)	Watson (1967)
Alpert–Haber Debilitating Anxiety	$r = .26, p < .01, N = 506$ (F)	Watson (1967)
Alpert–Haber Facilitating Anxiety	$r = -.15, p < .06, N = 142$ (M)	Watson (1967)
Alpert–Haber Facilitating Anxiety	$r = -.06$, ns, $N = 506$ (F)	Watson (1967)
Manifest Anxiety	$r = .38, p < .01, N = 142$ (M)	Watson (1967)
Manifest Anxiety	$r = .35, p < .01, N = 506$ (F)	Watson (1967)

*(M) = Males.   **(F) = Females.

productive to think in terms of coping styles, with their more active connotation of struggle and encounter.

In the data derived from correlations between I–E and measures of anxiety, the one reversal, though of a low magnitude, was with facilitative anxiety. If we examine a sample of the items from this scale (Alpert & Haber, 1960) perhaps some light may be shed upon differences in coping styles that are characteristic of internal- and external-control-oriented subjects:

> I work most effectively under pressure, as when the task is very important. Nervousness while taking a test helps me do better.
>
> When I start a test, nothing is able to distract me. [pp. 213–214].

Each of nine items like the above is either accepted or rejected by the subject and, in at least two studies, internals were more likely to agree with these items than externals. The latter, on the other hand, more often answered the items from the Debilitating Anxiety Scale in the affirmative than did internals. Examples of items from this scale are as follows (Alpert & Haber, 1960):

> Nervousness while taking an exam or test hinders me from doing well.
>
> In a course where I have been doing poorly, my fear of a bad grade cuts down my efficiency.
>
> During exams or tests, I block on questions to which I know the answers, even though I might remember them as soon as the exam is over.
>
> I am so tired from worrying about an exam that I found I almost don't care how well I do by the time I start the test. [p. 214].

Agreement with the facilitating anxiety items suggests what we commonly might describe as eagerness or motivation. The student acknowledges the arousing impact of examinations—he becomes nervous and unidirectional. In effect, he appears to be like a man at the starting line before a short dash—keyed up, hyperalert, and, once on the move, totally unconcerned about anything else. The conclusion—whether one wins or loses—becomes secondary to the preparation for and onset of action. The doing that is required in the challenge becomes primary. In essence, all cognitive-affective activity ceases but for the efforts demanded in the test.

In contrast, debilitating anxiety suggests the reverse. A student who admits to debilitating anxiety is stating that the task, test, or challenge is secondary to his feelings; that is, worry about ends and immediate affective responses are more prominent than the actual process of "doing." Thus, the student becomes "blocked," fearful, and perhaps even disinterested during the very period of testing. In search of an appropriate analogy one is reminded of *Zorba the Greek*, the novel by Nikos Kazantzakis, in which Zorba, the "servant," characteristically attacks challenges with a verve and enthusiasm that bewilders his more ruminative, artistocratic "boss." The latter obsessively worries and fails to accomplish his ambitions whereas Zorba plunges headfirst into one activity after another.

Most pertinent to the immediate discussion is the manner in which Zorba and his boss cope with failure and tragedy. The boss, who is a youthful, philosophically oriented writer, works in fits and starts. Every challenge, whether it be relevant to his work or social life, is engaged in with great hesitancy. In one series of episodes in which a young, attractive widow provides several "come hither" hints, considerable pushing from Zorba is required to encourage his youthful boss to respond. When the young man finally does respond to this and other challenges and eventually becomes witness to tragedy and failure, his response is to become maudlin about the inevitability of man's agony. Zorba, on the other hand, copes buoyantly with failure. He engages in vigorous dancing after suffering catastrophe in his creation of a complex irrigation project. In essence, Zorba teaches his boss that life is full of failure but that one must struggle on, fight, and resurrect oneself in the face of defeat.

To dance a vibrant Greek folk dance after failure is as if to say—"to hell with it—let's get on with living—there are other challenges to be encountered—other windmills with which to tilt." To call such a coping style denial or repressiveness would miss what is perhaps more important—Zorba always remains hopeful about tomorrow. Failure may be incurred in one project, but there are always other tasks, other commitments through which one can join the effortful pursuit of challenge. Today's failures can never be allowed to be so overwhelming as to preclude subsequent efforts. Resurgency, buoyancy, and humor would seem to be elements in a coping style that might result in less recall of failures but more preparation and readiness to engage in new challenges.

Though banal by comparison to the literary analogy, the dimensions of facilitative and debilitative anxiety offer a rough approximation to these opposites. In the former there is a sense of excitement in challenge, in the latter, a surrender and a shrinking away from encounter. That these two forms of anxiety are opposites is substantiated by the inverse relationship between them, which ranges from $-.37$, $p < .01$ (Alpert & Haber, 1960) to $-.77$ $p < .001$ (Butterfield, 1964). In turn, as we indicated previously, internal control expectancies are associated with greater facilitative and less debilitative anxiety, while external control expectancies are associated with the opposite.

In the preceding discussion, the inferred links between locus of control and psychopathology have been based on correlations between self-statements. In essence, we are observing a concurrence of descriptions; those who describe themselves as external in response to the I-E scale also describe themselves as more likely to become depressed or anxious. A second necessary approach is to ascertain whether locus of control is related to pathology as assessed by outside observers.

OBSERVER REPORTS OF PSYCHOPATHOLOGY

Harrow and Ferrante (1969) examined the relationship between locus of control and types of disorders among a sample of upper middle-class psychiatric patients. Diagnoses were independently extablished by two experienced clinicians. Patients who were diagnosed as schizophrenic were found to score in a more external direction than all nonschizophrenic patients. This finding replicated an earlier one reported by Cromwell, Rosenthal, Shakow, & Zahn, (1961).

The patient sample included a group of five patients diagnosed as manic, a type of pathology that is often characterized by the display of grandiosity. Harrow and Ferrante found that the manic patients had a mean score of 4.2 on the I-E scale, which was significantly more internal that the means of all nonmanic patients.

The patients were reassessed on the I-E scale after a six-week period at the clinical facility, with the expectation that there would be some shifts in I-E toward the internal end of the continuum. The first finding of interest was that schizophrenics did not display any increase in internality in contrast to other groups. Depressive patients, on the other hand, did change significantly toward greater internality from the first to second assessments. Other groups also exhibited shifts toward internality, though to a less degree than depressives. The single exception was manic patients who became more external, though the small number of subjects in this diagnostic category precluded statistical significance. In essence, the manics appeared to recover to some degree from an extreme internality (grandiosity) and became more cognizant of their limitations.

Although most patient groups decreased in externality and manics increased in externality, only schizophrenics remained relatively the same. The differences between schizophrenics and normals reported by Harrow and Ferrante have been found by other investigators. Cromwell et al. (1961) had found schizophrenics to be more external on four measures of the I-E dimension (James-Phares I-E scale, the Bialer-Cromwell scale, and two early prototypes of Rotter's I-E scale) and Cash and Stack (1973) found externality on the I-E scale to be associated with schizophrenia [$r = .57$, $p < .001$] and paranoia [$r = .59$, p $< .001$] on the MMPI.

Other investigators have examined the severity of psychopathology with relevance to the locus of control. Shybut (1968), for instance, found that severely disturbed psychiatric patients who had been rated for severity of psychopathology on the basis of disorders of thought, affect, behavior, and social adjustment were more external than moderately disturbed patients and normal persons. Smith, Pryer, and Distefano (1971) replicated Shybut's findings when severity of emotional impairment was assessed by psychiatric attendants using a behavioral adjustment scale. These investigators found that the severely impaired group was higher in external control expectancies than the mildly impaired group.

Lottman and de Wolfe (1972) have reported that locus of control is related to the process-reactive dimension of schizophrenia. Process schizophrenics exhibit little competence throughout their life span. Usually such patients are disorganized and deviant from earliest recorded observations. Reactive schizophrenics, in contrast, have often been competent until beset by a crisis that leaves them in a state of dismay. Such patients often recover with but little attention from the staff in clinical facilities, a period of respite seeming to suffice in their recovery. Comparing patients on the I–E dimension, process schizophrenics were found to be more external than either reactive schizophrenics or nonschizophrenic control subjects. The latter two groups did not differ from each other. The finding failed to be replicated, however, in a study by Cash and Stack (1973).

Palmer (1971) found that not only were psychiatric patients more external on Rotter's I–E scale than nonpsychiatric patients, but that a brief index of competence derived from education, marital status, and occupational level differentiated the most from least external within the psychiatric patient sample. In general, the more internal the patient, the more competent he seemed on the composite index.

Thus far, we may conclude that the admission of anxiety and/or depression, the diagnosis of schizophrenia, and rated severity of personal disorders are related to locus of control. Two studies remain to be discussed, however, in which the relation between pathology and locus of control was in the opposite direction. Goss and Morosko (1970) found that alcoholics scored in a more internal control direction than did the normative samples reported by Rotter (1966). As a secondary point of interest, Goss and Morosko also found within their alcoholic sample positive relationships between locus of control and anxiety, depression, and clinical pathology as assessed by the MMPI; that is, the more external the alcoholic, the more likely he was to respond in a pathological and dysphoric fashion on the MMPI.

Similar results among drug addicts have been reported by Berzins and Ross (1973). They found hospitalized narcotic addicts to be significantly more internal than a rather large sample of university students. Berzins and Ross attempted to explain their findings in terms of experienced self control via opiates; that is, the addict is said to achieve control over bodily states, anxieties, conflicts, and so on through his use of drugs and, therefore, comes to see himself as more internal perhaps than he had been prior to his addiction. Goss and Morosko contend that alcohol affords the alcoholic a similar means for regulating his feelings, thus resulting in a greater sense of personal control.

Since these studies were published there has been a groundswell of research pertaining to the linkage between locus of control, alcoholism, and the addictions. These studies have been well summarized in two review articles by Rohsenow and O'Leary (1978a,b). As Rohsenow and O'Leary have noted, there is considerable conflict in this literature. Evidence has been reported to the effect that externality is associated with alcoholism (Butts & Chotlos, 1973; Chess, Neuringer, & Goldstein, 1971; Nowicki & Hopper, 1974), with problem drinking (Naditch, 1975) and with hypochondriasis and acute adverse reactions to psychoactive drugs (Naditch, 1974). At the same time, other studies have suggested that alcoholics are more internal or equal to nonalcoholics with regard to locus of control (Donovan & O'Leary, 1975; Goss & Morosko, 1970; Gozali & Sloan, 1971; Gross & Nerviano, 1972) and that addicts similarly are more internal or equivalent to nonaddicts (Calicchia, 1974; Strassberg & Robinson, 1974).

In an attempt to explain these paradoxical findings, Rohsenow and O'Leary have raised questions concerning the heterogeneity that exists with alcoholic samples and the appropriateness of locus of control scales for these persons. It has been found that alcoholism can occur for a variety of reasons and can serve a number of purposes. Consequently, Rohsenow and O'Leary suggest that it is unlikely that any personality variable will be highly characteristic of such a diverse set of persons. In addition, since most alcoholic samples studied have been middle aged, the pertinence of most locus of control scales are questionable. That is, academic achievement or friendship making may be of little interest to the middle-aged alcoholic facing the dissolution of his home life and career.

To meet the need for assessing locus of control among alcoholics, Donovan and O'Leary (1978) have published an extensive description of the Drink-related Locus of Control Scale (DRIE) with reliability and validity data. Alcoholics who score as more external on the DRIE are found to be more depressed, more self-critical, more pessimstic with periodic thoughts of suicide, more indecisive and inhibited, and are found to be more deviate in their profile patterns on the MMPI than are internal alcoholics. Likewise external alcoholics are found to be more anxious and dissatisfied; to have more difficulties with interpersonal communication; and to have less adequate coping skills than internals, as assessed by the DRIE. The DRIE was compared with Rotter's I–E scale and the relationships with the DRIE were higher in most cases. In addition, the DRIE differentiated among alcoholics and nonalcoholics, whereas the I–E scale did not. As Donovan and O'Leary (1978) hope, they may have found a way to help resolve some of the conflicting data obtained from alcoholics. As will be noted in the assessment chapter, the development of measurement devices pertinent to given samples and problems may help to make locus of control more useful as a predictor of behavior in different settings with particular persons.

Though the paradoxical findings with alcoholics and addicts compel one to search for explanations, the suggestion that the momentary impulse control afforded by alcohol and other drugs influences perceived control as assessed by I–E scales seems specious. Alcoholics and drug addicts often are known to deny the fact that they have become dependent upon a drug. It is, consequently, not accidental that an important element in recovery for both alcoholics and drug addicts is the open admission of addiction. Perhaps the more internal responses of some addicts reflect a tendency to deny the very helplessness or slavishness to the drug in question that is so evident to everyone but the addict himself. It may also be this tendency to deny disability that accounts for the lower scores on MMPI indexes of dysphoria among some internal addicts, for it seems inconceivable that the addict does not suffer feelings of discontent with his increasingly failure-ridden life.

ADDITIONAL CONTRIBUTIONS

In the studies by Glass and Singer (1972) described in Chapter 1, two ego-relevant functions—frustration tolerance, as represented in the decision to persist despite failure, and vigilance, as demanded in proofreading—diminished significantly subsequent to an uncontrollable aversive experience. Likewise, the study of persons who had attempted to commit suicide reported by Melges and Weisz (1971) implicated another ego function, that of time binding, with locus of control. Individuals at the time of their suicide attempt reported a marked loss of awareness of the future as well as a loss of the sense of control.

These ego functions—frustration tolerance, attention, and time binding—are, within psychoanalytic theory, necessary for the maintenance of an integrated, nonpathological personality. Without the efficient and effective operations of the ego a person is more subject to what Freud described as dangers from within or without. As a consequence, he frequently suffers anxiety and erects protective defenses against anxiety-arousing dangers. These defenses, when marked, can so hinder an individual in his goal-directed activity that the resultant helplessness often eventuates in a diagnosis of psychopathology. In fact, Bibring (1953) has contended that the basic mechanism of depression is ''the ego's shocking awareness of its helplessness in regard to its aspirations [p. 43].'' Bibring views the surcease of activity among depressives as a surrender, not of the goals, but of the pursuit of them, because there is little hope that the pursuit will be effective.

In essence, a weakened ego affords poor prognosis, whether through a loss of ability to cope with external challenges or through the *awareness* of one's own weakness and vulnerability. The important point to be made here is that the ego skills noted above, as well as those described in research with information assimilation (DuCette & Wolk, 1973), hypothesis formation (Lefcourt, Gronnerud, & McDonald, 1973), and information seeking and utility (Davis & Phares, 1967; Phares, 1968), allow us to assert that an internal locus of control and ego strength are likely to coexist within the same persons. In fact, it is conceivable that a perception of internal control may be the phenomenological counterpart to ego strength.

Robert White (1965) had forged a similar link between what he refers to as a ''sense of competence'' and ego strength in theorizing about the sources of schizophrenia:

It is important . . . to make allowance for the child's action upon his environment, of the extent to which this action is apt to be successful, and consequently of the confidence he builds up that he can influence his surroundings in desired ways. I use the term sense of competence to describe this, and I think that one's sense of competence is an exceedingly important aspect of self-esteem. We can suppose that a placid child who has always received generous narcissistic supplies, without doing much to earn them will enjoy an agreeable level of self-esteem, provided he never enters a harsher environment. Self-esteem will be much more substantial, however, in the more active child who feels confident that he can elicit esteem from others by competent performances, by modulated assertiveness, or by personal charm. It is to this second person that we would attribute large ego strength. The first would strike us as too much at the mercy of his surroundings [p. 201].

White subsequently evokes a case for the position that schizophrenic withdrawal derives from a sense of incompetence:

The schizophrenic has not been able to reach, or at least to maintain, a bearable level of confidence that he can influence others so that they will engage with him on an equal basis, listen to him, understand him, respect him, and given him some of the things he wants from human interaction. Not having the confidence, being constantly forced into submissive, avoidant, and other helpless roles, he has not been able to maintain self-respect, has come to dislike people, and has quite possibly not dared to love anyone [p. 208].

In brief, White contends that a sense of helplessness or, in the present terms, an external control orientation, results in dissatisfaction during social interaction. The person who feels unable to succeed in obtaining desired ends in social interactions will come to a point where those interactions are perceived as aversive. The withdrawal of persons suffering with schizophrenia is, then, interpreted as avoidance of events that are perceived as offering displeasure.

A second point of some interest discussed by White is his differentiation of "confidence" from self-esteem. Where esteem is defined in terms of the value with which one is held by others or by himself, confidence reflects the expectancy held regarding one's ability to determine his fate through the use of personal skills. This differentiation lends some precision to the locus of control construct. Locus of control and self-esteem are not identical, though an internal locus of control should make positive self-esteem a more likely and frequent occurrence.

Another differentiation that may be profitable to consider is that between specific and more generalized expectancies of control. Valins and Nisbett (1971) have presented case reports as well as data deriving from elaborate investigation the reveals the salutary effects of shifting patients' causal attributions from internal to external sources. In one case discussed by these authors, a man who feared that he was a homosexual was helped to overcome his anxiety and depression by being instructed in how he had misconstrued his own "normal" behaviors. In essence, he was taught that what he had considered abnormalities deriving from personal proclivities were actually natural derivatives from mistaken perceptions of his own body; that is, his difficulties were not "personal" or intrinsic to his character but accidents of perception. This externalization, so to speak, served to lessen the patient's consequent burden of guilt and self-derogation.

In this and other instances discussed by Valins and Nisbett, patients' attributions of causality are the object of therapeutic intervention. Patients are encouraged to shift attributions of cause, sometimes to external, sometimes to internal sources, depending on the circumstances involved in the case at hand. These reattributions are most often of a singular nature—the reconstrual of a drug effect, a symptom, or a reaction. In each case, the misattribution has left the patient believing that he is incapable of dealing with his problems. Therapy, while at the same time encouraging a specific external attribution, can oddly enough serve to reinstate the general sense of being able to act. In social learning terms, shifts in specific expectancies from internal to external can be said to at times encourage the return of confidence or generalized expectancies of internal control. If a person's confidence has faltered, for instance, because he has aspired to goals that are beyond his grasp, then it would seem likely that a lowering of aspirations to a more attainable level may help a person regain faith in his abilities and consequently become more ready to accept other challenges. Thus, specific expectancies or attributions of causality may at times be the obverse of generalized expectancies of control. That discriminations need to be drawn between events that are controllable and those that are not, if one is to maintain an internal locus of control, appeals to common sense. Its therapeutic value may be appreciated in noting the similarity with the prayer adopted by Alcoholics Anonymous from a sermon by Reinhold Niebuhr: "O God, Give us the serenity to accept what cannot be changed, courage to change what should be changed, and wisdom to distinguish the one from the other."

CONCLUSIONS

While some areas of uncertainty remain, there is good reason to believe, on the basis of the research reviewed, that external control orientation and abnormal personal functioning are correlated. One ambiguity is the direction of causality—does being ineffective and defensive generate a sense of helplessness; or, the converse, does helplessness generate defensiveness? In all probability the relationship is circular and perpetuated through a vicious circle, though there is little empirical data available to allow for certainty regarding this conjecture.

Second, little information is available as to the coping mechanisms that might allow internals to accept failure with more grace than externals. If forgetting is not the internal's device for specifically coping with failure, then what enables him to persist despite failure? We have guessed at the idea of residual hope among internals: Given another opportunity, it might be possible to rectify to-day's errors. The formulation is appealing that internals possess resilience because of a tendency not to take defeats as final.

Third, the puzzling results with reported tendencies of internals to forget require empirical and theoretical explanation. We may guess that a busy and involved individual is more likely to forget much that he judges to be trivial each day, and we may assume that it is the internal more than the external who is likely to be the active and engaged person.

It may be concluded then that there is enough convergence of theoretical and empirical data to support the assumption of correlation between locus of control and psychopathology. What is needed are more factual details to fill in the gaps related to specific questions of how and why.

9 The Social Antecedents of Locus of Control

INTRODUCTION

In recent years there has been a widening interest in the social origins of locus of control and like constructs. Though research pertaining to social origins has been on the increase, there is some lack of incisiveness as well as of conclusiveness in the results obtained thus far. Nevertheless, some consistency can be found in the evidence deriving from diverse sources.

In this chapter, research specifically concerned with familial antecedents of locus of control is reviewed, as well as those investigative efforts dealing with a closely related construct, contingency awareness. Much of the research in this area has consisted of correlational findings—comparisons of scores obtained upon measures of locus of control from children, and scores pertaining to child-rearing practices of parents. Despite the apparent consistency of methods, however, there is considerable diversity both in terms of the measurement of locus of control and in terms of how child-rearing methods are inferred. In some cases, children are asked to describe their homes; in others, young adolescents are asked to recall what their homes were like when they were younger children. In some cases, parents have been observed while they interacted with their children, sometimes in laboratory settings, occasionally in their own homes. In other cases parents have been interviewed about their current parenting methods and attitudes; in still others, they have been asked to recall their parenting behaviors that occurred several years prior to the study in question. Although the variety of approaches is considerable, some relatively consistent findings have been obtained that appeal to common sense. Nevertheless, the reader will quickly grasp the fact that this is still an area ripe for exploration, with more questions to be asked than to be answered.

FAMILIAL ORIGINS

Among the earliest studies aimed at an examination of familial determinants of locus of control were those by Chance (1965) and Katkovsky, Crandall, and Good (1967). Chance interviewed the mothers of a select sample of university lab schoolchildren who had completed Crandall's Intellectual Achievement Responsibility Questionnaire (described in Chapter 6). The interview consisted of questions from Schaefer and Bell's Parent Attitude Research Instrument (PARI, 1958) as well as an extended inquiry regarding independence training. The latter inquiry asked the mothers at what ages they expected their children to become capable of performing various acts. Chance found that the more internal the boys on their total IAR scores, the more likely it was that they had mothers who had expectations for early independence [$r = .47$, $p < .01$]. Secondly, the more educated the mother [$r = .45$, $p < .05$] and the less concern the mother had about controlling her son [$r = .48$, $p < .01$], the more internal her son was likely to score on the IAR questionnaire. As will also be noted in certain other studies, these relationships were not obtained with girls. Each of these correlations found with males was statistically insignificant in the female sample.

Katkovsky, Crandall, and Good (1967) conducted their study with families participating in the Fel's Research Institute's Longitudinal Study of Human Development. As in Chance's study, the children's locus of control was assessed by the IAR. Given the unique nature of the Fel's Institute, however, it was possible for these investigators to make ratings of parental behavior in the home rather than to rely upon parents' self-reports. Maternal behavior was rated on nine scales of which four proved to be consistently relevant to IAR scores. These were "babying," "general protectiveness," "affectionateness," and "approval instead of criticism."

Babying referred to the extent of parental nurturance, ranging from the imposition of help despite the child's lack of need or desire for it, to a refusal of help when requested. High ratings could be said to reflect "overhelp," low ratings, the withholding of help. Observed maternal babying was found to be strongly related to children's IAR scores [$r = .64$, $p < .001$], the more internal children having the more babying mothers. Most particularly, babying was related to I−, internality for failure [$r = .68$, $p < .001$]; the correspondent relationship with I+, internality for success, was of a lesser though still significant magnitude [$r = .44$, $p < .01$].

General protectiveness was defined as the degree to which parents sheltered their children or exposed them to difficulties, discomforts, and hazards. High ratings indicated sheltering, low ratings, exposure. As with babying, this measure was related to total IAR scores [$r = .64$, $p < .001$] and again, the relationship with I− [$r = .67$, $p < .001$] was stronger than with I+ [$r = .49$, $p < .01$].

Affectionateness was defined in terms of warmth and affection versus rejection and hostility. High ratings indicated affection, low, hostility. Total IAR scores correlated significantly with affectionateness [$r = .38, p < .05$], though it was largely the I− half of the IAR, that accounted for this relationship. I− was significantly correlated with maternal affectionateness [$r = .46, p < .01$]. The relationship with I+ was insignificant.

The fourth variable, approval versus criticism, pertained to the degree to which parents offered the child praise and approval as opposed to criticism and disapproval. High ratings indicated approval, low ratings, disapproval. Overall IAR scores were related to this dimension [$r = .57, p < .001$], indicating that an internal locus of control among children was associated with having parents who were more approving than they were critical. However, unlike the other three ratings of maternal behavior, there were marked sex differences in the obtained relationships. For boys, total IAR scores and approval-criticism produced an $r = .63, p < .01$; the equivalent correlation for girls was .41, $p < .10$. For boys, approval-criticism was related to I+ [$r = .45, p < .05$] and even more so to I− [$r = .65, p < .001$], whereas for girls the same correlations were .29 and .39 respectively, both of which are statistically insignificant.

Five other rated behaviors were unrelated to the children's IAR scores. These were "restrictiveness of regulations," "severity of punishment," "clarity of policy of regulations and enforcements," "coerciveness of suggestions," and "accelerational attempts."

In addition to the rated home behaviors, the Fel's investigators interviewed and tested both the mothers and fathers of 20 girls and 20 boys. The rather lengthy interviews (2½ hours) were rated for each of four variables:

1. Affection—the amount of overt affection and acceptance that the parents seemed to feel and reported expressing toward their child;
2. Nurturance—the frequency and quality of emotional support and instrumental help given the child by the parent;
3. Dominance—the frequency and intensity of the parents' attempts at influence and control of the child through the establishment and enforcement of rules and regulations;
4. Rejection—the parents' dissatisfaction with the behaviors and personality of their child and the frequency and intensity of their direct criticisms and punishments.

The test completed by the parents was a "Parent Reaction Questionnaire" that assessed the parents' reactions to their child's achievement behaviors in four areas: intellectual, physical skill, mechanical, and artistic achievement.

For the 20 boys there were few if any relationships between their parents' interview ratings and their own IAR scores. Only maternal nurturance even approached being a correlate of IAR scores [$r -.44, p < .10$]. For girls, however parental rejection whether by mothers [$r = -.61, p < .01$] or fathers [$r = -.42, p < .10$] was associated with scores indicating an external locus of control. Otherwise, the results with the questionnaire were sparse. Paternal negative reactions to children's achievement behaviors were inversely related [$r = -.41$, $p < .01$], whereas positive reactions tended to be positively associated with total IAR scores [$r = .27$, $p < .10$]. As a point of interest, I+ (internality for success) was more highly related to paternal positive reactions [$r = .35$, $p < .05$], especially for girls [$r = .59$, $p < .01$], than the total IAR score.

From home observations, interviews, and questionnaires then, the results suggest that the "child's belief in internal control of reinforcements are related to the degree to which their parents are protective, nurturant, approving, and non-rejecting [p. 774]." The maintenance of a supportive, positive relationship between parent and child seems more likely to foster a child's belief in internal control than is a relationship characterized by punishment, rejection, and criticism.

Despite the relative congruence among the findings within this investigation, it is noteworthy that the directly observed maternal behavior proved to be more highly related to children's IAR scores than were the self-report measures obtained from either parent. This may be due to the self-consciousness aroused among parents when they are questioned about their child-rearing behavior. It is not difficult to imagine the apprehension attendant upon having one's parental adequacy assessed. To be a poor parent can be tantamount to an admission of personal inadequcy, an odious thing for this largely middle class sample.

Given the limitations of parental self-reports, several investigators who have used such data have corroborated the findings from the more direct observations of parental behavior noted above. Davis and Phares (1969) compared parents' attitudes about child rearing, children's reports of parental behavior, and the parents' own locus of control scores with those of their children. The subjects were university-age students who were asked to recall their parents' behavior. Rotter's I–E scale was used as the measure of locus of control, and the subjects included in the study were all chosen from the extremes of that dimension. The investigators' guiding hypothesis was that parental restrictiveness and directiveness would inculcate external control expectancies in children whose opportunities to test and experience the consequences of their own behaviors would thereby be curtailed.

Davis and Phares found that extreme internals recalled their parents as having had more positive involvements with them, with less rejection, hostile control, inconsistent discipline, and less withdrawal from them than did extreme externals. As with the results of the Katkovsky et al. (1967) study, however, independently assessed parental attitudes were found to be largely unrelated to children's I–E scores, though some interesting interactions with the sex of parent were noted. For instance, fathers of internals were found to have been more indulgent and less protective than had been their spouses, whereas fathers of externals had been less indulgent and more protective than their wives. Such data suggest that the evaluation of parental interactions and complementarities may be valuable targets for developmental research aimed at elucidating the antecedents of locus of control.

A dissertation by Shore (1967) revealed a pattern of results that was similar to the previously described studies. Shore assessed young children with Bialer's (1961) and Battle and Rotter's (1963) locus of control measures and also obtained the children's perceptions of their parents' behavior. As well, parents' self-reported attitudes regarding child rearing were collected. Similar to the previously discussed studies, children's locus of control scores were more related to their own descriptions of parental behavior than to their parents' self-reports. Children who perceived their parents as exercising more psychological control, as being less warm and less intrinsically accepting, scored in a more external direction than did children who described their parents in the opposite terms. The magnitude of the relationships between Bialer's locus of control measure and each "perception of parent" variable were as follows: with control [$r = .22$, $p < .01$]; with warmth [$r = .43$, $p < .01$]; and with intrinsic acceptance [$r = .46$, $p < .01$]. In contrast, only one parental attitude, the father's internality with regard to child rearing per se, was related to Bialer's locus of control scores [$r = .21$, $p < .01$].

In each of the aforementioned studies, then, parental attitudes regarding child-rearing activities proved to be the least useful information for predicting children's locus of control scores. On the other hand, children's reports about the warmth and nurturance experienced within their homes was associated with their locus of control scores. Only in the study by Katkovsky et al. (1967) were more direct observations obtained and these substantiated the reports obtained from the children themselves.

In more recent years there have been a number of investigations reported that help to confirm earlier findings while raising questions concerning particular details. Johnson and Kilmann (1975), for one, found that the recall of parental overprotectiveness and restrictiveness among university students was associated with externality on Rotter's I–E scale. Likewise, Nowicki and Segal (1974) found that perceived parental nurturance was associated with internality assessed by the NOSIE. As an interesting point, paternal nurturance was primarily associated with internality among females, but maternal nurturance proved of greater importance for male's internality.

In the latter study, parental I–E scores were estimated by the subjects and these ascribed scores proved to be highly related to the subjects' own I–E scores; this was particularly so among male subjects. Similar findings were reported by Ollendick (1979), who obtained parents' I–E scores that were compared with those of their fourth-grade children. Mothers' I–E scores proved to be related to those of their daughters' [$r = .33$, $p < .01$] as well as to measures of their daughters' anxiety. For sons, on the other hand, intelligence, achievement test scores, and behavioral adjustment were each related to maternal I–E scores, though their own I–E scores were not. As a further point, those children who had two external parents were considerably higher in anxiety and lower in intelligence measures than children who had either one or both parents classified as internals.

Finally, a study by Rohner, Chaille, & Rohner (1980) indicated that internality, assessed by the NOSIE, was positively related to age (8–12 years) but only among those who rated their parents as accepting. For those who perceived their parents as rejecting, no such trend was found with age.

The overall findings, deriving as they do from different age samples, tested with a diversity of locus of control measures and procedures for ascertaining familial experiences, are impressive in their relative consistency. Warmth, supportiveness, and parental encouragement seem to be essential for the development of an internal locus of control. Katkovsky et al. (1967) conjectured that "the security provided by the loving, nonthreatening parent is especially necessary for the child to be able to internalize the responsibility for the negative reinforcements he receives. Conversely, a mother's rejecting, primitive, and dominating behavior encourages her daughter to believe that factors outside her own control are responsible for her rewards in intellectual situations [p. 774]." That parental protectiveness, babying, affection, and approval are related to the development of an internal locus of control indicates that a certain degree of insulation must exist around a child, an insulation from the more aversive experiences, if it is to develop a sense of itself as a causative agent.

It has been suggested by some psychiatrists (Gardner, 1971) that exposure to traumatic, incapacitating events during early childhood interferes with subsequent reality testing and thus encumbers the learning of basic skills that are components of such important activities as reading. In view of the research pertaining to locus of control, it is possible to add to Gardner's formulation that for a child to develop into a reality testing adult, one who is aware of his capabilities and limitations, he needs to be reared in a home in which he is relatively sheltered from aversive stimulation that could intimidate him and thus decrease his sense of freedom to explore his milieu. In becoming less exploratory the child would have too constricted a range of experiences from which to discover his particular talents.

In recent years evidence has accumulated to add substance to Gardner's assertion. For example, experiencing the break up of the family, a major trauma for any child, has been found to be associated with the development of an external locus of control which, in turn, may interfere with reality testing and the development of competence. Both Hetherington (1972) and Duke and Lancaster (1976) found father-absent children to be more external than those from intact homes. Similarly, Cook, Novaco, and Sarason (1980) found that marine recruits from intact homes were more internal than were those from homes in which divorces or separations had occurred [$F = 7.13$, $p < .008$, 1/545].

Finally, in longitudinal investigations concerned with attachment processes in infancy and early childhood, Sroufe (1979) has found that security in the relationship between caregivers and children of 15 months of age is associated with competence in interactions with peers at the age of 3½ years, and later with curiosity and resilience when the children were five years of age. The security provided by caregivers was defined in terms of the mother's availability, responsiveness to signals, and reliability with regard to emotional comforting. Security rated in early childhood was associated with confidence, skill development, and the capability of affective involvement in later years as was reflected in the children's enthusiasm, persistence, and effectiveness when encountering challenges. Whereas Sroufe (1979) has not explicitly related his findings to those reported in the literature concerned with locus of control, it is evident that a certain degree of similarity exists. The development of internal control expectancies with its concomitant development of basic skills requires the kind of nurturant, protective home free of traumatic, incapacitating events that characterizes secure attachments.

Theoretical Considerations of Familial Influences

Despite the appeal of the above formulations it would be a marked oversight to ignore a number of questions generated by the data presented thus far. For instance, it may be asked how a "babied" child, one who is overindulged by a hyper-responsive parent, can develop a sense of himself as an active source. It is likely that he receives social reinforcement on a random, if overabundant schedule and therefore may fail to perceive a connection between the occurrence of social reinforcements and his behavior. Alfred Adler described the debilitating effects of pampering and neglect, the former of which corresponds to the common definition of babying. Adler (Ansbacher & Ansbacher, 1956) believed that if children were overindulged or neglected they were equally likely to develop misguided "fictions" about life, and these were frequently in the form of exaggerated feelings of inferiority and helplessness. Pampered children were said to be as thwarted in their development as were neglected children in that they were deprived of the opportunity to learn how to act so as to cause the occurrence of desired outcomes. Both pampered and neglected children, then, through lack of experience with contingent reinforcement, may fail to explore and discover the relationships between acts and outcomes from which beliefs in the order of causal sequences develop. Nonreinforcement for one and indiscriminate reinforcement for the other may result in exaggerated feelings of helplessness, or an extremely external locus of control.

Nurturance and babying, therefore, must be distinguished from the indiscriminate reinforcement implied by the term pampering if the research described in this chapter is to be in harmony with Adler's sensible formulations. Other theorists such as Erich Fromm (1956) offer some help in drawing this distinction. Fromm has discussed "mother love" in a way that clarifies the difference between nurturance that encourages growth and development and the more stultifying aspects of pampering:

> In motherly love . . . the relationship between the two persons involved is one of inequality; the child is helpless and dependent on the mother. In order to grow, it must become more and more independent, until he does not need mother any more.

Thus the mother-child relationship is paradoxical and, in a sense tragic. It requires the most intense love on the mother's side, and yet this very love must help the child to grow away from the mother, and to become fully independent. It is easy for any mother to love her child before this process of separation has begun-but it is the task in which most fail, to love the child and at the same time to let it go-and to *want* to let it go [pp. 33-34].

Implied in Fromm's writing pertinent to love is a temporal element that can perhaps define the differences between nurturance, babying, and pampering. Nurturance may be defined as that "intense love" required of parents to enable their children to securely pass through their more vulnerable years. However, this safety and security can become arresting if the parents do not later accept the movement toward independence that safety engenders. A. H. Maslow (1954) has discussed a similar point of view from the perspective of motivation theory. The more expansive motives, curiosity and exploration through the desire for self-actualization, rest upon more basic foundations such as safety and security that are established in the earlier interactions between children and their families. In effect, the warm and protective home that has been found to be associated with the development of an internal locus of control may be described as one where the child is protected in his early years but not squelched; where he is sheltered from the excessive frustrations that can easily occur when a child is young and relatively helpless that, in turn, can engender a more fearful approach to life's challenges. That children with an internal locus of control recall their homes as more warm and nurturant settings than do external children may also indicate the acceptance with which their own movement toward independence was greeted. It is a moot point whether persons would recall their homes as warm when their attainment of independence was thwarted by parental overindulgence. The themes of many novels, particularly those of Philip Roth, depict the anguish and anger of children reared in such smothering homes.

Recent Empirical Advances

Virginia Crandall (1973) has presented a unique set of data concerning familial antecedents of locus of control that are of immediate relevance to the above discussion. Crandall's data is exceptional in that they are comprised of locus of control measures assessed during young adulthood, home observations of maternal behavior during the first ten years, and interviews with subjects during early adolescence.

With this uncommon set of longitudinal data, Crandall expressed considerable surprise to find that "coolness" and "criticality" on the mother's part was often positively associated with internal locus of control scores obtained in young adulthood. Crandall tempered her response to this reversal of the highly replicated warmth-internality correlations as follows: "I do not mean to imply that these maternal and familial predictions were composed of cruel rejection, devastating criticism, severe neglect or extreme family pathology, for these are rare in the Fels sample. I only mean to indicate that from the moderate range of these behaviors displayed in our sample, those on the "negative" end were associated with adult internality [p. 11]."

In addition to this emphasis on the "moderate range of behaviors" Crandall attributed some of the difference between her results and those of others to the ages at which locus of control was assessed. As Crandall states:

> It may be that warm, protective, supportive maternal behaviors are necessary for the assumption of personal responsibility during childhood, but in the long run, militate against internality at maturity. Perhaps internality at later developmental stages is best facilitated by some degree of maternal 'coolness' criticality, and stress, so that offspring were not allowed to rely on overly indulgent affective relationships with their mothers, but were forced to learn objective cause-effect contingencies, adjust to them, and recognize their own instrumentality in causing those outcomes [p. 11].

Among the correlates of locus of control scores, independence training proved to be one of the most reliable. Mothers of internals were more likely to have "pushed their children toward independence, less often rewarded dependency, and displayed less intense involvement and contact with them (p. 12)." Though the ages at which locus of control and independence training were most highly related differed between sexes "nevertheless, the internal adult has at some time during childhood experienced a greater push out of the nest than the external adult [p. 12]."

Crandall's conclusions are resonant with the theorizing of Fromm as noted above. The child is thought to need some degree of security that is afforded by a nurturant home but also the freedom to explore his world. This, as Crandall states, is facilitated by some distance and criticality on the part of his parents:

> In childhood, then, when offspring are most dependent on parental acceptance, it may be that the assumption of internality, especially for failure, is expedited if the maternal push toward independence is embedded in a warm, supportive maternal-child relationship. At maturity, however, after the offspring no longer need rely on such maternal emotional support, then some previous lack of affectionate behavior and close involvement in childhood seem to be interpreted as part and parcel of a general maternal assist to help them stand on their own feet [pp. 12–13].

When Crandall finally addressed herself to the question of why the maternal "push from the nest" is so helpful for the development of an internal locus of control, her response is close to some of the previous discussions in this chapter: "I would like to suggest that its function is to put the child into more active intercourse with his physical and social environment so that there is more opportunity for him to observe the effect of his own behavior, the contingency between his own actions and ensuing events, unmediated by maternal intervention (p. 13)."

Other investigators have confirmed Crandall's thesis regarding independence training. Wichern and Nowicki (1976), for example, found that seventh-grade internals perceived their mothers as being more lax than had externals, and that the mothers of internals reported that they had allowed their children greater independence at an earlier age than had the mothers of externals. In three other studies in which parent and child interactions have been directly observed, analogous findings have been obtained. Loeb (1975) observed parents as they interacted with their blindfolded children who were attempting to build a tower of blocks. Parental remarks were coded as being either suggestive, in which case the parents offered possible choices, or as directive, in which case the parents clearly directed their children as to what they should do. The parents of externals were found to decidedly give more directions than suggestions, a predilection that was repeated during the administration of a "family Rorschach." These data bear similarity to those reported by Wichern, Gordon, and Nowicki (1981), who found that as children worked on jigsaw puzzles with their mothers, more help and interference was forthcoming from the mothers of externals, though greater attention was paid by the mothers of internals. In response, external children were less cooperative and yet more help seeking than were internal children. Similarly, Chandler, Wolf, Cook, and Dugovics (1980) observed the interactions between parents and their children while the latter were engaged in block and rocket building tasks. The parents of internals were found to be less authoritarian but more authoritative, more accepting and rewarding of independence, and offered more suggestions than directions and more positive than negative statements while their children worked on the puzzles than did the parents of external children.

These results with directiveness suggest that parents who leave more room within which children may maneuver with self-respect, by providing choices and a degree of autonomy, have children who score in a more internal direction on locus of control scales. It is perhaps in the homes where nurturance is provided yet independence is encouraged where the child can become aware of himself as an agent, or as will be described below, where he can more readily become aware of the contingencies between his behaviors and his outcomes.

CONTINGENCY AWARENESS

An independent construct with some relevance to the literature concerning the origins of locus of control is referred to as "contingency awareness." Though research with contingency awareness is also at a neophyte stage of development, it lends some substance to the conjecture regarding the circularity between locus of control and intelligence. Though theoretically far removed from the more phenomenological, self-reflecting aspects of locus of control, the molecular perception of links between self-generated activity and resulting environmental changes referred to as contingency awareness seems to be that kind of building block of which locus of control is composed.

John Watson (1966, 1967, 1972; Watson & Ramey, 1972) began his investigations of contingency awareness with direct observations of his own newborn child. Given the limited mobility of a two-month-old infant, Watson focused upon eye fixation as an available behavior that was potentially an instrumental act for an infant. Watson extended his arms toward his infant so that his closed fists were about a foot apart and about two feet from the child's eyes. On any one day Watson would open and close one of his hands upon being visually fixated by his infant. The other fist was held immobile regardless of fixation. The occurrence of hand opening, then, was contingent with the infant's looking at the fist that was active on that specific day. Included in this sequence were a day's trials in which the fist that opened did so when the infant fixated on the immobile fist.

What Watson discerned in his 11 days of observation was a growing ease of learning and an accompanying display of positive affect. On the 10th day, he recorded the following observations (Watson, 1966):

Observation 1: As O [observer] prepared to begin the session S [subject] seemed to show signs of heightened arousal and interest. O therefore decided to begin the game without covering his face. This proved to cause no competing distraction save for an occasional glance now and then (face covering was never again instituted). A game was played to the left and then one to the right. Both of these contingencies were rapidly adjusted to by S.

Notable here was the observation that S no longer seemed to fixate on anything while looking away between fixations on the fist as had been the case in previous games. S now looked away in a continuous arch which returned to the fist.

Observation 2: Given S's apparent mastery of the basic game, O changed the nature of the contingency in an attempt to eliminate a tropistic explanation of S's behavioral adjustments. The new game involved opening and closing the left fist when S fixated on the right fist. At first, S had great difficulty. He distributed his fixations overwhelmingly to the left following each occasional fixation on the right which released the left fist reward. This unadaptive pattern continued until O gave up hope and instituted a "shaping" procedure. The shaping involved having the left fist opening contingent upon fixating to the right of the left fist. The required distance to the right was slowly increased till it coincided with the position of the right fist. The shaping was successful and was completed within 3 to 5 minutes. After a few minutes of stable responding to this "peripheral reward" game, the contingency and reward positions were reversed. The new contingency was learned slowly but required no shaping.

Observation 3: At the beginning of this session, S's apparent delight and "ready attention" was so marked that O noted the feeling of confronting a "sophisticated" subject. Learning was judged to have occurred for both a basic game and a peripheral reward game [p. 129].

These observations by Watson merely indicated that a child of but a couple of months of age could learn sequences of events. The infant's eye fixations did not really determine the outcomes, though in the child's mind this is not inconceivable. Consequently, Watson would have been hard pressed at this point to conclude that what had been observed indicated at some level that the child had attained an awareness of his causative powers. However, other subsequent observations (Watson, 1966) of his child did lend some credibility to these early speculations.

Observation 4: The subject was observed successfully turning from his stomach to his back on the first occurrence of this act. He was immediately returned to his original prone position. He reestablished a near-successful position and after a bit of a struggle finally rocked past the fulcrum of balance with a swinging movement of his leg. He was again returned to prone position. His speed of turning was faster than previously. Again he was returned to prone position and this time his turning was essentially instantaneous. Again he was replaced and again he turned immediately.

While the sequence of increasing articulation of behavior in Observation No. 3 surely would have done no more than exhilarate O's paternal pride under other circumstances, in the setting of the present case O could not help considering an hypothesis of transfer. If the previous learning games had increased the temporal limits of S's contingency awareness, this could have contributed to the rapid mastery of turning following its initial occurrence.

Observation 5: Following the seemingly complete mastery of a few fixation learning games, S was provided a structured but yet natural contingency situation. A cradle gym was hung in front of S while he was seated in the bouncing chair. The gym was at a distance which would allow S's occasional extended arm movements to contact the gym. Within 20 minutes it appeared that S had clearly established a stable response to striking the gym as its movement ceased. S's eyes were fixed on one of the shiny supportive springs of the gym.

Observation 6: During the preceding six days, fixation games were played and two new variations were introduced. One variant provided a vocal "beep" from O when the designated fist was fixated by S. The other variation provided tactile stimulation to S's legs for correct fist fixation. Learning seemed to be clearly apparent under both of these new modalities of reward.

On this occasion S was seated in his bouncing chair near the table where O and Mrs. O were finishing dinner. Suddenly O noted that S was making gross contortive archings of his body (similar to a wrestler's "bridging" exercise) which when relaxed caused the bouncing chair to react with extensive bouncing. While O, worried about the neurological implications of these periodic contortions, Mrs. O proposed that the bouncing effects of this behavior might be rewarding the response. It was true that S had previously "enjoyed" being bounced, but he had never systematically bounced himself. O then proposed that if Mrs. O's hypothesis was correct, S should eventually refine his behavior if the notion of least effort had any merit.

Observation 7: At this time S was systematically bouncing his chair by use of rhythmic arm and leg movements.

Observation 8: Now S was bouncing the chair consistently with use of rhythmic leg movement alone. These latter observations are presented here simply to illustrate what may be the potential breadth of generalization of a young infant's contingency awareness which has been heightened by experience with artificial contingencies. Obviously the behavior may only be the consequence of a fortunately endowed subject who is enjoying an early advance into Piaget's stage of "secondary circular reactions," which supposedly begins normally around the 4th month of age. Yet given the somewhat unusual history of this particular infant, the proposition of generalization is not untenable [pp. 130–131].

Watson's initial observations were quite suggestive even if they were the overamplications of a proud parent. However, the rudiments of generalization from the effect of providing early contingent experiences proved compelling enough to have stimulated a series of studies which have added substance to Watson's claim for the importance of contingency awareness. Before describing the research that followed upon Watson's initial observations it is instructive to read his theoretical description of contingency awareness that resulted from his first study (Watson, 1966):

If an organism is to learn to produce rewards in its natural setting, it needs more than just the behavior which effects the occurrence of rewards. In addition, it must be at least functionally aware of the contingency existing between its behavior and the rewarding stimuli. Without such awareness, the organism would be destined to wait until its stream of behavior emitted the appropriate response. Moreover, the frequency of emission of that response relative to any other would remain unchanged by either the number of times the reward was elicited or its present desirability. If there exists some awareness that the occurrence of a reward is contingent on the occurrence of a particular available response, the organism is in a position to increase the rate of reward by increasing the rate of the appropriate response. In general then, "contingency awareness" refers to an organism's functional knowledge that the nature of the stimuli received is sometimes affected by the nature of the behavior the organism is emitting. More specifically, contingency awareness refers to an organism's readiness to react adaptively in a contingency situation and to an organism's sensitivity in the perception of contingency situations when they occur.

In the nicely mechanistic language of computer terminology, one might describe contingency awareness as the organism's tendency to scan or read back its memory records of response output and stimulus input and to select that behavior emitted just prior to the reception of the rewarding stimulus. From this perspective, the following two things might be expected to affect the speed of learning in any contingency situation: (1) the tendency to scan the memory record; and (2) the accuracy of the memory record regarding which behavior preceded the occurrence of the reward. Scanning without memory or memory without scanning would be of no consequence for learning. For the purpose of this discussion, then, both factors will be subsumed in the concept of contingency awareness.

An organism possessing a high degree of contingency awareness is set to learn. It is set to record response-output and stimulus-input data, as well as being set to eventually scan this record whenever a rewarding stimulus is received. In computer terms, the "learning instruction" reads: Find and repeat the response which preceded the reception of the rewarding stimulus [pp. 123–124].

In essence, Watson has described in molecular terms the steps in the process of developing a sense of instrumentality. To appropriately repeat a given activity requires an awareness of previous action-outcome sequences; that is, a child must be able to recall his prior actions that caused a given outcome, and to know that those actions were related to those outcomes if he is to repeat the sequence.

To explore these conjectures in a more deliberate and controlled fashion, Watson and his colleagues (Watson & Ramey, 1972) constructed an elaborate device for use in an infant's crib. Electrically controlled mobiles connected to pressure-sensing pillows were constructed so that small head movements upon the pillow activated the mobiles, turning them through a full 90° rotation. Infants were enabled by this device to control the rotation of the mobiles which were suspended a foot and a half above their heads. These mobiles were placed in the homes of a number of infants whose mothers monitored event recorders to ascertain the number of times the infant activated the mobile within each daily 10-minute period. Watson and Ramey arranged to have two control groups to compare with the contingency aware sample. In one control group the mobiles rotated but not in response to the infant's head movements; in the other, the mobile was fixed in position so that in fact it was an "immobile."

Subsequent comparisons of head movements indicated that the two control groups did not differ from one another either at the starting or final sessions. As is evident from Figure 11, there was no marked increase in head movements for either control group.

In contrast, the infants for whom the mobile rotated contingent upon their own activity increased their head movements from the first to the final trials, as had been anticipated. These data lend support for Watson's conjectures about the utility of contingency awareness as an explanatory construct. The only difference between the experimental and control groups was in the potential for perceiving contingency between head movements and the activation of the mobile. Therefore it is reasonable to conclude that the infants who produced the increasing number of head movements did so with some level of awareness that these movements were necessary antecedents of the mobile rotation.

Another observation in this study was of some interest. As had Watson's own infant, many of the contingent-aware infants in this larger study exhibited positive affect in response to their causal activity. Though they did not collect such data systematically, Watson and Ramey (1972) noted that "the overall consistency of reports strongly suggests that the experimental infants had a very different 'socio-emotional' reaction to their contingency mobiles than did the controls to their stabiles or non-contingent mobiles. . . . it appeared that the experimental babies blossomed into smiling and cooing after a few days of exposure to the contingency mobile [p. 222]."

FIGURE 11   Pillow responses per 10-minute session across two weeks for the experimental and two control groups. (△) Contingent, N = 18; (●) noncontingent, N = 11; (○) stabile, N = 11.

Consequently, Watson and Ramey (1972) concluded that "the infants' reactions to the response-contingent stimulation appear to be of two kinds. The infant reacts intellectually by moving forward to what Piaget . . . describes as the sensory-motor stage of secondary circular reactions. Additionally, he reacts 'socio-emotionally' by displaying vigorous smiling and cooing in the contingency situation [p. 226]."

The provision of contingency experience, then, is regarded as an accelerator of cognitive and affective responses for which Watson has contended (Watson, 1967) the infant is constitutionally prepared. Watson has suggested that the human infant is ordinarily deprived of this acceleration largely because he lacks the behaviors which commonly elicit contingent stimulation from his milieu.

In another study employing the contingent versus noncontingent mobile apparatus, Watson (1972) found replication of the contingency effect and some limits in the infants' ability to discern contingency. If any noncontingent movement occurred in even a small number of trials then the infants did not perform as predicted. Only with 100% contingent conditions did the increase in movements and affect displays occur as anticipated.

In his later work in which Watson (1979) has explored the conditions which affect the development of contingency awareness, confirmation has been found for the effects of contingency awareness upon activation. Suomi (1980) has reviewed and evaluated much of this research in a rather stimulating chapter in which he also discusses his own and others' research into the study of social responsiveness among subhuman primates as an extension of the contingency awareness paradigm. Others such as Goldberg (1977) and Ramey, Starr, Pallas, Whitten, and Reed (1975) have discussed the role of contingent interactions between caregivers and children in helping to account for the development of social competence on the one hand, and the failure to thrive on the other.

Finally, in a study by Yates, Kennelly, and Cox (1975), university students classified as to their locus of control were queried with regard to whether they had experienced rewards and punishments contingently within their families. Internals were found to view their parents as having been contingently punishing more than had externals. In turn, contingently punishing parents were perceived as loving parents by all subjects while noncontingently punishing parents were generally viewed as rejecting parents. As an interesting aside, the contingency of rewards was not related to evaluations of parents nor to locus of control scores.

In this study by Yates et al. (1975), a bridge between the locus of control and contingency awareness literatures would seem to have been established with enough commonality in findings to encourage further exploration of this linkage.

CONCLUSIONS

In John Watson's work with contingency awareness it is possible to see some convergence with locus of control research. Stephens (1973) had earlier asserted than an internal locus of control may be an antecedent of much that is referred to as intelligent behavior. Watson, too, seems prepared to argue that the perception of contingency may be a necessary step in the transition from one developmental stage to another. If these investigators are correct in positing an antecedent role to causal perceptions in generating intelligence-reflecting activity then this area of research focusing upon the origins of locus of control will undoubtedly become a target of progressively increasing activity.

The research pertaining to familial origins of locus of control seems to indicate that an attentive, responsive, critical, and contingent milieu is a precursor of the development of an internal locus of control. Likewise, as has been described in Chapter 2, the less responsive and less opportune milieu surrounding the poor, the ostracized and the deprived creates a climate of fatalism and helplessness that is reflected in the scores that individuals obtain on locus of control measures. Lower socioeconomic status, membership in denigrated minority groups, and nonvoluntary quasi-incarceration share commonality in affording minimal contingency between quality of effort and quality of reward, and in generating more external control expectations. The extent of this covariation is evident in the data reported by Stephens and Delys (1973b), who found not only that preschool children from poor homes were more external than middle class children, a common enough finding, but that within lower class children, those from homes assessed as above the poverty line were less external than those from homes rated as below the poverty line.

Access to opportunity for contingent responses, then, whether in the home or the larger social milieu, seems to be essential in the development of locus of control. The contingent responsiveness intrinsic to a nurturant but nonsuffocating home, and to a responsive and fair milieu, seems to be the necessary ingredient for the growth of internal control expectancies that research has uncovered thus far.

10 Changes in the Locus of Control

INTRODUCTION

With the exception of studies such as Glass and Singer's (1972) that concern momentary changes in a person's sense of control, the larger number of investigations discussed thus far contain descriptions of locus of control that make it appear as if it were a stable attribute. Especially in view of the longitudinal data discussed in the preceding chapter, the reader may presume that the locus of control construct is viewed as a trait or even as a typology by its users. With subjects commonly classified as internals or externals, it could not be argued that this impression is a gross misinterpretation. The difficulty, however, inheres less in the construct itself than in our language, which encourages concision on the one hand and an animate subject within each sentence on the other. If group differences are to be described, the more accurate phrasing, "those who report (on a given scale) that they perceive events as being largely contingent upon their personal efforts at the present time, as opposed to those who feel more fatalistic about the manner in which outcomes occur," would prove to be too cumbersome to allow for concise expression. Consequently, we are more often confronted with statements suggesting that there are people who *are* internals and others who *are* externals who will, as a result of these *identities,* differ on any number of associated dimensions. It is one purpose of this chapter to attempt to dispel this ready perception of locus of control as a trait, or worse, a typology with all the connotations of intractability and fixedness that those terms imply.

An individual's locus of control is often inferred from momentary expressions of his sense of causality which, if solicited at different points in time, may be relatively consistent. However, it must be kept in mind that empirical events such

148

as expressions of causal expectations are but referents of the locus of control construct and not the construct itself. Locus of control is not a characteristic to be discovered within individuals. It is a construct, a working tool in social learning theory that allows for an interpretation of remarks made by people in response to questions about causality. The remarks, expressions, and behaviors indicative of beliefs about causality are the events that psychologists observe and test for reliability, and measures such as Rotter's locus of control scale are simply devices created to elicit those expressions of belief. Whether scales such as Rotter's provide adequate opportunity for different persons to give reliable and valid indications of their causal beliefs is a moot point and will be the subject of the following chapter. However, it is to be understood that the responses given to locus of control-related questionnaires are not identical to the construct locus of control, nor perhaps to those phenomenologically real and private thoughts of individuals pertaining to causality. They are but rough approximations of what is believed to be a person's expectancies about control.

Though this brief prolegomenon may strain the reader's patience somewhat, it seems to be necessary, for if locus of control were thought to be a trait, consistent and inherent in the person being observed, then evidence regarding change would logically lead one to question the very legitimacy of the locus of control construct. Second, if the construct were to be confused with particular measurement devices, the error variance associated with the imperfections of any psychometric tools would be mistakenly attributed to theoretical limitations of the construct.

However, if the position is adopted that people do not *have* traits such as a locus of control, as if it were a possession, but rather are said to construct interpretations of events, some of which pertain to causality, then it will be less disconcerting to encounter both stability and change in these constructions. People do change their minds or constructions about many things, though they as often revert to prior positions or remain steadfast in their positions despite sometimes overwhelming reasons for changing. It is easier, though, to comprehend both the stability and changes of our constructions if they are regarded as constructions rather than as traits, or other less variable internal attributes.

Likewise, if we remain aware that measurements are but crude approximations of the operations of a construct, it will not be as disappointing when changes in these measures or correlations with other theoretically relevant scales do not reach very high magnitudes. No measures will ever account for every last individual quirk possible, so that data reflecting upon personality characteristics should not be expected to conform completely to theoretical expectations.

Interest in the processes that can alter one's locus of control is self-evident. In previous chapters, the research discussed revealed that an external locus of control is an impediment to coping with challenges and is associated with negative feelings. The shifting of one's locus of control from an external to a more internal position would seem to be a natural goal for professional psychologists whose aims are often to revive their patients' flagging efforts in pursuit of satisfactions they have foresaken as hopeless. Erwin Singer (1965) has stated that "the single proposition which underlies all forms of psychotherapy: the proposition that man is capable of change and capable of bringing this change about himself . . . were it not for this inherent optimism, this fundamental confidence in man's ultimate capacity to find his way, psychotherapy as a discipline could not exist, salvation could come about only through divine grace [p. 16]."

Similarly, Hilde Bruch (1974) has written that "the task of therapy in general terms, is to assist a patient in the development of a center of gravity so that he experiences himself as self-directed . . . free to assert himself and to pursue satisfaction in terms of his own goals of living [Bruch, 1974, p. 141]."

Granted the professional interest in processes that can alter control expectancies, this chapter will focus upon those events, natural, accidental, and deliberately contrived, that have been explored as potential influences for change of an individual's locus of control.

NATURAL AND ACCIDENTALLY OCCURRING CHANGES

Among the most obvious sources of change in the perception of causality are those associated with age. This author had the opportunity of observing this age-related locus of control phenomenon in a discussion with one of his then five-year-old daughter's friends. The children had been playing house. Knowing the occasional squabbles that resulted from having to choose between the roles each was to play, I asked my daughter's friend whether she had been "the mommy" or "the baby" on that day. She answered with an immediate and gleeful "the mommy." Asked if she preferred being "the mommy" to "the baby," she answered with an instantaneous "yes." My quizzical "why" elicited no uncertainty: "Because I get to boss around the baby." "Isn't it as much fun being the baby?" was my naive retort: "No, I don't like to be bossed around."

To be the mommy who directs and determines events in play is obviously preferred by these children, both of whom, incidentally, are the youngest in their respective families. To be young, especially the youngest, means to feel more helpless or external with regard to one's wishes. To acquire a status associated with being older, even in play, becomes an important source of satisfaction. The easily observed modelling of children after those who are but a few years older than themselves no doubt reflects this valuing of age and the belief that one becomes more capable of obtaining desired satisfactions as one becomes older.

A study by Penk (1969) lends empirical support for this hypothesized relationship between age and locus of control. Penk found chronological age to be positively correlated with internality as assessed by Bialer's locus of control scale [$r = .27$, $p < .01$]. This replicated an earlier finding reported by Bialer (1961) in which an $r = .37$, $p < .01$ was obtained between chronological age and locus of control scores. Bailer had also included a measure of mental age derived from the Peabody Picture Vocabulary Test, which was found to be related to locus of control scores, $r = .56$, $p < .01$. When Bialer partialled out mental age, the relationship between chronological age and locus of control diminished substantially, leaving a partial $r = .02$. On the other hand, mental age and locus of control remained strongly related [$r = .47$, $p < .01$] when chronological age was partialled out.

Penk also included the Peabody test in his battery and likewise found a relationship between mental age and locus of control [$r = .26$, $p < .01$]. Though Penk did not examine the pattern of his results for effects deriving from partialling procedures, it is reasonable to assume that had he done so he might have obtained results similar to Bialer's. It may therefore be concluded that chrological age per se is not the most salient aspect of maturation with regard to locus of control. Rather, it is the growth of mental age, the extent of vocabulary development and usage that become associated with a sense of being able to determine the shape of one's life.

One other study reveals complementary findings with regard to the passage of time, if not growth, and locus of control. Harvey (1971) found that the longer a person held an administrative position in the upper echelons of government, the more internal he scored on Rotter's locus of control scale. Mean scores on Rotter's scale were 5.4 for administrators holding their statusful positions for 11 years or more and 7.2 for those with but 1 to 10 years' experience, the difference being significant [$p < .05$] even within this generally internal sample.

Though none of these results are "within" or repeated measures as they would have to be to more conclusively test the hypothesis that growth and/or upward mobility in status is associated with shifts in locus of control toward the internal direction, the results do lend some credence to that position. However, in an excellent critical review of the literature pertaining to development and locus of control, Weisz and Stipek (in press) have contended that no clear statements can be drawn from the extant research findings. Having surveyed the results from 33 studies using 12 different measures of locus of control, Weisz and Stipek found that about half reported increases in internality with age, about half had mixed results or no changes, and only a few reported a decline with age. After a close examination of these studies Weisz and Stipek argued that: 1. some findings were probably artifacts of scale characteristics; 2. others may reflect developmental effects or constructs other than perceived control; and 3. in many assessment devices perceived contingency and perceived self-competence are confounded such that developmental predictions become difficult. This latter point derives from the fact that although *perceived competence* may increase as one matures, *perceived contingency* may decline with maturity. As persons develop, they may become more familiar with a variety of events, outcomes, and situations so that they come to make finer discriminations with regard to the potential controllability or contingency of those events. Weisz and Stipek (in press) have provided enough evidence in their cogent review to convince this writer that little can be concluded in this area, though it is still appealing to assume that perceived competence at least could increase with age given the increased likelihood of successes in the pursuit of goals that more mature individuals should experience.

In addition to these studies concerning the passage of time and natural changes in status as determinants of change in locus of control, two more serendipitous findings have been reported that reveal the effects of contemporary events upon individuals' perceptions of causality. Both studies presented locus of control data that were obtained shortly after public events that were pertinent to control expectancies. One report (Gorman, 1968) contained scores upon Rotter's locus of control scale that had been administered on the day following the 1968 Democratic National Convention. Gorman's students were largely supporters of Eugene McCarthy and consequently were highly disappointed and, perhaps, disillusioned with the political process in which they had been so roundly defeated. Though Gorman did not have repeated measures with the locus of control scale, the scores he obtained on that day were more external [$M = 11.56$, $t = 5.2$, $p < .001$] than the national norms for university students at that time.

More convincing because of the availability of comparison groups was a study by McArthur (1970). Rotter's scale had been administered to a group of Yale undergraduates on the day following a lottery that the United States government conducted to determine draft eligibility for the armed services. Students who were 19 years or older, and therefore affected by the lottery, scored in a more external direction on the locus of control scale than control subjects to whom the scale had been administered prior to the lottery. More important, when those who were favorably affected by the lottery were contrasted with those who were not, the difference in locus of control scores was again significant. Those who were virtually eliminated from draft consideration scored in a more external control direction [$M = 15.5$] than did those who retained the same draft eligibility [$M = 10.22$]. Only the favorably-affected students differed from the freshman class and control groups; the nonaffected were not different from the comparison samples.

McArthur (1970) described the social context of the lottery so that the meaning of the results become clear:

> Prior to the lottery, most college students probably believed the odds were that they would have to serve in the armed forces after graduation unless they went to jail, left the country, or managed to secure a deferment until they reached the age 26. Hence the lottery clearly brought good luck to individuals . . . for this meant that they would probably not have to serve in the army—a real change from their prelottery draft status. On the other hand, the lottery did not as clearly bring bad

luck to individuals . . . for their draft status remained relatively unchanged in comparison to their prelottery status [p. 317].

Both of these studies convey an important point: Locus of control scores shift with relevant environmental events. In these cases the shifts were toward the external whereas the age-related studies assumedly change toward the internal end of the continuum. The opposite directions are sensible if one considers the ramifications of the different events. With increases in mental age, chronological age, and length of time in positions facilitating effectiveness, individuals may come to perceive themselves as more able to determine the events about them. That is, reinforcements are seen as occurring more in response to personal efforts and/or abilities than they had been previously. Political disappointment, however, especially to those who were so committed, as were Eugene McCarthy supporters, creates an impression that the world is unmanageable. Despite political footwork and financial outlays, the Greek tragedy seemed foreordained. In effect, events were beyond control so that participants suffered feelings of impotence that were reflected in more external control scores. Unlike Gorman's study, McArthur's reported upon changes coincident with good fortune. In a sense, those eliminated from the draft could be thought of as enjoying undeserved good fortune. Though opposite in direction, the events described in each study were noncontingent upon personal characteristics, and the results were the same. Noncontingent highly valued reinforcements, then, can generate shifts toward a more external locus of control.

Whether these shifts were of any permanence is unanswerable with the data that were presented in these studies. However, it is at least possible to conclude that internal states can be created by environmental occurrences such that individuals will shift in their expressions of the perception of control.

One further study of more clinical relevance illustrates the shifting of locus of control with changing life events. Ronald Smith (1970) examined locus of control scores of a number of clients who appeared at a crisis intervention center in a neuropsychiatric facility. Smith reasoned that since an acute crisis entails feeling temporarily overwhelmed by negative influences, such clients should report that they feel helpless or external. However, as crises become resolved, a return to a more internal locus of control should be evident. With a six-week period of treatment focusing upon crisis management, Smith found that locus of control scores did decline from the external to the internal significantly. Where crisis clients shifted in locus of control scores from a high at admission [$M = 10.08$] to a low after six weeks [$M = 7.12$], noncrisis psychiatric admissions remained fairly consistent [$M = 9.63$ and 8.86] for the equivalent test administrations. As one might have expected, then, acute crises are typified by feelings of helplessness at coping with important events. Such helplessness is reflected in locus of control scores that may therefore be taken as a rough barometer of one's sense of being able to cope.

DELIBERATELY CONTRIVED AND BEHAVIORALLY ASSESSED CHANGES

Several investigators, like Smith, have attempted to use locus of control as a criterion or outcome measure for studies pertaining to behavior modification and psychotherapy. In many of these studies, locus of control scales have been employed as the primary assessment devices, a procedure that is not without special difficulties. Common sense would suggest that if a person were seeking help he would be ill advised to speak of himself as competent and/or in potential control of his life events. It is more likely that helplessness and a deference toward the helping other would be displayed because these are more appropriate to help seeking. Likewise, upon discharge from treatment, many clients, either through gratitude to a helpful therapist or through a wish to justify termination of the therapeutic relationship, might wish to express more of an internal orientation.

Fortunately, a few investigators have reported data of a less potentially reactive sort. That is, they have focused upon behavioral changes from which shifts in locus of control have been inferred. Since these are the rarer and more compelling sort of data, these studies will be discussed in somewhat greater detail than those in which scale measures have served as the sole criteria of change.

Research in Educational Settings

Gunars Reimanis (1971) has presented data from three separate investigations in which deliberate attempts were made to alter locus of control among students of different age groups. One study dealt with children from the first and third grades in elementary school. Children for the experiment were selected on the basis of locus of control scores derived from the Battle-Rotter cartoon test, Bialer's scale, and a teacher's rating. Those in the lowest quartile, the most external, were assigned to experimental and control groups.

Reimanis held weekly meetings for three months with the teachers of the experimental-group children in which he discussed the means of modifying classroom procedures to encourage children to develop feelings of internal control. Reimanis (1971) explains that these teachers knew the identity of the "experimental children" and as time permitted "gave these children more individual attention with respect to learning about their behavior consequences and consistency in the environment around them [p. 6]." The later training sessions were devoted to clarifying reinforcement principles by which teachers could identify what was actually reinforcing for each child. Subsequently, they tried to use this information to point out behavior-effect contingencies to their pupils.

Later, the Battle-Rotter cartoon measure was readministered to the pupils. The experimental group showed a significantly greater change toward internality than did control-group children. Furthermore, experimental-group children demonstrated more classroom behavior associated with an internal locus of control than did control group children:

> The experimental children appeared to know and be interested in what they were doing. They were more a part of their class projects and the teachers could rely on them more. At the beginning of the sessions these children were quite different. Some did not appear to be part of the class. Some showed inappropriate behaviors in the class. Some showed complete lack of interest in classroom activities. And some demanded constant attention from the teachers [p. 7].

Though these change data were based on small samples, and academic achievement a year later failed to reflect these changes, the initial results proved to be encouraging if uncertain as to cause and permanence.

A second investigation by Reimanis (1971) was conducted with groups of community college students. Experimental and control groups were selected from the most external 20% of the student population. One sample received group and another, individual counselling sessions aimed at altering the student's locus of control. In the group counselling sessions the counselor confronted students with questions such as "What could you have done about it?" or "What do *you* want to do?" Reimanis also had the counselor attempt to replace external control reflecting statements ("I am in college because my father wants me to be an optometrist") with internal ones ("I want to learn more about people"). Individual counselling sessions encouraged discussion about vocational and educational goals and raised questions for subjects about the problems they were experiencing with their goal ambitions (Reimanis, 1971):

> At each external response the student gave, the counselor interrupted and asked the students to analyze the statement: Why did he say what he said and what could have been done to prevent what happened? The attempt again was to replace an external response made by the student with an internal one. In addition, the student was encouraged to transfer the internal thoughts to future events. That is, now that he knows what he could have done, what will he do in the future? [p. 9].

Experimental group subjects who had received group or individual counselling displayed an increase in internality but no change in locus of control scores was found among control subjects. More importantly, it was noted from the counselling records that most of the experimental—group subjects began to model the counselor's style of questioning and to talk more about their own responsibility for continuing with their education and solving interpersonal problems. In addition, behavioral indications of internality such as taking a new apartment, changing study programs, seeking out course instructors to ascertain status and needs for improvement were noted among the experimental-group subjects.

In one last sutdy Reimanis examined the effects of achievement motivation training courses among college students. In these courses, students participated in game-like situations in which they were able to explore their levels of aspiration and thoughts about achievement. The Rotter scale was administered before the training sessions, immediately after, again after one to two months had elapsed, and then again seven months later.

Students showed a significant increase in the internal direction following achievement training. Though this increase dissipated somewhat with time, male students retained a significant increase in internality after seven months. However, the equivalent increase that had initially been found among females dissipated in that time. Reimanis conjectured that this may have been due to a lesser concern with academic achievement among females.

Altogether, Reimanis' three studies are suggestive in that they each reveal similar changes in locus of control scores and behaviors relevant to locus of control. However, each of these studies contain weaknesses: small sample sizes, possible experimenter bias effects, and "Hawthorne effects," which prohibit the drawing of clear conclusions. Only in conjunction with other investigations do Reimanis' studies gain credence as demonstrations of changing perceptions of control.

The most ambitious of those studies pertaining to behavioral changes relevant to locus of control is indubitably one by Richard deCharms, whose work focuses upon "personal causation," a similar if somewhat different construct than locus of control. DeCharms (1972) defines personal causation as

> the initiation by an individual of behavior intended to produce a change in his environment. When a person initiates intentional behavior, he experiences himself as having originated the intention and the behavior. He is the locus of causality of the behavior and he is said to be intrinsically motivated. Since he himself is the originator, we refer to the person as an origin.
>
> When something external to the person impels him to behavior, he experiences himself as the instrument of the outside source, and the outside source is the locus of causality. He is said to be extrinsically motivated. Since the person is impelled from without we refer to him as a pawn. We sometimes talk of people as primarily pawns implying that they more characteristically see themselves as pushed around by outside forces. Conversely, we refer to people as primarily origins implying that they characteristically see themselves as originating their own behavior [pp. 96–97].

The similarity of deCharms' origin-pawn dimension with that of internal-external control is evident, though there are shades of differences between them. Where locus of control pertains more to the perception of contingencies between actions and outcomes, the origin-pawn dimension focuses more upon the perception of one's self as a subject or object of actions. Nevertheless, the congruities are more salient than are the differences between these constructs, especially with regard to behavioral referents. For a fuller description of the similarities and differences between the constructs the reader is referred to deCharms (1981).

In a rather ambitious study, deCharms (1972) established training programs specifically aimed at encouraging origin behaviors in the schools. His thesis was that to enable a person to behave like an origin the person must be helped "a) to determine realistic goals for himself; b) to know his own strengths and weaknesses; c) to determine concrete action that he can take now that will help him to reach his goals; and d) to consider how he can tell whether he is approaching his goal, that is, whether his action is having the desired effect [p. 97]."

Black teachers from inner city schools, with black pupils who were largely from lower class homes, comprised the samples for this investigation. Experimental-group teachers were paid to attend a week-long residential personal causation training course prior to meeting their classes in the fall. Among the course objectives, teachers were instructed in ways to promote origin rather than pawn behavior.

During the year, subsequent to the initial week's training, teachers met regularly with the researchers to design classroom exercises that emphasized self-concepts, achievement motivation, realistic goal setting and the origin-pawn concept. The latter exercises stressed internal, realistic goal setting, planning, personal responsibility, feelings of personal causation, and self-confidence.

The first result of interest pertained to the way that the children came to see their teachers and the classroom atmosphere. The children were asked a series of questions dealing with the amount of initiative that would be welcome or acceptable within their own classrooms. Children who had trained teachers perceived their classrooms as more encouraging of origin behavior than did children with untrained teachers. These statistically significant differences were obtained from 46 classrooms, 12 children in each class being sampled for their perceptions of classroom atmosphere. With this rather extensive sampling, differences for both the seventh- and eighth-grade samples would have to be regarded as indicating considerable success for the training program.

Second, the effects of the teacher's training upon student behavior were evaluated in several ways. One set of data derived from content analyses of stories that the children created in each of three grades. The most fascinating aspect of these data is that they were of a longitudinal nature; that is, the same students were assessed during successive grades (fifth through seventh). Children's stories were scored for each of six origin-pawn categories: internal goal setting, internal determination of instrumental activity, reality perception, personal responsibility, self-confidence, and internal control, so that scores ranging from 0 to 6 for each of the six stories were obtained each year from the students.

As is evident in Figure 12, origin scores obtained during each grade provided rather striking confirmation of deCharms' effectiveness in shaping up origin-like thought samples. The curve labelled D (bottom right) reflects control-group origin scores. Children with untrained teachers did not change throughout the

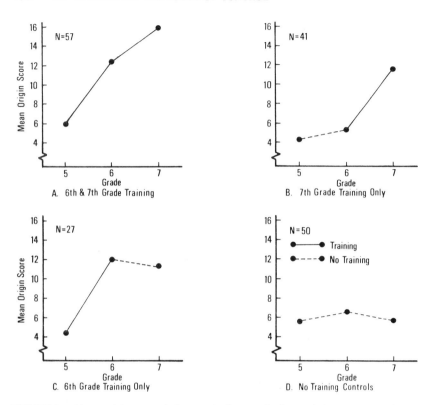

FIGURE 12   Mean origin score before and after motivation training. (From DeCharms, 1972.)

three years in which assessments were made. Curve C (bottom left) reflects origin scores of students who received the benefits of training during the sixth but not during the seventh grade. After training there were decided increases in origin scores that did not decline in the following year, though no further training was offered. However, there were also no further increases in origin scores. Curve B (top right) illustrates origin scores from a group that received training in the seventh but not during the fifth or sixth grades. Here, it becomes increasingly clear that origin scores change with training. Curve A (top left) shows the cumulative effects of receiving continuous causation training throughout both the sixth and seventh grades. Origin scores increased following each year of training.

These data are fascinating for their detailed, step-by-step effects. Whenever training was offered, origin scores subsequently increase [$p < .001$ in each case]. Whenever training was not provided, there were no changes in origin scores. Clear evidence was obtained, then, that personal causation training affected the ways in which children produced imaginative stories. After training, the characters in the stories more often were described as setting their own goals, determining their own instructional activity, as being more realistic, taking more responsibility for their actions, and as being more self-confident.

In addition to the thought-sample data, deCharms noted that children in the experimental group became more moderate in their risk-taking behavior during spelling games that entailed choosing more words to spell from lists that were of more appropriate levels of difficulty. Most meaningful for the particular samples under observation, deCharms found that the usual increasing discrepancy between performances by these inner city school children and national norms for achievement tests had been arrested by personal causation training; that is, students who underwent the special training offered by teachers who were involved in the personal causation program did not lose ground in achievement scores as they proceeded from the fifth to the seventh grades, whereas control-group children exhibited the more typically increasing discrepancy from national norms. Additionally, experimental-group children averaged fewer absences than the untrained control-group children.

In subsequent studies (Koenigs, Fiedler, & deCharms, 1977; Shea & de-Charms, 1976), some replications of the above findings have been obtained. Koenigs et al. (1977) found that teachers with more complex cognitive styles were more apt to encourage pupil influence in the classroom, which in turn resulted in a greater perception of an origin climate among pupils. In those classes where pupil influence and perceived origin climates were higher, academic achievement was also higher. Shea and deCharms (1976), in addition, found that teachers' locus of control scores were related to both the encouragement of pupil initiatives and academic achievement. That is, internal teachers helped to facilitate pupil achievement more successfully than did external teachers.

Other investigators have found locus of control scores shifting toward the internal end of the continuum following eight weeks of a sports fitness summer camp (Duke, Johnson, & Nowicki, 1977) and eight hours of a life planning workshop (Lynch, Ogg, & Christensen, 1975). Finally, in research deriving from the attribution literature, Carol Dweck has demonstrated the impact of causal reattribution upon behavior that can be said to reflect self-determination. Dweck and Reppucci (1973) had initially found that Seligman's "learned helplessness phenomenon" could be engendered among children when, with a particular experimenter, they suffered continuous unavoidable failures. A number of these children subsequently failed to complete problems administered by the "failure experimenter" when those problems were, in fact, solvable. These failures occurred despite the fact that the children had solved almost identical problems previously administered by the "success experimenter." In addition, these investigators found that the greatest decrements in performance following failure were evident among children who were assessed as externals on the IAR questionnaire, or among those who, when they did attribute the cause of their outcomes to internal characteristics, did so to ability (stable-internal) rather than to expenditure of effort (variable-internal). Children who persisted despite failures were more apt to attribute outcomes to effort than they were to the stable characteristic, ability.

Given the positive value of persistence in the face of failures for achievement behavior, Dweck (1975) subsequently experimented with a process of causal reattribution in an attempt to produce that very persistence that had been associated with the tendency to attribute cause for outcomes to effort. Dweck obtained a small sample of children who were adjudged by school personnel to be helpless, in the sense of being passive before challenges which they were capable of achieving. These children were found to differ considerably from "nonhelpless" children both with regard to IAR questionnaire scores and measures of failure avoidance, thus validating the judgments offered by the teachers and guidance counsellors. Dweck then contrasted two training procedures that were designed to alter the failure avoidance behavior expected of helpless children. One procedure was designed to teach the children to assume responsbility for their failures, but with attributions made to effort rather than ability. The other procedure, on the other hand, provided an "enriched diet" of success experiences. When Dweck interpolated failure experiences among the long sequences of successes enjoyed by all of the children, she found that the children who experienced the success diet deteriorated rapidly in their performances. However, those who had received reattribution training maintained or improved in their performance following failures and were found to continue verbalizing the fact that insufficient effort rather than inability was responsible for failures.

Dweck's investigation is compelling for several reasons. First of all, her subjects were real failure avoidant children whose behavior coincided with that of children who had experienced experimentally induced learned helplessness in the first study. Perceiving that external attributions were associated with a ready capitulation to failure, and that internal stable attributions also serve to perpetuate avoidant behavior, Dweck chose to train her "helpless children" to perceive internal-variable characteristics as being responsible for their failures. Although this approach drew appropriately upon the results of her first study, it also capitalized upon the element of hope, or a belief in the possibility of change that is implied in variable-internal attributions. Failure due to inability is more apt to be thought of as insurmountable whereas ascribed lack of effort invites challenge for change. Dweck's success in generating persistence among helpless children attests to the wisdom of her choice. Within this study, then, there was a sophisitcated selection of the criterion variable (persistence despite failure) and a wise use of a more refined subcategory of perceived causality. Hopefully, more therapy relevant research will make use of similar refinements.

Dweck's work has been expanded upon (Dweck & Goetz, 1978) and extended to the realm of sex differences (Dweck & Bush, 1976). Throughout these studies, most particularly that by Diener and Dweck (1978), Dweck's research has indicated that particular attributions following failure experiences are associated with performance decrements and that training at reattribution may be one fruitful means of altering the performances of seemingly helpless children.

These investigators have shown that behavioral as well as indirect verbal indicators of locus of control can be altered by training programs directed at increasing an individual's sense of personal causation or control. Each has conducted his or her research in educational settings where the concern was largely with achievement relevant activity, and they have demonstrated the efficacy of educational approaches to changing students' perceptions of causality.

Research in Clinical Settings

Another successful alteration of locus of control was reported in a case study that used completely behavioral criteria. John Masters (1970) discussed a case study in which an "adolescent rebellion" was reduced in severity by therapy that focused upon the reconstrual of causality. The client was a young adolescent who, while inebriated, had attempted to steal a neighbor's car. That very evening he was apprehended and placed in a detention home where he became agitated and destroyed the furnishings in his cell. From subsequent clinical interviews it was discovered that the youth had been mildly depressed for about a year and that his relationship with his family had become strained to the point where some physical violence occurred. Briefly, the client described himself as "put upon" or as a pawn of his parents' wishes. Masters (1970) described his therapeutic approach as follows:

> The client's initial perception of the relationship between himself and his parents was one in which the parents were the almighty controllers. He interpreted commands (which may actually have been requests) to mow the lawn or wash the car as infringements on his personal freedom. As these examples were brought out during therapy, it was pointed out that they could be used to his advantage. It was argued that parents learn to reward what they label "good son behavior." This category of behavior includes a large number of distinctly menial chores which by many adolescents are considered degrading. It was then argued that they *are* degrading if one falls into the pattern of performing them blindly or playing the game without being aware of the rules. However, such behaviors could also be performed intentionally and "contingently" as a method for controlling parental behavior.
> A series of behaviors were planned in order to demonstrate this hypothesis. On one day it was decided that GB was to mow the lawn without being asked and then to report in detail the effect of his maneuver on his family. The initial report was that his father had difficulty responding, that he thanked BG, and subsequently he seemed less likely to enter into verbal arguments. It was interpreted to GB that he had become "master" of this game and had turned some tables. Instead of the father's argument, "I pay for the food in this house, you earn your keep by mowing the lawn, etc.," GB had placed his father at a disadvantage by performing some work (equivalent to "I pay for the food"), but had not asked anything in return.

However, the father now felt obligated, and GB had very effectively controlled the father's arguing behavior as well by removing a primary inciting stimulus from the father's repertoire. He also had prevented his father from commanding (requesting) him to mow the lawn by his early performance of that task, thus removing an oppressive stimulus from his own environment.

Gradually the above procedure was applied to various good son behaviors such as washing the car or helping out in the family business. The results were consistently positive. Most notable were a reduction in friction between GB and his father and early restoration of the use of the family car which had been denied following the attempted care theft. Tangential to the planning of manipulative good son behaviors were discussions concerning behaviors likely to produce friction. For example, after the use of the car was restored, it was noted that care should be taken in getting home on time, since otherwise the client's father would "automatically" become angry. It was stressed that the father was the foil in this game, since his anger was automatic and unwitting. GB, however, would be the master since he could predict his father's behavior and thus control it by failing to provide the necessary stimuli (coming home late). Getting home on time would also control the father's future behavior concerning late night privileges and future use of the car. The point of the therapeutic argument was always to describe the emission of good son behavior as an effective method for the control of parental behavior [p. 215].

Therapy, then, consisted primarily of the verbal reinterpretation of events that otherwise remained the same, which, in turn, caused actual changes in the family environment and in the youth's morale. Feedback some eight months after therapy termination revealed that the client was doing well in school and was in good spirits.

Masters has provided a detailed close up of youth in crisis, and reports observations that are congruent with the findings of Smith (1970) regarding crisis clients. The youth described by Masters initially reported feeling very much like an object or pawn and, as such, was highly agitated and antagonistic toward his parents, "the controllers." Where Smith noted that crisis resolution was accompanied by a shift toward internality, Master's purposefully reoriented client exhibited improved morale and coping behavior along with the assumed shift in locus of control that Masters had engineered.

These studies by Reimanis, de Charms, Dweck, and Masters are among the few that have not relied entirely upon changes in scale scores to ascertain the effectiveness of therapeutic techniques. The larger number of investigators have used locus of control scales before and after treatments to contrast the shifts in perceptions against control groups that have received either less adequate or no treatments. Though these studies offer some further information regarding methods for changing perceptions of causality, they are subject to more criticisms than the behaviorally focused investigations noted above, due to the more likely biasing of responses by their clients.

SCALE ASSESSED CHANGES

Foulds (1971) found that college students who were engaged in quasi-group therapy that emphasized affective expression, awareness of personal freedom, and responsibility, become more internal on Rotter's locus of control scale. Foulds repeated this experiment with three successive samples with the identical results. A second study by this same investigator and his colleagues (Foulds, Guinan, & Warehime, 1974) reported similar shifts in locus of control scores subsequent to a marathon group session characterized as experiential-gestalt in orientation. Diamond and Shapiro (1973) also found shifts toward internality on Rotter's scale after encounter group experiences in two successive studies, each of which had three experimental and one control group. In each study, control groups remained stable in locus of control scores whereas experimental subjects exposed to one or another form of encounter group experience shifted toward internality.

A number of other studies further illuminate the change process. One investigation by Gillis and Jessor (1970) indicated that there were no changes in locus of control scores among hospitalized psychiatric patients who had received brief psychotherapy in comparison to an untreated control group. However, when patients were subsequently classified as to whether or not they had improved in therapy, those adjudged ''improved'' did demonstrate the predicted shift in their locus of control scores. The simple provision of psychotherapy per se was not found to be an all-powerful determinant of change in locus of control scale scores. However, the fact that patients who improved, even with brief psychotherapy, shifted toward internality on locus of control measures encourages the interpretation that such a change in the perception of causality is one element of successful psychotherapy. Support for this interpretation can be found in another study investigating the impact of a short-term therapy. Parks, Becker, Chamberlain, and Crandall (1975) helped college students to eliminate self-defeating behaviors within a four-week period. Locus of control scores became more internal for therapy subjects than for matched control subjects, a difference that remained stable at a four month follow up. The conclusions to be drawn from these studies are congruent with Singer's supposition noted earlier, that the aims of psychotherapy are dependent upon a restoration of self-determination.

Another therapy study (Dua, 1970) compared the effects of a behavioral action-oriented form of therapy with those of a reeducative psychotherapy. The subjects were female university students who came to the university counselling center expressing a concern about their relative inability to relate with others. Subjects were assigned to one of three matched groups, two of which received treatment and one (the control group) in which subjects were placed on a waiting list. One treatment consisted of an action program. Dua explains (1970): ''The main emphasis in this method was first to direct the subject to define the interpersonal problem in behavioral terms and then to establish a sequence of specific actions to expand the subject's repertoire of specific behaviors. Tangible actions were suggested by the therapist that would lead the subject to change his actual behavior vis-a-vis the significant other [p. 568]." In contrast, the reeducative program involved discussions "of the subject's affects and attitudes toward the significant other that might be cultivated or changed and suggestions were made about new concepts and constructs that could be adopted about oneself in relationship to the significant other [p. 569]." Control subjects, on the other hand, were placed on a waiting list that delayed treatment for six weeks, the length of time expended in the treatment programs. Rotter's locus of control scale was administered before and after the six-week treatment or waiting periods. Girls who received the action-oriented treatment were found to have increased in internality from their pretreatment locus of control scores; and their post-treatment scale scores were significantly more internal than those of either the reeducative treatment or control subjects. Though girls in the reeducative group shifted somewhat toward internality, they did not differ significantly from the untreated control subjects.

Dua's action-oriented treatment was evidently more effective than his reeducative efforts insofar as changes in the perceptions of control are concerned. This is not too surprising in view of the greater likelihood that cognitive rehearsals and consideration of alternative approaches for interacting with others would have occurred in the action-oriented treatment. Such active exercises bear rough similarly to the kinds of learning tools used in deCharms' personal causation training.

Nowicki and Barnes (1973) designed a quasi-therapy program in which contingent reinforcement and effectance training were intrinsic elements. The setting was a summer camp provided for deprived inner city adolescents. The camp was described as being highly structured, with emphasis placed upon contingent reinforcement for good or poor performances. Nowicki and Barnes had access to seven successive groups of adolescents, with each group ranging in size from a low of 27 to a high of 54. In addition, for an eighth week, selected students from the first seven weeks were invited back for another week-long stay at the camp.

Although diverse, the camp activities stressed cooperation in the pursuit of group goals, the groups being formed by residence in particular cabins. To accomplish these group achievements a number of conservation projects were undertaken by each group. During these projects campers were socially reinforced for each of their efforts, and at the end of the week actual deeds by individuals were recounted during a public ceremony (Indian council).

All of the campers were administered the Nowicki-Strickland locus of control scale at the beginning and at the end of each week of camp. An overall comparison based on all eight groups was highly significant, indicating that campers expressed some shift toward internality after the week's camping experience. Similar to deCharms' finding that internality or a sense of being an origin increased cumulatively with additional training toward that end, Nowicki and Barnes found that the youngsters who returned for the extra week's session revealed further shifts toward internality. That is, these children began their extra week with "pretreatment" locus of control scores that were already more internal than any of the "pretreatment" groups; and still they revealed further shifts toward internality. In essence, the more experience with challenge and contingent reinforcement, the more internal youngsters were likely to feel. .

Jerome Frank (1976) has described a research investigation in which he and his colleagues (Liberman, 1978) obtained measurements of mastery or "powerlessness" as well as discomfort and improvement throughout a treatment program in which patients were led to attribute successful performing to their own efforts or to the effectiveness of a placebo drug that was administered throughout treatment. Successful performances on tasks, said to be related to their improving health (reaction time, recognition of tachistoscopically presented stimuli, and arousability as revealed by a quasi-GSR) were prearranged such that all patients succeeded but differed with regard to attributions for their success. Three months after the 10 training sessions had been completed, patients were reevaluated for improvements, powerlessness, and discomfort. All patients showed some improvement, registered less discomfort, and scored in the direction of greater mastery. However, after the three-month lapse, self-attributors were found to have maintained their improvement more than those provided with placebos as the cause for their improvements. As an interesting aside, those patients who were initially more internal showed greater improvement with the self-attributed improvement than with the placebo condition whereas externals exhibited the opposite pattern, improving more with the placebo than the self-attribution. Although not germane to the content of this chapter, it is of note that several other investigators have found similar interaction effects with regard to therapy and educational methods. Internals seem to thrive in more self-directed settings whereas externals seem to prefer greater structure and external direction (Abramowitz, Abramowitz, Roback, & Jackson, 1974; Best, 1975; Best & Steffy, 1975; Freidman & Dies, 1974; Kilmann, Albert, & Sotile, 1975).

One other brief set of findings bears discussion here. Most of the therapy studies discussed thus far have been with persons suffering from some deficits for which ameliorists have attempted to provide compensatory training. Researchers with interest in the effects of poverty, however, have often spoken of the benefit of becoming a helper as opposed to a "helpee." Frank Riessman (1962), for one, has written of the increases in self-esteem accrued through the helping of others and has demonstrated this phenomenon in therapy programs with certain deprived individuals. As indicated earlier in this chapter, evidence has been found that experience in positions that allow effectiveness is associated with greater internality (Harvey, 1971). To help others is, in a very real sense, being effective. Whether in an advisory or counselling capacity, a helper actively seeks to affect another and sometimes can see the explicit results of his efforts. Consequently, it can be hypothesized that the learning of skills that enable a person to become an effective helper should result in a greater sense of internal control. Two studies bear out this hypothesis. Gottesfeld and Dozier (1966) found that the more experience that "community stimulators" had within their "Massive Economic Neighborhood Development" program in East Harlem, the more internal were their scores on Rotter's locus of control scale. Likewise, Martin and Shepel (1974) found that nurses who requested and subsequently received some training in personal counselling skills exhibited a significant shift toward internality on James' locus of control scale. Their training consisted of three elements: methods for developing helping relationships, identifying and exploring problems, and creating plans of action. Role-playing was used as an instructional device and the nurses learned how to seek information and encourage potential help-seekers in problem solving. Considerable feedback was available throughout the training procedures so that these nurses were able to assess their own potential effectiveness as counsellors.

Given all of this ready, contingent feedback it was no surprise that these nurses exhibited significant shifts toward internality. Accompanying these changes was a correlated increase in scores on a measure designed to assess their likelihood for engaging in facilitative therapeutic interventions. The correlation between post-training locus of control scores and therapeutic potential [$r = .56$, $p < .01$] was substantial. As a testament to the effectiveness of that training, this same correlation between locus of control and therapeutic potential before training was negligible and statistically insignificant [$r = .16$].

CONCLUSION

Research with both naturally occurring and contrived events has revealed that locus of control scores assessed by scalar and/or behavioral means are susceptible to influence. People change in their customary causal attributions if they encounter experiences that meaningfully alter the contingencies between their acts and perceived outcomes. Though a number of studies have been cited in this chapter, it is obvious that there is considerable room for further information. With the exception of deCharms' study, for instance, there is little evidence regarding long-term persistence of observed changes. Though there seems to be considerable consistency in the research on changes in perceptions of control, many of the studies discussed in this chapter could be criticized for potential contaminating effects, whether they be the "Hawthorne effect," experimenter bias, or demand characteristics, each of which can play havoc with designs involving pre- versus post-treatment assessments.

More critical, perhaps, are the lack of both clear descriptions of the therapeutic approaches and the systematic use of varied criteria in many of the studies that have been conducted thus far. From the research reviewed here it can be concluded that the more action-oriented therapies that stress the learning of and effecting of contingent results seem to be the optimal approaches for changing clients' perceptions of causality. Whether these findings derive from the more clearly explicated task demands or therapist expectancies is not evident at the moment. Though this author is prone to accept the suggestion that behavior modification procedures aimed at increasing contingency awareness are apt to be effective at shifting clients' perceptions of control, there will remain gnawing doubts that can only be assuaged by more extensive and precise research that controls for all of those highly contaminating influences that often serve to give us the results we already anticipate.

11 | The Assessment of Locus of Control

INTRODUCTION

The history of psychology is replete with examples of constructs that have been granted prominence for a brief period of time only to be subsequently discarded and forgotten. However, given the limits of human innovations in describing recurrent phenomena, reinstatements of discarded constructs also occur, albeit with differences in language and assumptions. One contributing factor to the common decline of interest in many an adequate construct derives from the mistaken tendency to identify a construct with some singular measurement device: Anxiety, a construct that is central to several theoretical positions, becomes defined by Taylor's manifest anxiety scale; repression becomes synonymous with Byrne's repression-sensitization scale; authoritarianism with the California F scale, and so on. In each of these instances a measure became, for many investigators, the definition of the construct, and subjects' scores on those instruments came to be taken as indications of the presence or absence of given traits; that is, individuals scoring high on an anxiety scale are said *to be* highly anxious or *to have* high anxiety.

This tendency to equate constructs with their measurement devices occurs naturally. Typological phrasing is a simple condensation that allows for the communication of considerable information. To say "high anxious subjects will ..." conveys in highly condensed form the more cumbersome, if accurate, "persons who answered a large proportion of items on a scale that assumedly contains independent items adjudged to be relevant to feelings of apprehension or dread will...." Unfortunately, the casting of scale scores into condensed nominal classifications can have the effect of reifying the relationship between scale scores and constructs that, in turn, can eventually erode interest in the construct when the scales lose their utility or fail to afford the precise predictions required for clinical concerns. The awareness that many measurement devices are not meant to be more than crude approximations of an individual's position with respect to a particular construct is easily lost in the pursuit of research employing group statistics with limited criteria.

As most psychology students come to know, there are a host of "error" variables that can contribute to inaccuracy in any measurement device and therefore lessen the utility of that device for measuring actions or cognitions pertinent to a particular construct. Even a tape measure may prove to be inaccurate for the precise measurement required in some work; and if such reliable tools as tape measures can fail to provide enough precision, then the difficulties inherent in assessing the more metaphorical constructs of personality should be legion. Examiners of personality are faced with variations in habitual expressiveness, cooperativeness, the desire to appear well before others, self-delusions, to say nothing of the problems of task-demands, the perceived relationship of test performance to decisions to be made about the person, and so on.

For personality researchers and clinical psychologists these difficulties are of primary importance. Theoretical models and their derivative constructs are invented to describe important personal phenomena that are of focal interest to mental health, psychopathology, and social problems. To test the utility of a given construct, crude devices are often created to approximate the relative positions of individuals on that dimension. The results are then used to predict behavior on some constructed criterion that bears analogy to a "real-life" relevant phenomenon. If success in predictions abound, the measuring device becomes widely adopted and slowly assumes an identity with the construct that it was devised to assess. However, the construct has meaning within a theoretical network that may have important clinical implications. Given the salience of a particular construct for clinicians, the acceptance of the tool bearing the name of that construct for clinical applications can occur all too easily, and it is in this leap from the demonstration of utility in nomothetic research to clinical purposes that difficulties abound. Clinical prediction requires much data from convergent and divergent sources to raise the probability levels of any prediction. Demonstration research that explores the possible utility of constructs does not require such exactitude. Low-magnitude significant results suffice for demonstration purposes but lead to a large number of failures in the exact location of subjects with respect to a given dimension, the very task of the clinician.

Locus of control research, like most research in personality, suffers from these same difficulties and confusions. Rotter's scale, as well as other measures of locus of control, are often taken as if they were equivalents of the construct. Scores on particular measures may be used appropriately for classifying subjects *as if* they were more or less external in orientation, but the very process of classification has often led investigators into believing that people *are* internals or externals, or, even worse "internalizers" or "externalizers"—worse because such terms imply processes that are not immediately relevant to the locus of control construct.

One of the first incentives for creating a new locus of control scale grew from the desire to assess control perceptions among children. Rotter himself, with Battle, (Battle & Rotter, 1963) devised one such test that was modelled after Rosenzweig's (1945) Picture Frustration Test. Children were asked to provide answers for characters in a series of cartoons that were later scored for causal attribution. Bialer (1961) was also an early contributor in creating a locus of control scale suitable for children.

It was with the presentation of the Intellectual Achievement Responsibility Questionnaire (Crandall, Katkovsky & Crandall, 1965), however, that questions regarding assessment aims were first given emphasis. In their paper, Crandall et al. (1965) raised three issues pertinent to their assessment device, one being the question of generalization. Rotter's scale was originally devised to assess control expectancies in different reinforcement areas (achievement, dominance, affiliation, etc.), but factor analysis revealed only one general factor. Consequently, with repeated item analyses, the scale was eventually reduced to 23 items that were viewed as being fairly homogeneous. Despite this scalar homogeneity, Crandall and his colleagues did not feel there had been a substantial demonstration that beliefs across reinforcement areas were consistent. In addition, since the Crandalls were engaged in a research program exploring the antecedents of achievement behavior, they were interested in developing a measure that primarily involved achievement reinforcements. With the presentation of their specific reinforcement area locus of control scale, the question of generalizability became salient.

A second problem raised by Crandall et al. (1965) pertains to the sources of external control; that is, in a more general scale such as Rotter's, a variety of external coercers are mentioned as potential forces arrayed against self-direction. Luck, fate, impersonal and personal forces are offered as agents of external control. Crandall et al. (1965) chose to focus upon "significant others," parents, teachers, and peers, as the sources of external control. This restriction upon particular, known agents derived from Crandall et al.'s interests in the natural development of autonomy within the child's world. Most important for the present discussion, however, is the point that Crandall and his coworkers raised, the question as to the particular agents of control, which has become a central issue for some investigators.

A third point stressed by Crandall et al. (1965) concerns the type of reinforcement—positive versus negative. It was argued by these investigators that attributing responsibility for success can be independent of the way in which individuals interpret their failures. Consequently, the Crandalls' locus of control measures, the IAR, was devised to provide separate scores for the response to success and to failure. As have the previous two points, this discrimination in type of outcome has been subsequently explored by other investigators with some success.

In this relatively early paper, then, three issues were raised as being of some importance for investigation with locus of control scales: the generalizability across reinforcement areas, the specification of agents of external control, and the type of reinforcement involved. Each of these aspects has been amplified by certain investigators who have often developed their own devices to correct for perceived shortcomings in other assessment tools.

THE ISSUE OF GENERALIZATION

Generalization Across Persons

The first studies directed toward the issue of generalization were less focused upon reinforcement areas than they were on the ways in which minority groups differentiated between themselves and others with regard to locus of control. Gurin, Gurin, Lao, and Beattie (1969) contended that blacks were more likely than whites to draw distinctions in the ways in which outcomes were determined for themselves as opposed to the culture at large. As these authors indicated, Rotter's scale contains some items that solicit beliefs about the causes of outcomes for people in general, and some that explicitly refer to the respondent's own life situation. Gurin et al. (1969) factor analyzed Rotter's scale along with several additional items pertaining to personal efficacy and racial ideology. Contrary to Rotter's earlier findings with a primarily white subject sample, Gurin et al. (1969) found separate factors for personal as opposed to general causality:

> The items loading on Factors I and II (Control Ideology and Personal Control) are distinguishable in terms of whose success or failure is referred to in the question. The five items with the highest loadings on Factor II are all phrased in the *first person*. The student who consistently chooses the internal alternative on these five items believes that he can control what happens in his own life. He has a strong conviction in his own competence or what we have called a sense of *personal control*. In contrast, only one of the items loading on Factor I explicitly uses the first person. Referring instead to people generally, these items seem to measure the respondent's ideology or general beliefs about the role of internal and external forces in determining success or failure in the culture at large. Endorsing the internal alternative on these items means rejecting the notion that success follows from luck, the right breaks or knowing the right people, and accepting the traditional Protestant Ethic explanation. Such a person believes that hard work, effort, skill and ability are the important determinants of success in life. We have called this factor a measure of the respondent's *control ideology*. [p. 35].

The first factor, "control ideology," includes items 16, 11, 6, 23, 7, 10, 26, 20, and 18 from Rotter's locus of control scale, the order being from the highest to the lower loadings on this factor. The second factor, "personal control," contains items 13, 9, 28, 25, and 15, also in the order of loading magnitude (see Appendix). This isolation of two factors within Rotter's scale was subsequently put to practical test by Gurin et al. (1969) and again by Lao (1970). Gurin et al. (1969) found that

> students who are strongly internal in the personal sense have higher achievement test scores, achieve higher grades in college, and perform better on an anagrams task. . . . In contrast students who are strongly internal in the sense of believing that internal forces are the major determinants of success in the culture at large (ideological) perform *less* well than the more externally-oriented students [pp. 43–44].

In addition, Gurin et al. found that externality on the control ideology factor was associated with readiness to participate in social action and the likelihood of choosing careers that had been atypical for blacks. Lao (1970) found similar patterns of results, with personal control predicting academic achievement and control ideology allowing the prediction of social action and civil rights activity.

These findings obtained with black students reveal some limitations in the generalizability of control expectancies. In essence, the black experience provides for some disjunction between the ways in which one perceives one's own and others' experiences; and this is particularly evident in black perspectives upon causality. Similar cases can be made for other groups. Sex differences commonly obtained in locus of control research may partially derive from different perceptions of personal control and control ideology among women.

Generalization Across Reinforcement Areas

A second group of studies pertaining to the generalization issue have focused upon the realm of the reinforcement area. These studies have differentiated between those reinforcements that are directly experienced occurrences in one's private life and those indirect societal events that would more often require concerted effort by groups. Mirels (1970) was the first of many to report finding two factors in Rotter's scale, one concerning felt mastery over the course of one's life, and the other, the extent to which individuals feel they can exert impact on political institutions. The items from Rotter's scale loading, in order of magnitude on Factor I (felt mastery), were 25, 11, 15, 16, 23, 18, 5, and 10. Factor II, dubbed "system control" by later investigators, contained items 17, 22, 12, and 29 (see Appendix).

The early factor studies did not offer much data of immediate utility. Mirels concluded his own work with a statement calling for studies that might reveal the potential utility of the differentiation suggested by factor analytic results. As will be evident in subsequent discussion, validity research with the different factors has been limited. Nevertheless, the work of Gurin et al. (1969), Lao (1970), and

Mirels (1970) did indicate that there is less than total consistency in the way people perceive events. Locus of control is not to be thought of as a general variable ranging in extremes from total impotence to omnipotence. Rather, the world of events can at least be subdivided for realm of reinforcement on the one hand, and persons for whom attributions are made, on the other.

Subsequent investigators have reported finding similar outcomes from factor analytic procedures. MacDonald and Tseng (1971), for example, found the same two factors in Rotter's locus of control scale with a male sample as had Mirels. However, MacDonald and Tseng found that although the personal control factor accounted for 15% of the variance obtained with the scale, the social system control factor accounted for a rather small 4 to 5% of the variance. In addition, when these investigators tested a female sample, they found a third factor comprised of items that pertained to social as opposed to achievement reinforcements. Items 4, 5, 7, 20, and 26 characterize this separate factor and largely concern the controllability of being liked and/or separated.

Joe and Jahn (1973) have presented similar data with respect to the personal control and social systems control factors and David Reid and Ed Ware (1973) expanded upon these findings by adding items to the original Rotter scale that should have theoretically loaded upon each of the two factors. These latter investigators found support for the assumed reliability of these factors. Items pertaining to the control of more distant world affairs loaded on the social system control factor, whereas the more personal items loaded on the personal control factor.

Reid and Ware (1973, 1974) followed up their own investigation with other studies focusing upon multidimensionality within locus of control measures. In one study, these investigators found that responses to items pertaining to beliefs about control of impulses, drives, and emotions were independent from either the personal control or social systems control factors of Rotter's locus of control scale. On the other hand, the differences between items of control attributed to self and to others as reported by Gurin et al. (1969) were not found. These results, particularly with regard to impulse control, led these researchers to suggest that it was plausible to speak of many independent areas with regard to perceived control.

In support of their contention regarding the utility of a multidimensional approach, Reid and Ware (1974) reported some validity date for the use of separate factors. Personal and social system control were used as differential predictors of causal attributions made in response to two situations, one of which lent itself to a personal, and the other to a system control interpretation. Both personal and social system control were related to causal attributions made about a student who discussed his academic failures on a prepared videotape presentation. Subjects who scored as more internal on either personal or social systems control held the student responsible for his failure experience. However, only social system control was associated with causal attributions made about a videotaped interview that portrayed a person who had been evicted from his apartment because of a bylaw concerned with the number of occupants allowed in a single residence. At the same time, the study found that only social system control was related to political cynicism on the one hand, and political participation on the other. Personal control was not related to the more politically relevant criteria.

Abramowitz (1973) has likewise found that social system control is related to political attitudes whereas personal control is irrelevant to those same political concerns. Given the lack of relationship between personal control and political attitudes Abramowitz concluded, as did Reid and Ware, that considerable predictive power may be lost when the items from both factors are combined without attention being paid to the pertinence of the particular factor to given criteria.

Enough confirmatory evidence has been reported that it is now plausible to speak of a variety of specific areas of control. One investigator has, in fact, isolated four separate factors within Rotter's locus of control scale. Barry Collins (1974; Collins, Martin, Ashmore, & Ross, 1973) separated each single forced choice item from Rotter's scale into two items such that the scale became a 46-item Likert scale. In addition to finding that the internal and external items were not highly related to each other, he reported finding four factors after the rotation of his matrix. The factors were labelled "difficulty of world," "unjust world," "predictability-luck," and "political responsiveness." Though Collins acknowledges that each of these factors would be functional equivalents for Rotter's social learning orientation, in that each factor would contribute toward or against instrumental activity, Collins asserted that sources of unpredictability in the world are meaningfully distinguishable and relatively uncorrelated.

In response to these data confirming the multidimensional character of locus of control scales, this writer has contended (Lefcourt, 1973) that the discovery of multidimensionality is not surprising, and that the problems attending such discovery are more in the way that subsequent investigators will use diverse factors than as criticisms of the robustness of locus of control as a personality construct. Similar arguments have been offered by Rotter (1975).

Locus of control measures have been devised that differentiate among reinforcement areas or between persons' perceptions of themselves and others. Investigators such as Oscar Parsons (Parsons & Schneider, 1974) and Walter Mischel (1975) have both found some profit in ascertaining contrasts in the perception of control for one's self and others. The task that is of the greatest importance now, involves the systematic selection of specific factors to be studied; that is, there is not much additional benefit to be derived from the continuous factor analyzing of given locus of control measures, though confirmations of Mirel's work (Viney, 1974) and analyses such as those by Tyler, Gatz, and Keenan (1979) have been of some value. At the present time it is most apt that investigators have taken to devising specifically aimed locus of control measures for theoretically relevant criteria. Instead of simply rediscovering multidimensionality, investigators have begun to assess perceived control for specific reinforcement areas.

In the first of a two-volume set edited by this author (Lefcourt, 1981a) detailed descriptions have been provided of research programs in which specific targetted locus of control measures have been created. Since the scales and normative data are presented in that volume, they will not be repeated in this book. However, a brief survey of the programs will provide some idea of the new directions to be found in the literature concerned with the assessments of locus of control.

Reid and Ziegler (1981) have created a scale referred to as The Desired Control Measure. Derived from a survey conducted among a sizable sample of the elderly, the scale elicits both the concern for and the expectation of control for those outcomes or events that were commonly found to be desired by the elderly. Examples of those desired experiences are going out when the person wants to, being able to do chores by oneself, maintaining health, etc.

Reid and Ziegler have used their scales successfully in a series of studies, managing to predict adjustment and illness among the elderly a year after initial assessments (Reid, Hass, & Hawkings, 1977; Reid & Ziegler, 1977; Ziegler & Reid, 1979).

Another program of research is that by Paulhus and Christie (1981). These authors have constructed scales concerned with each of three spheres of control—the nonsocial environment (Personal Efficacy Scale), the social environment (Interpersonal Control Scale), and the larger political milieu (Sociopolitical Control Scale). With this battery, Paulhus and Christie have been able to differentially predict criteria relevant to each scale such as voting behavior, interpersonal assertiveness, and the preference for skill-demanding tasks.

Wallston and Wallston (1981) have developed health-focused locus of control scales that are already well-known in the literature. Originally described in two publications (Wallston, Maides, & Wallston, 1976; Wallston, Wallston, Kaplan, & Maides, 1976), these scales have already seen wide use in the literature concerned with health and behavioral medicine.

This author has described his own goal-specific locus of control research in several places (Lefcourt, 1979; 1981a; Lefcourt, VonBaeyer, Ware, & Cox, 1979). The initial work concerned the locus of control for achievement and affiliation, two goal areas of importance for young university students. Other attempts at studying goal- or area-specific locus of control in our labs have concerned work (Lewandowski, 1979) and marital satisfaction (Miller, 1981). With regard to marriage, locus of control has been found to be related to marital satisfaction and the degree of intimacy experienced with one's spouse.

Hill and Bale (1981) have constructed two scales pertaining to mental health: The Mental Health Locus of Control Questionnaire concerning the responsibility for progress in therapeutic encounters and The Mental Health Locus of Origin Scale, which assesses etiological beliefs about the development of mental illness. These scales would seem to have promise for explaining the development of particular types of pathology as well as the behaviors exhibited during therapy. Other specific-area locus of control scales that have been developed concern the drinking behavior of alcoholics (Donovan & O'Leary, 1978; Worell & Tumilty, 1981); weight management (Saltzer, 1978; 1981); and achievement (Wong, Watters, & Sproule, 1978).

As the above makes evident, much investigative effort is currently being expended in the study of the locus of control for specific goals or areas, a development that argues well for the continued use of the construct in research.

AGENTS OF EXTERNAL CONTROL

The second point emerging from the original Crandall et al. (1965) contribution pertained to the agents of external control. Shortly after the publication of the Crandall article in which the IAR measure was presented, Hersch and Scheibe (1967) published an article concerned with the reliability and validity of Rotter's locus of control measure. In that paper, Hersch and Scheibe reported certain data with adjective check lists that led them to suggest that externality was considerably less homogeneous than was internality. In all, 23 adjectives were checked significantly more often by internals than externals such that internals were found to present a fairly coherent self-portrait. Characteristics assigned to themselves by internals were: "clever, efficient, egotistical, enthusiastic, independent, self-confident, ambitious, assertive, boastful, conceited, conscientious, deliberate, persevering, clear-thinking, dependable, determined, hard headed, industrious, ingenious, insightful, organized, reasonable, and stubborn [p. 612]." In complete contrast, only one adjective was checked more often by externals—"self pitying." Hersch and Scheibe (1967) concluded, therefore, that there may be greater diversity in the meaning of externality:

> One may be an external individual because he is in fact physically or intellectually weak in relation to those around him. On the other hand, a person may describe himself as an external because he is in a highly competitive social situation, where the actions of others may have great relevance for the success of his own effort. . . . If a person believes in luck or fate, and if he further believes that these external forces are on his side, he may accurately describe himself as an external. Further, a person may develop feelings of persecution, with or without reason [p. 613].

These differences among external forces bear some similarity to those factors reported by Collins and his colleagues (1973). However, among locus of control investigators, Hannah Levenson has exerted the most effort toward examining the utility of assessing diverse agents of control. In the process, she has created a three-factor measure of locus of control that consists of "internality," "control by powerful others," and "control by chance" scales. She has used these scales with some success in predicting specific criteria. For instance, Levenson was able to predict political involvement with her "control by chance" scale but neither "internality" or "control by powerful others" proved to be relevant to her criterion (Levenson, 1974). Those who believed that events occur in chance fashion were less apt to become politically involved in an antipollution group. As a further point of interest, even among active members of the antipollution group, those who believed in the potency of chance were less knowledgeable about pollution than their less chance-controlled counterparts.

In addition to social action, Levenson has explored the ramifications of her scale measures among institutionalized populations (Levenson, 1973a). Patients diagnosed as psychotic or neurotic were tested at monthly intervals with Levenson's scales. On initial testing, patients scored higher on control by powerful others and chance forces than normal adult samples, though neurotics were much closer to the normal samples than were psychotics. After the second month of hospitalization, patients diagnosed as paranoid scored higher on control by powerful others than did all other patients. Finally, with therapy as the intervening occurrence, internality scores shifted toward the internal end of the continuum, whereas control by chance and powerful others remained constant. Levenson (1974) has also found her factors operating differentially among prison inmates. Belief in the control by powerful others was found to be related to the time spent in prison and the frequency of solitary confinement. Inmates who scored high external on the powerful others scale had been disciplined with solitary confinement six times more frequently than inmates who had lower expectations of control by powerful others. Internality and beliefs regarding control by chance were irrelevant to these criteria.

Levenson (1974) suggests that the belief in control by powerful others is similar in nature to the social system control factor of Mirels (1970) and others. Her contribution, then, rests in the demonstration of the utility of employing her factored scales as well as in advancing the conception that beliefs in internal control are differentiable from beliefs in the efficacy of chance or powerful others, and that it is possible for all three to coexist independently within individuals.

Early support for Levenson's tripartite division of locus of control came from a study by Kleiber, Veldman, and Menaker (1973). These investigators administered each of Rotter's 23 forced choice items as 46 Likert scale items similar to the way that Collins presented the scale to his subjects. Originally, paired items were relatively uncorrelated, ranging in magnitude of correlations from .14 to − .47 where high magnitude, negative correlations were expected. Most significantly, a factor analysis of the 46 item scale produced three factors: 1) disbelief in luck or chance; 2) system modifiability; and 3) individual responsibility for failure. Obviously, these three factors bear some similarity to Levenson's chance, powerful others, and internality scales, respectively.

Levenson (1981) has reviewed the work that has been completed with her three factor scale. A surprisingly large number of investigations have made use of her scales or drawn upon them to help create newer measures such as the Health Locus of Control scales.

As with specificity of reinforcement, there is evidence supporting the utility of assessing the impacts of specific controlling agents. However, it should be evident to the reader that there has not been anything like an exhaustive search for possible external forces that could be evaluated with respect to particular criteria. It would not seem untoward if one were to attempt to delineate a host of possible external forces that might affect outcomes in specific reinforcement areas. An example for such a project is available in Weiner's work pertaining to achievement behavior. As discussed previously, Weiner has described a variety of external and internal forces that can be grouped into categories of stable and unstable sources of control, whether internal or external. It should be possible to do a similar job with reinforcement areas other than achievement, and it may be in such a pursuit that the findings of Levenson and others will reach fruition.

TYPE OF REINFORCEMENT—POSITIVE VERSUS NEGATIVE

The third area of concern originally discussed in the Crandall paper is that of the type of reinforcement, positive or negative. As was indicated in Chapter 6, research related to achievement activity has revealed that control expectancies relevant to failure may be considered separately from control expectancies for success. Both Crandall et al. (1965) and Mischel, Zeiss, & Zeiss (1974) have found that locus of control for failure and for success may be relatively independent from each other, and that each may afford the prediction of specified events which the other does not. As noted previously, Mischel et al. (1974) found that a measure of internality for success experiences predicted persistent efforts in activity directed toward the attainment of desired goals, whereas an equivalent measure of internality for failure was better at predicting behavior aimed at avoiding aversive consequences.

A number of other experimenters (Antrobus, 1973; DuCette, Wolk, & Soucar, 1972; Meyer, 1970) subsequently reported data suggesting that contrasts between the locus of control for success and for failure within the same individuals offers valuable information for behavioral predictions. Most notably, DuCette et al. (1972) reported the data from two studies in which they were able to predict the occurrence of "nonadaptive behavior" from what was referred to as "atypical patterns in locus of control." Lower class black children in one investigation, and lower IQ children in another study, all of whom were defined as problem children, were found to have rated themselves as more internal for success than they were for failure on Crandall's IAR scale. This was in direct opposition to problem children who were white, had high IQs, and who scored as more internal for failure than for success.

DuCette et al. (1972) concluded that these pattern discrepancies were comprehensible in that problem children were likely to be less sensitive to the environmental feedback they would probably experience and thus would seem to be less apt to learn from their experiences. As DuCette et al. (1972) have expressed it: "In both cases, the problem child by his discrepancy between the assumption of responsibility for positive and negative events has systematically reduced the amount of meaningful feedback he can obtain about himself. The argument being presented . . . is that such reduction in feedback, via these atypical patterns of locus of control, in the long run, might produce maladjusted behavior [p. 296]."

Although it may be argued that the more normal state of affairs is one in which the locus of control for positive and negative events is symmetrical, the research by DuCette et al. (1972), along with that by Crandall et al. (1965) and Mischel et al. (1974) indicates that much valuable data may emerge from the consideration of separate measures of positive and negative reinforcement control expectancies.

This conclusion has received strong support in the investigations by Gregory (1978; 1981). After noting that locus of control scales were often more effective in predicting responses to aversive than to positive situations, Gregory set out to investigate the predictive power of locus of control scales pertinent to positive and negative outcomes respectively. Using the procedures from the decision time study of Rotter and Mulry (1965) noted earlier, Gregory (1978) found that persons who were assessed as being internal for both positive and negative outcomes did not differ in the time they spent making decisions in reward or punishment conditions. Likewise, those who were symetrically external did not differ with conditions. However, those who were internal for positive and external for negative outcomes spent more time working under reward than punishment conditions; the opposite pattern was obtained from those who were more external for negative and internal for positive outcomes. When these same data were analyzed opposite Rotter's I–E scale, on the other hand, where positive and negative events are not equally represented, there were no differences discernable in predicting decision times in the reward conditions as a function of locus of control. In the punishment condition, however, internals were found to spend more time in decision making than externals, and more time in comparison to themselves in the reward condition.

These data, along with preceding work by DuCette et al. (1972) and others indicate that the disaggregation of locus of control scales can be profitably pursued with differentiations drawn between positive and negative outcomes.

CONCLUSIONS

If one were now to summarize the current status of assessment tools used in the study of locus of control, it would be possible to conclude that there is enough evidence to encourage investigators to both continue in their use of existing devices and to develop newer, more criterion-specific measures. If the investigator's purposes are to expand upon the nomological network within which locus of control may operate, then devices such as Rotter's scale, Crandall's IAR, or Nowicki and Strickland's I-E scales may suffice despite the failings inherent in each of them. However, if one were seeking to use the construct to make sense of more clinical problems where precision is an issue, then due consideration should be given to the construction of measures that are appropriate to the given problem. Examples of ingenuity in this activity have become abundant, ranging from scales focused upon a broad range of behaviors subsumed under the headings of achievement or health to some that are hyper-specific such as the efficacy scales of Bandura (Bandura, Adams, Hardy & Howells, 1980).

Though other researchers have offered criticism of the locus of control construct and scales referring to ideological biases in the measuring instruments (Fink & Hjelle, 1973; Mirels & Garrett, 1971; Thomas, 1970), to the social desirability of internal control beliefs (Cone, 1971; Hjelle, 1971; Joe, 1972), and even more critical, to the verbal facility required for comprehending item meanings (Gorsuch, Henighan, & Barnard, 1972), though these findings have been opened to question (Halpin & Ottinger, 1981), the major criticisms or advice to investigators in this area pertains to the ways in which devices are selected and used. Two studies have exemplified the wisdom of using the locus of control construct as a moderating variable within a social learning formulation. Wolk and DuCette (1973) found that predicted correlations between achievement motivation and achievement-related behaviors were to be found largely among internal subjects. For instance, the positive correlations expected between a measure of achievement motivation and the preference for intermediate risk was .53 [$p < .05$] among internals in one study and .44 [$p < .01$] in a second study. In contrast, the same correlations among externals were −.07 and .10 in each study, respectively. Here, the interaction between value and control expectancy is revealed as a powerful way to enhance the prediction of specified criteria.

A second powerful illustration of the way in which the sophisticated use of Rotter's locus of control measure can lead to good differential predictions was provided in a study by Naditch and DeMaio (1975). In this article, Naditch and DeMaio described what they referred to as a means/ends motivational framework. Briefly, these authors reasoned that "locus of control should relate to competence only in areas that are important to that person, i.e., areas where competence is related to important goals endorsed by that person [p. 3]." To test this assumption, Naditch and DeMaio obtained self-reported measures of competence in four separate goal areas, assessments of interest in each area, and the locus of control scores from a sample of over 300 public school children. The four competence areas chosen—school achievement, social popularity, sports achievement, and doing things well at home (home achievement)—were derived from informal interviews with the school children.

Naditch and DeMaio (1975) found confirmation for the interaction between interest value and locus of control upon reported competence for each of the first three areas among male students:

Among males correlations between locus of control and self-reported academic competence, national battery test scores, and grade point average were not statistically significant among subjects in the bottom two-thirds of the distribution of the goal value of academic performance. For those students in the top third of the goal value distribution, i.e., those students for whom academic success represented a highly valued outcome, there were significant correlations between locus of control and self-reported academic competence ($r = -.40$, $p < .01$). [p. 552].

Likewise, with regard to social competence the "correlations between locus of control and self-reported social competence were insignificant for people less interested in social competence, and significantly correlated among those subjects for whom social competence was more highly valued ($r = -.32$, $p < .01$) [p. 553]." With regard to sports competence, similar findings were reported: "Correlations between locus of control and sports competence were not significant among people for whom sports competence did not represent a valued outcome, but were significantly correlated among those people for whom performance in sports was important ($r = -.72$, $p < .05$) [p. 553]."

Though the findings with female students did not replicate the above, let it suffice to say that at a crude level of assessment, Naditch, as well as Wolk and DuCette, demonstrated the power of using locus of control measures in interaction with assessments of values and interests. In neither case did these authors devise more precise measures of locus of control. It is perhaps in the development of such specific measures, and the use of them within value X expectancy frameworks, as exemplified in the work by Reid and Ziegler (1981), that we can anticipate finding improvements in precision and clinical prediction that may save the locus of control construct from the waning of interest that is so common among personality constructs.

12 Implications of Research

OVERVIEW

At this point it would seem appropriate to address ourselves to the question of what generalizations may be drawn from this literature about the perception of control. It has been a continuous fear among researchers in this area that the dimension of locus of control is simply a euphemism for "good guys-bad guys," with internality being a substitute for "intelligent, bright, and successful," and externality for "dull, inadequate, and failure ridden." In each data realm that we have explored, the findings, in fact, would lead one to believe that the locus of control dimension is an accurate euphemism for such extreme qualities. An intelligent inquiry, however, would include questions as to the reality of beliefs in control, to the problems of grandiosity and delusions of omnipotence, and to the realization that there is much in the way of life experience that must be accepted as inevitable and beyond man's ken. The creation of gods, idols, and other powers attest to man's awareness that he is indeed a limited creature, one that suffers infirmities and threats to his existence that are beyond any reasonable hope of control.

In view of the obvious constraints upon man's self-direction, theorists such as Rotter (1966) have hypothesized that locus of control measures should have a curvilinear relationship with assessments of maladjustment. In other words, individuals who feel themselves to be entirely at the mercy of external circumstances should be no more aberrant in their daily functioning than persons who believe that they are responsible for each and every important event that occurs throughout their lifetime. In the latter case, we approach those pathological processes that would be associated with paranoia, ideas of reference, delusions of grandeur, and so on, whereas the former would seem to be more relevant to depression, withdrawal, apathy, and retreatism.

Why then, it may be asked, has an internal locus of control most usually been found to be a positive asset and externality a deficit, in the research conducted thus far? The answer to this question may be simpler than one might assume. The measurement tools and criterion situations that have been used in most experiments have focused upon events that are largely in the range of conrollability for the subjects examined. Achievement reinforcements are often realistically contingent upon the efforts of middle-class North American children. Consequently, internality with regard to achievement-related events is appropriate, and therefore a good prognostic indicator of achievement-facilitating behavior.

No one has yet constructed devices, to this writer's knowledge, that ascertain control beliefs about events that are extremely improbable and commonly believed to be beyond control. Only in the separate factor of "system control," the expression of beliefs about the contingency between individual action and changes in large systems, do we even approach an assessment of less probable event control. With the myth of the democratic New England town meetings and labor movements still fresh in memory, however, North Americans continue to prize the assumption that individuals can count in remote social events, even if alienation and anomie in large faceless organizations tends to erode that myth. Granted that this myth still persists, if with less general faith in its verisimilitude, system control does not fully qualify as an inappropriate control expectation, especially among privileged middle-class university students. Consequently, an accurate statement of the research to date must take into account the fact that most research has concerned controllable outcomes and that the "realism" of control expectancies should be considered as new outcome areas are investigated.

If we define realistic limits and boundaries within which the locus of control variable should have its greatest utility, we may be better able to draw appropriate conclusions from the research literature. To begin with, locus of control is not to be regarded as an omnibus trait similar to competence or intelligence, which pertains to each and every facet of human endeavor. Rather, it can be more fruitfully defined as a circumscribed self-appraisal pertaining to the degree to which individuals view themselves as having some causal role in determining *specified events.*

Some of the research that we have discussed explored the ramifications of more generalized appraisals or expectancies deriving from cumulative experience with goal striving. Other studies have focused upon more specific self-appraisals relevant to the pursuit of particular goals. Results from both sorts of studies allow us to conclude that the manner in which individuals appraise themselves with regard to causality makes a considerable difference in the ways that many life experiences will be confronted, and we have chosen to describe those ways with the term "vitality."

If we summarize the bulk of the findings discussed in this book, it would be fair to conclude that internal control expectancies about personally important events that are to some reasonable degree controllable, will be related to signs of vitality—affective and cognitive activity that indicates an active grappling with those self-defined important events. Where fatalism or external control beliefs are associated with apathy and withdrawal, the holding of internal control expectancies presages a connection between an individual's desires and his subsequent actions. As such, locus of control can be viewed as a mediator of involved commitment in life pursuits. If one feels helpless to affect important events, then resignation or at least benign indifference should become evident, with fewer signs of concern, involvement, and vitality.

Good examples that can convey the essence of this generality linking perceived causation and vitality are contained in James Fenimore Cooper's novel, *The deerslayer* and Leonid Andreyev's *The seven that were hanged.* Cooper (1910) described a scene in which Deerslayer is bound tightly to a tree and surrounded by an execution squad of his enemies, the Huron Indians. The warriors of this tribe cut at Deerslayer's flesh repeatedly with varying accuracy and ferocity so that his torso becomes gashed and oozing with blood. Despite their intimidating tortures, Deerslayer reveals progressivly *less* rather than *more* fear than the warriors had anticipated. His stoical countenance proves to be a disappointment if not a threat to the assumed fearsomeness of his captors. Consequently, his assailants pause in their execution ceremony and begin discussing the situation:

"I see how it is", he said. "We have been like the palefaces when they fasten their doors at night, out of fear of the red-man. They use so many bars, that the fire comes and burns them before they can get out. We have bound the Deerslayer too tight; the thongs keep his limbs from shaking, and his eyes from shutting. Loosen him; let us see what his own body is really made of."

The proposal of the chief found instant favor; and several hands were immediately at work cutting and tearing the ropes of bark from the body of our hero. In half a minute Deerslayer stood as free from bonds as when, an hour before, he had commenced his flight on the side of the mountain. Some little time was necessary that he should recover the use of his limbs, the circulation of the blood having been checked by the tightness of the ligatures; and this was accorded to him. It is seldom men think of death in the pride of their health and strength. So it was with Deerslayer. Having been helplessly bound, and, as he had every reason to suppose, so lately on the very verge of the other world, to find himself so unexpectedly liberated, in possession of his strength, and with a full command of limb, acted on him like a sudden restoration to life, reanimating hopes that he had once absolutely abandoned. From that instant all his plans changed. In this he simply obeyed a law of nature; for while we have wished to represent our hero as being resigned to his fate, it has been far from our intention to represent him as anxious to die. From the instant that his buoyancy of feeling revived, his thoughts were keenly bent on the various projects that presented themselves as modes of evading the designs of his enemies; and he again became the quick-witted, ingenious, and determined woodsman, alive to all his own powers and resources. [pp. 349-350].

In Cooper's discerning commentary we can see the connection between efficacy and vitality. When one believes that hope is possible, that there is some opportunity to act in one's own behest, then he becomes more "determined" and "alive to all his own powers and resources," or in a word, vital.

In *The seven that were hanged,* Leonid Andreyev (1918) portrayed the behavior of seven persons awaiting their executions. One of these persons, Vasily Kashirin, is described in terms that have pertinence to our discussion of control and vitality:

Under the same roof and to the same melodious chant of the different hours, separated from Sergey and from Musya by a few empty cells, but as isolated as if he alone had existed in the whole universe, the unhappy Vasily Kashirin was finishing his life in anguish and terror.

Covered with sweat, his shirt adhering to his body, his formerly curly hair now falling in straight locks, he went back and forth in his cell with the jerky and lamentable gait of one suffering atrociously with a toothache. He sat down for a moment and then began to run again; then he rested his forehead against the wall, stopped, and looked about as if in search of a remedy. He had so changed that one might think he possessed two different faces, one of which, the younger, had gone nobody knows where, to give place to the second, a terrible face, that seemed to have come from darkness.

Fear had shown itself suddenly to him, and had seized upon his person as an exclusive and sovereign mistress. On that fatal morning, when he was marching to certain death, he had played with it; but that evening, confined to his cell, he had been carried away and lashed by a wave of mad terror. As long as he had gone freely forward to meet danger and death, as long as he had held his fate in his own hands, however terrible it might be, he had appeared tranquil and even joyous, the small amount of shameful and decrepit fear that he had felt having disappeared in a consciousness of infinite liberty, in the firm and audacious affirmation of his intrepid will, leaving no trace behind. With an infernal machine strapped around his waist, he had transformed himself into an instrument of death, he had borrowed from the dynamite its cruel reason and its flashing and homicidal power. In the street, among the busy people preoccupied with their affairs and quickly dodging the tramcars and the cabs, it seemed to him as if he came from another and an unknown world, where there was no such thing as death or fear.

Suddenly a brutal, bewildering change had taken place. Vasily no longer went where he wanted to go, but was led where others wanted him to go. He no longer chose his place; they placed him in a stone cage and locked him as if he were a thing. He could no longer choose between life and death; they led him to death, certainly and inevitably. He who had been for a moment the incarnation of will, of life, and of force, had become a lamentable specimen of impotence; he was nothing but an animal destined for the slaughter. Whatever he might say, they would not listen; if he started to cry out, they would stuff a rag in his mouth; and, if he even tried to walk, they would take him away and hang him. If he resisted, if he struggled, if he lay down on the ground, they would be stronger than he; they would pick him up, they would tie him, and thus they would carry him to the gallows. And his imagination gave to the men charged with this execution, men like himself, the new, extraordinary, and terrifying aspect of unthinking automata, whom nothing in the world could stop, and who seized a man, overpowered him, hanged him, pulled him by the feet, cut the rope, put the body in a coffin, carried it away, and buried it. [pp. 63–65].

Kashirin is said not to have feared death when he had actively chosen to become a suicidal revolutionary. However, when he ceased to be the active determiner of his fate, to be the conscious center of his own world, his terror became almost palpable. As Andreyev wrote: ''His consciousness went out like the dying embers that one scatters on the hearth, it froze, like the body of a man just dead in which the heart is still warm while the hands and feet are already cold [p. 68].''

Where Cooper has described how vitality varies with changes in hope and a belief in one's efficacy, Andreyev has described the depersonalization and withdrawal that occasions the loss of choice and self-direction. Both authors, then, convey the manner in which self-direction is experienced as a primary source of affect and vitality.

Until this point we have largely been in the process of summarizing and looking backward at the sequence of research discoveries that have led us to recognize the value of the locus of control construct. We have concluded that the perception of control is a useful construct that allows us to comprehend a diversity of human characteristics that we have subsumed under the term ''vitality.'' Now our attention should be drawn to a number of reservations that researchers need to bear in mind when employing the locus of control construct.

First, the locus of control construct per se should not be expected to account for a lion's share of the variance in most situations. The perception of control is but a single expectancy construct. Other interacting variables of equal, if not greater, importance include the value of the reinforcements in question, as well as the expectancy that one will obtain that desired reinforcement, whether by one's own or external forces.

Second, people are not totally internals or externals. The terms are used as expressive short cuts and are not meant to imply that perception of control is a trait or a typology. The perception of control is a process, the exercise of an expectancy regarding causation; and the terms internal and external control depict an individual's more common tendencies to expect events to be contingent or noncontingent upon their actions.

Third, if one wishes to use the perception of control as a powerful predictor, then it will most always be profitable to design one's own assessment devices for the criterion of interest. This is similar to stating that people are not so much to be characterized as internals and externals as they may be said to hold internal and external control expectancies about different aspects of their lives. If one were concerned about a particular aspect, such as the ability to maintain close intimate relationships, then the perception of control of love and affection responses would be more salient than would control expectancies pertaining to achievement. To summarize this point, one would always do well to add an ''of what'' after the phrase perception of control.

Fourth, we must always bear in mind that there are many confounding elements in the term ''control.'' It has been contended by some that the construct was originally misnamed, that control was never the central issue, but rather that contingency was at the core of the construct. The term control connotes successful manipulation. The construct, locus of control, on the other hand, focuses upon the perceived contingency of events, whether they be positive or negative outcomes. In addition to the confounds associated with the term control, other researchers such as Ivan Steiner (1970) have drawn distinctions between ''outcome'' and ''decision freedom,'' both of which have pertinence to locus of control. The perception of control may be differentiated between beliefs regarding one's freedom to select a goal (decision freedom), and beliefs regarding the way goals are accomplished once they have been adopted (outcome freedom). Other researchers have illustrated how various locus of control measures are replete with such confounds and some investigators have attempted to refine their assessment tools so as to measure only a simple aspect of control.

At the same time that those concerned with control explore the various contaminants and confusions in the literature, those concerned with learned helplessness have also taken to noting which other characteristics and variables can alter the assumed relationship between helplessness and depression. Though it is not my intention to criticize those who continually work at drawing finer differentiations between facets of the control literature, there is a dnager that the appeal of the analytic process could come to overshadow the more compelling pursuit of seeking the ramifications of control.

Perceived contingency is not identical to perceived efficacy. Yet, it is doubtful that the latter would exist without the former. Likewise, the freedom to choose options would seem a cruel farce if the freedom to act were denied or impossible. In other words, though differentiations are possible, the functional significance of the control variables may inhere in their convergence. Vitality may reflect efficacy and perceived contingency and outcome freedom and decision freedom and so on.

At this point we may ask if there is enough evidence to continue to support this catholic view, that there is a unifying theme across the literature concerned with control. A recent review article by Suzanne Thompson (1981) encourages us to believe in the affirmative. After presenting the various definitions and types of control involved in those investigations in which control has been used as an experimentally manipulated variable, Thompson (1981) was able to extract some unifying themes—that the effects of control derive from its limiting of the maximum of aversive experiences, and that man's potential sufferings are alterable by the meanings assigned to those experiences that threaten to destroy him. When Deerslayer discovered that he was free to act, the hopelessness of his condition changed. He was no longer faced with the inevitable—limitless torture and the infinity of death. If killed while escaping, his death would have been sudden and only briefly painful, whereas the torture planned for him would have been continuous and increasing beyond endurance until death.

For Kashirin also, the active death of the revolutionary was to be brief. In addition, his death was to be meaningful, in service to a cause. With the expectation of execution by his captors, however, meaning evaporated and, during the period of detention, he was no longer able to affect the important events of his life. Here, the loss of efficacy led the hero to dread the inescapable and to exhibit a deterioration of self that Andreyev noted (1918) when he wrote, "A man had disappeared from the world."

Despite the various classifications, then, that can be delineated within the spectrum of the control literature its thrust is relatively clear. Though work must continue in the direction of refinements from attribution research, and from unravelling the confounds in measures and conceptions, the direction of research should retain the potential of illuminating how man can grapple with the burdens of his life and even his death.

Appendices

These appendices comprise several scales that have been used in the assessment of locus of control. With each scale some normative data are presented to enable potential users to draw comparisons with their own samples. The scales are presented, however, not in the expectation that readers will come to rely upon these particular measures, but that they may be encouraged to examine these devices and the results obtained with them with a somewhat more discerning eye.

The scales presented are as follows:

1. Bialer's Locus of Control Questionnaire (Bialer, 1961);
2. Crandall's Intellectual Achievement Responsibility Questionnaire (Crandall, Katkovsky, & Crandall, 1965);
3. Dean's Alienation Scales (Dean, 1969);
4. James' I–E Scale (James, 1957);
5. Nowicki–Strickland Locus of Control Scale (Nowicki & Strickland, 1973);
6. Reid–Ware Three-Factor I–E Scale (Reid & Ware, 1974);
7. Rotter's I–E Scale (Rotter, 1966); and
8. Stanford Preschool I–E Scale (Mischel, Zeiss, & Zeiss, 1974).

In addition, I have included a new and untried device from our labs (Lefcourt, Reid, & Ware) which has been constructed to allow for a more open-ended assessment of values, expectancies, and locus of causation. This device is included because it may prove useful as a framework from which more goal-relevant locus of control measures may be derived.

APPENDIX I:
BIALER LOCUS OF CONTROL QUESTIONNAIRE*

In the administration of the questionnaire, the subject is asked to respond with "yes" or "no" to each item. The letter "f" indicates that a "yes" response is scored as internal control. The letter "p" signifies that an answer of "no" is scored as internal control. The scale is scored in terms of the total number of responses in the direction of internal control.

Children's Locus of Control Scale

Instructions

This is not a test. I am just trying to find out how kids your age think about certain things. I am going to ask you some questions to see how you feel about these things. There are no right or wrong answers to these questions. Some kids say "yes" and some say "no." When I ask the question, if you think your answer should be yes, or mostly yes, say "Yes." If you think the answer should be no, or mostly no, say "No." Remember, different children give different answers, and there is no right or wrong answer. Just say "Yes" or "No," depending on how *you* think the question should be answered. If you want me to repeat a question, ask me. Do you understand? All right, listen carefully, and answer "Yes" or "No."

1p. When somebody gets mad at you, do you usually feel there is nothing you can do about it?

2f. Do you really believe a kid can be whatever he wants to be?

3f. When people are mean to you, could it be because you did something to make them be mean?

4f. Do you usually make up your mind about something without asking someone first?

5f. Can you do anything about what is going to happen tomorrow?

6f. When people are good to you, is it usually because you did something to make them be good?

7f. Can you ever make other people do things you want them to do?

8f. Do you ever think that kids your age can change things that are happening in the world?

9f. If another child was going to hit you, could you do anything about it?

10f. Can a child your age ever have his own way?

11p. Is it hard for you to know why some people do certain things?

12f. When someone is nice to you, is it because you did the right things?

---

*From Bialer (1961).

Norms for the Bialer Locus of Control Scale

Subjects	N	Mean	SD
Normals—white, male	13	18.1	2.17
Schizophrenics—white, male	15	14.4	3.89
(Cromwell, Rosenthal, Shakow, & Zahn, 1961)			
6th and 8th grade—selected on basis			
of sex, social class, ethnic group			
from five metropolitan schools.			
Negro—middle class	16	15.8	4.4
Negro—lower class	23	18.3	3.4
White—middle class	20	15.0	4.4
White—lower class (Battle & Rotter, 1963)	21	16.4	3.5
Undergrads	108M	17.23	2.29
(A. P. MacDonald, Unpublished paper)	72F	17.41	2.12
Total:	180	17.31	2.21

13f. Can you ever try to be friends with another kid even if he doesn't want to?

14f. Does it ever help to think about what you will be when you grow up?

15f. When someone gets mad at you, can you usually do something to make him your friend again?

16f. Can kids your age ever have anything to say about where they are going to live?

17f. When you get in an argument, is it sometimes your fault?

18p. When nice things happen to you, is it only good luck?

19p. Do you often feel you get punished when you don't deserve it?

20f. Will people usually do things for you if you ask them?

21f. Do you believe a kid can usually be whatever he wants to be when he grows up?

22p. When bad things happen to you, is it usually someone else's fault?

23f. Can you ever know for sure why some people do certain things?

APPENDIX II: THE CRANDALL
INTELLECTUAL ACHIEVEMENT RESPONSIBILITY QUESTIONNAIRE*

Internal alternatives are designated by an I. Positive-events items are indicated by a plus sign, and negative events by a minus sign following the I. A child's score is obtained by summing all positive events for which he assumes credit, and his I^- score is the total of all negative events for which he assumes blame. His total I score is the sum of his I^+ and his I^- subscores.

*From Crandall, Katkovsky, and Crandall (1965).

The IAR Scale

1. If a teacher passes you to the next grade, would it probably be
   (a) because she liked you, or
   I^+(b) because of the work you did?

2. When you do well on a test at school, is it more likely to be
   I^+(a) because you studied for it, or
   (b) because the test was especially easy?

3. When you have trouble understanding something in school, is it usually
   (a) because the teacher didn't explain it clearly, or
   I^-(b) because you didn't listen carefully?

4. When you read a story and can't remember much of it, is it usually
   (a) because the story wasn't well written, or
   I^-(b) because you weren't interested in the story?

5. Suppose your parents say you are doing well in school. Is it likely to happen
   I^+(a) because your school work is good, or
   (b) because they are in a good mood?

6. Suppose you did better than usual in a subject at school. Would it probably happen
   I^+(a) because you tried harder, or
   (b) because someone helped you?

7. When you lose at a game of cards or checkers, does it usually happen
   (a) because the other player is good at the game, or
   I^-(b) because you don't play well?

8. Suppose a person doesn't think you are very bright or clever.
   I^-(a) Can you make him change his mind if you try to, or
   (b) are there some people who will think you're not very bright no matter what you do?

9. If you solve a puzzle quickly, is it
   (a) because it wasn't a very hard puzzle, or
   I^+(b) because you worked on it carefully?

10. If a boy or girl tells you that you are dumb, is it more likely that they say that
    (a) because they are mad at you, or
    I^-(b) because what you did really wasn't very bright?

11. Suppose you study to become a teacher, scientist, or doctor and you fail. Do you think this would happen

I^-(a) because you didn't work hard enough, or

   (b) because you needed some help and other people didn't give it to you?

12. When you learn something quickly in school, is it usually

   I^+(a) because you paid close attention, or

     (b) because the teacher explained it clearly?

13. If a teacher says to you, "Your work is fine," is it

     (a) something teachers usually say to encourage pupils, or

   I^+(b) because you did a good job?

14. When you find it hard to work arithmetic or math problems at school, is it

   I^-(a) because you didn't study well enough before you tried them, or

     (b) because the teacher gave problems that were too hard?

15. When you forget something you heard in class, is it

     (a) because the teacher didn't explain it very well, or

   I^-(b) because you didn't try very hard to remember?

16. Suppose you weren't sure about the answer to a question your teacher asked you, but your answer turned out to be right. Is it likely to happen

     (a) because she wasn't as particular as usual, or

   I^+(b) because you gave the best answer you could think of?

17. When you read a story and remember most of it, is it usually

   I^+(a) because you were interested in the story, or

     (b) because the story was well written?

18. If your parents tell you you're acting silly and not thinking clearly, is it more likely to be

   I^-(a) because of something you did, or

     (b) because they happen to be feeling cranky?

19. When you don't do well on a test at school, is it

     (a) because the test was especially hard, or

   I^-(b) because you didn't study for it?

20. When you win at a game of cards or checkers, does it happen

   I^+(a) because you play real well, or

     (b) because the other person doesn't play well?

21. If people think you're bright or clever, is it

     (a) because they happen to like you, or

   I^+(b) because you usually act that way?

22. If a teacher didn't pass you to the next grade, would it probably be

     (a) because she "had it in for you," or

   I^-(b) because your school work wasn't good enough?

23. Suppose you don't do as well as usual in a subject at school. Would this probably happen
   I⁻(a) because you weren't as careful as usual, or
   (b) because somebody bothered you and kept you from working?

24. If a boy or girl tells you that you are bright, is it usually
   I⁺(a) because you thought up a good idea, or
   (b) because they like you?

25. Suppose you became a famous teacher, scientist or doctor. Do you think this would happen
   (a) because other people helped you when you needed it, or
   I⁺(b) because you worked hard?

26. Suppose your parents say you aren't doing well in your school work. Is this likely to happen more
   I⁻(a) because your work isn't very good, or
   (b) because they are feeling cranky?

27. Suppose you are showing a friend how to play a game and he has trouble with it. Would that happen
   (a) because he wasn't able to understand how to play, or
   I⁻(b) because you couldn't explain it well?

28. When you find it easy to work arithmetic or math problems at school, is it usually
   (a) because the teacher gave you especially easy problems or
   I⁺(b) because you studied your book well before you tried them?

29. When you remember something you heard in class, is it usually
   I⁺(a) because you tried hard to remember, or
   (b) because the teacher explained it well?

30. If you can't work a puzzle, is it more likely to happen
   I⁻(a) because you are not especially good at working puzzles, or
   (b) because the instructions weren't written clearly enough?

31. If your parents tell you that you are bright or clever, is it more likely
   (a) because they are feeling good, or
   I⁺(b) because of something you did?

32. Suppose you are explaining how to play a game to a friend and he learns quickly. Would that happen more often
   I⁺(a) because you explained it well, or
   (b) because he was able to understand it?

33. Suppose you're not sure about the answer to a question your teacher asks you and the answer you give turns out to be wrong. Is it likely to happen

Norms for the Crandall IAR
Questionnaire

Subjects	N	Mean	SD
Boys			
Grade 3	44	23.16	3.80
4	59	24.83	3.00
5	52	24.04	3.69
6	93	24.74	4.57
8	68	25.38	3.51
10	90	25.27	4.62
12	52	24.38	3.71
Girls			
Grade 3	58	23.22	4.00
4	44	24.75	3.81
5	47	24.36	3.96
6	73	26.93	3.71
8	93	26.64	3.86
10	93	26.50	3.93
12	57	27.33	2.98

(a) because she was more particular than usual, or
Γ⁻(b) because you answered too quickly?

34. If a teacher says to you, "Try to do better," would it be
(a) because this is something she might say to get pupils to try harder, or
Γ⁻(b) because your work wasn't as good as usual?

APPENDIX III:
DEAN'S ALIENATION SCALE(S)*

Below is a keyed copy of the Dean Alienation scale. The letter to the left of each item indicates whether it belongs to the Powerlessness, Normlessness, or Isolation subscale; scores are usually reported separately.

Public Opinion Questionnaire

Below are some statements regarding public issues, with which some people agree and others disagree. Please give us your own opinion about these items, i.e., whether you agree or disagree with the items as they stand.

---

*From Dean (1969).

Please check in the appropriate blank, as follows:

___A (Strongly Agree)
___a (Agree)
___U (Uncertain)
___d (Disagree)
___D (Strongly Disagree)

I   1. Sometimes I feel all alone in the world.

   _5_ A _4_ a _3_ U _2_ d _1_ D

P   2. I worry about the future facing today's children.

   _5_ A ___a ___U ___d ___D

I   3. I don't get invited out by friends as often as I'd really like.

   _5_ A ___a ___U ___d ___D

N   4. The end often justifies the means.

   _5_ A ___a ___U ___d ___D

I   5. Most people today seldom feel lonely.

   _1_ A _2_ a _3_ U _4_ d _5_ D

P   6. Sometimes I have the feeling that other people are using me.

   _5_ A ___a ___U ___d ___D

N   7. People's ideas change so much that I wonder if we'll ever have anything to depend on.

   _5_ A ___a ___U ___d ___D

I   8. Real friends are as easy as ever to find.

   _1_ A ___a ___U ___d ___D

P   9. It is frightening to be responsible for the development of a little child.

   _5_ A ___a ___U ___d ___D

N   10. Everything is relative, and there just aren't any definite rules to live by.

   _5_ A ___a ___U ___d ___D

I   11. One can always find friends if he shows himself friendly.

   _1_ A ___a ___U ___d ___D

N   12. I often wonder what the meaning of life really is.

   _5_ A ___a ___U ___d ___D

P   13. There is little or nothing I can do towards preventing a major "shooting" war.

        _5_ A __a __U __d __D

I   14. The world in which we live is basically a friendly place.

        _1_ A __a __U __d __D

P   15. There are so many decisions that have to be made today that sometimes I could just "blow up."

        _5_ A __a __U __d __D

N   16. The only thing one can be sure of today is that he can be sure of nothing.

        _5_ A __a __U __d __D

I   17. There are few dependable ties between people any more.

        _5_ A __a __U __d __D

P   18. There is little chance for promotion on the job unless a man gets a break.

        _5_ A __a __U __d __D

N   19. With so many religions abroad, one doesn't really know which to believe.

        _5_ A __a __U __d __D

P   20. We're so regimented today that there's not much room for choice even in personal matters.

        _5_ A __a __U __d __D

P   21. We are just so many cogs in the machinery of life.

        _5_ A __a __U __d __D

I   22. People are just naturally friendly and helpful.

        _1_ A __a __U __d __D

P   23. The future looks very dismal.

        _5_ A __a __U __d __D

I   24. I don't get to visit friends as often as I'd really like.

        _5_ A __a __U __d __D

Mean Powerlessness Scores

	N	Scores
Columbus, Ohio (men), stratified sample, 1955.	384	22.65
Denison University, Introductory Sociology, 1962 (men)	62	23.75
Denison University, Introductory Sociology, 1965 (women)	93	24.91
Iowa State University, Social Psychology, 1971 (men)	16	24.63
Iowa State University, Social Psychology, 1971 (women)	24	24.60

APPENDIX IV: THE JAMES
INTERNAL–EXTERNAL LOCUS OF CONTROL SCALE*

The James internal–external scale is a 60-item questionnaire. The higher the score the individual obtains, the more external his orientation. (Only even numbered items are scored.)

Instructions

Below are a number of statements about various topics. They have been collected from different groups of people and represent a variety of opinions. There are no right or wrong answers to this questionnaire. For every statement there are large numbers of people who agree and disagree. Please indicate whether you agree or disagree with each statement as follows:

Circle SA if you strongly agree   = 3
Circle A   if you agree   = 2
Circle D   if you disagree   = 1
Circle SD if you strongly disagree   = 0

Please read each item carefully and be sure that you indicate the response which most closely corresponds to the way which you personally feel.

1. I like to read newspaper editorials whether I agree with them or not.
2. Wars between countries seem inevitable despite efforts to prevent them.
3. I believe the government should encourage more young people to make science a career.
4. It is usually true of successful people that their good breaks far outweigh their bad breaks.

*From James (1957).

5. I believe that moderation in all things is the key to happiness.
6. Many times I feel that we might just as well make many of our decisions by flipping a coin.
7. I disapprove of girls who smoke cigarettes in public places.
8. The actions of other people toward me many times have me baffled.
9. I believe it is more important for a person to like his work than to make money at it.
10. Getting a good job seems to be largely a matter of being lucky enough to be in the right place at the right time.
11. It's not what you know but who you know that really counts in getting ahead.
12. A great deal that happens to me is probably just a matter of chance.
13. I think that people spend too much time watching television these days.
14. I feel that I have little influence over the way people behave.
15. It is difficult for me to keep well-informed about foreign affairs.
16. Much of the time the future seems uncertain to me.
17. I think the world is much more unsettled now than it was in our grandfather's times.
18. Some people seem born to fail while others seem born for success no matter what they do.
19. I believe there should be less emphasis on spectator sports and more on athletic participation.
20. It is difficult for ordinary people to have much control over what politicians do in office.
21. I tend to daydream more than I should.
22. I feel that many people could be described as victims of circumstances beyond their control.
23. Movies do not seem as good as they used to be.
24. It seems many times that the grades one gets in school are more dependent on the teacher's whims than on what the student can really do.
25. Money shouldn't be a person's main consideration in choosing a job.
26. It isn't wise to plan too far ahead because most things turn out to be a matter of good or bad fortune anyhow.
27. At one time I wanted to become a newspaper reporter.
28. I can't understand how it is possible to predict other people's behaviour.
29. I enjoy smoking cigarettes and will continue to be a smoker.
30. When things are going well for me I consider it due to a run of good luck.
31. I believe the federal government has been taking over too many of the affairs of private management.
32. There's not much use in trying to predict which questions a teacher is going to ask on an examination.
33. I get more ideas from talking about things than reading about them.
34. Most people don't realize the extent to which their lives are controlled by accidental happenings.

Norms for the James Internal–External Scale

Subjects	N	Mean	SD
Normals	13	51.7	7.66
Schizophrenics	15	42.3	4.98
(Cromwell, Rosenthal, Shakow, & Zahn, 1961)			
Undergrads	33F	41.6	8.8
(Rotter, Simmons, & Holden, 1962)	31M	37.68	8.1
Undergrads–half male and half female	80	37	12
(Lotsof, James, Drucker, & Blount, 1964)			
Physically Disabled	30	41.6	3.3
Non Disabled	30	40.3	3.57
(Lipp, Kolstoe, James, & Randall, 1968)			
Undergrads	108M	43.09	9.24
(A. P. MacDonald, unpublished)	72F	44.19	11.18

35. At one time I wanted to be an actor (or actress).
36. I have usually found that what is going to happen will happen, regardless of my actions.
37. Life in a small town offers more real satisfactions than life in a large city.
38. Most of the disappointing things in my life have contained a large element of chance.
39. I would rather be a successful teacher than a successful businessman.
40. I don't believe that a person can really be a master of his fate.
41. I find mathematics easier to study than literature.
42. Success is mostly a matter of getting good breaks.
43. I think it is more important to be respected by people than to be liked by them.
44. Events in the world seem to be beyond the control of most people.
45. I think our country should take a more active role in world affairs.
46. I feel that most people can't really be held responsible for themselves since no one has much choice about where he was born or raised.
47. I like to figure out problems and puzzles that other people have trouble with.
48. Many times the reactions of people seem haphazard to me.
49. I rarely lose when playing card games.
50. There's not much use in worrying about things—what will be, will be.
51. I think that everyone should belong to some kind of church.
52. Success in dealing with people seems to be more a matter of the other person's moods and feelings at the time rather than one's own actions.
53. One should not place too much faith in newspaper reports.
54. I think that life is mostly a gamble.

55. I am very stubborn when my mind is made up about something.
56. Many times I feel that I have little influence over the things that happen to me.
57. I like popular music better than classical music.
58. Sometimes I feel that I don't have enough control over the direction my life is taking.
59. I sometimes work at difficult things too long even when I know they are hopeless.
60. Life is too full of uncertainties.

APPENDIX V: THE NOWICKI–STRICKLAND LOCUS OF CONTROL SCALE*

The Nowicki–Strickland Locus of Control scale is a paper and pencil measure consisting of 40 questions which are answered either yes or no by placing a mark next to the question. The higher the score the more external the orientation.

Nowicki–Strickland Scale

(Y) 1. Do you believe that most problems will solve themselves if you just don't fool with them?
(N) 2. Do you believe that you can stop yourself from catching a cold?
(Y) 3. Are some kids just born lucky?
(N) 4. Most of the time do you feel that getting good grades means a great deal to you?
(Y) 5. Are you often blamed for things that just aren't your fault?
(N) 6. Do you believe that if somebody studies hard enough he or she can pass any subject?
(Y) 7. Do you feel that most of the time it doesn't pay to try hard because things never turn out right anyway?
(Y) 8. Do you feel that if things start out well in the morning that it's going to be a good day no matter what you do?
(N) 9. Do you feel that most of the time parents listen to what their children have to say?
(Y) 10. Do you believe that wishing can make good things happen?
(Y) 11. When you get punished does it usually seem it's for no good reason at all?
(Y) 12. Most of the time do you find it hard to change a friend's (mind) opinion?
(N) 13. Do you think that cheering more than luck helps a team to win?

*From Nowicki and Strickland (1973).

(Y) 14. Do you feel that it's nearly impossible to change your parent's mind about anything?

(N) 15. Do you believe that your parents should allow you to make most of your own decisions?

(Y) 16. Do you feel that when you do something wrong there's very little you can do to make it right?

(Y) 17. Do you believe that most kids are just born good at sports?

(Y) 18. Are most of the other kids your age stronger than you are?

(Y) 19. Do you feel that one of the best ways to handle most problems is just not to think about them?

(N) 20. Do you feel that you have a lot of choice in deciding who your friends are?

(Y) 21. If you find a four-leaf clover do you believe that it might bring you good luck?

(N) 22. Do you often feel that whether you do your homework has much to do with what kind of grades you get?

(Y) 23. Do you feel that when a kid your age decides to hit you, there's little you can do to stop him or her?

(Y) 24. Have you ever had a good luck charm?

(N) 25. Do you believe that whether or not people like you depends on how you act?

(N) 26. Will your parents usually help you if you ask them to?

(Y) 27. Have you felt that when people were mean to you it was usually for no reason at all?

(N) 28. Most of the time, do you feel that you can change what might happen tomorrow by what you do today?

(Y) 29. Do you believe that when bad things are going to happen they just are going to happen no matter what you try to do to stop them?

(N) 30. Do you think that kids can get their own way if they just keep trying?

(Y) 31. Most of the time do you find it useless to try to get your own way at home?

(N) 32. Do you feel that when good things happen they happen because of hard work?

(Y) 33. Do you feel that when somebody your age wants to be your enemy there's little you can do to change matters?

(N) 34. Do you feel that it's easy to get friends to do what you want them to?

(Y) 35. Do you usually feel that you have little to say about what you get to eat at home?

(Y) 36. Do you feel that when someone doesn't like you there's little you can do about it?

(Y) 37. Do you usually feel that it's almost useless to try in school because most other children are just plain smarter than you are?

(N) 38. Are you the kind of person who believes that planning ahead makes things turn out better?

The Nowicki–Strickland
Locus of Control Scale

Subjects	N	Mean	SD
Males			
grade 3	44	17.97	4.67
grade 4	59	18.44	3.58
grade 5	40	18.32	4.38
grade 6	45	13.73	5.16
grade 7	65	13.15	4.87
grade 8	75	14.73	4.35
grade 9	43	13.81	4.06
grade 10	68	13.05	5.34
grade 11	37	12.48	4.81
grade 12	39	11.38	4.74
Females			
grade 3	55	17.38	3.06
grade 4	45	18.80	3.63
grade 5	41	17.00	4.03
grade 6	43	13.32	4.58
grade 7	52	13.94	4.23
grade 8	34	12.29	3.58
grade 9	44	12.25	3.75
grade 10	57	12.98	5.31
grade 11	53	12.01	5.15
grade 12	48	12.37	5.05

(Y) 39. Most of the time, do you feel that you have little to say about what your family decides to do?

(N) 40. Do you think it's better to be smart than to be lucky?

APPENDIX VI: THE REID–WARE
THREE-FACTOR INTERNAL–EXTERNAL SCALE*

The Reid–Ware scale is a 45-item forced choice questionnaire composed of the following three factors: self-control, social systems control, and fatalism. The higher the score the more external the individual. There are 13 filler items.

Belief Survey

This questionnaire is a measure of personal belief: obviously there are no right or wrong answers. Each item consists of a pair of alternatives lettered (A) or (B). Please select the one statement of each pair (and only one) which you more

---

*From Reid and Ware (1974).

strongly believe as far as you are concerned. Be sure to select the one you actually believe to be more true rather than the one you think you should choose or the one you would like to be true. To ensure anonymity, please use a fictitious name when signing this questionnaire.

Please answer these items carefully, but do not spend too much time on any one item. Be sure to find an answer for every choice. Circle the letter of the statement (A or B) which you choose.

In some cases you may discover that you believe both statements or neither one. In such cases be sure to select the one you more strongly believe to be the case as far as you are concerned. Also try to respond to each item independently when making your choice: do not be influenced by your previous choices.

1. (A) Various sports activities in the community help increase solidarity amongst people in the community.
   (B) Various sports activities in the community can lead to rivalry detrimental to the solidarity of the community.

2. (A) War brings out the worst aspects of men.
   (B) Although war is terrible, it can have some value.

SSC E 3. (A) There will always be wars no matter how hard people try to prevent them.
   (B) One of the major reasons why we have wars is because people do not take enough interest in politics.

SC E 4. (A) Even when there was nothing forcing me, I have found that I will sometimes do things I really did not want to do.
   (B) I always feel in control of what I am doing.

SSC E 5. (A) There are institutions in our society that have considerable control over me.
   (B) Little in this world controls me, I usually can do what I decide to do.

6. (A) I would like to live in a small town or a rural environment.
   (B) I would like to live in a large city.

Fatalism 7. (A) For the average citizen becoming a success is a matter of hard work, luck has little or nothing to do with it.
E (B) For the average guy getting a good job depends mainly on being in the right place at the right time.

8. (A) Patriotism demands that the citizens of a nation participate in any war.
   (B) To be a patriot for one's country does not necessarily mean he must go to war for his country.

Fatalism   9. (A) In my case getting what I want has little or nothing to do with luck.

E   (B) It is not always wise for me to plan too far ahead because many things turn out to be a matter of good or bad fortune anyhow.

SC E 10. (A) Sometimes I impulsively do things which at other times I definitely would not let myself do.

(B) I find that I can keep my impulses in control.

Fatalism E 11. (A) In many situations what happens to people seems to be determined by fate.

(B) People do not realize how much they personally determine their own outcomes.

12. (A) College students should be trained in times of peace to assume military duties.

(B) The ills of war are greater than any possible benefits.

Fatalism E 13. (A) Most people do not realize the extent to which their lives are controlled by accidental happenings.

(B) For any guy, there is no such thing as luck.

SSC   14. (A) If I put my mind to it I could have an important influence on what a politician does in office.

E   (B) When I look at it carefully I realize it is impossible for me to have any really important influence over what politicians do.

Fatalism E 15. (A) With fate the way it is, many times I feel that I have little influence over the things that happen to me.

(B) It is impossible for me to believe that chance or luck plays an important role in my life.

SC   16. (A) When I put my mind to it I can constrain my emotions.

E   (B) There are moments when I cannot subdue my emotions and keep them in check.

17. (A) Every person should give some of his time for the good of his town or country.

(B) People would be a lot better off if they could live far away from other people and never have to do anything for them.

SSC E 18. (A) As far as the affairs of our country are concerned, most people are the victims of forces they do not control and frequently do not even understand.

(B) By taking part in political and social events the people can directly control much of the country's affairs.

SC E 19. (A) People cannot always hold back their personal desires; they will behave out of impulse.

(B) If they want to, people can always control their immediate wishes and not let these motives determine their total behavior.

Fatalism E 20. (A) Many times I feel I might just as well decide what to do by flipping a coin.

(B) In most cases I do not depend on luck when I decide to do something.

21. (A) Our federal government should promote the mass production of low rental apartment buildings to reduce the housing shortage.

(B) The best way for our government to reduce the housing shortage is to make low interest mortgages available and to stimulate the building of low cost houses.

SSC E 22. (A) I do not know why politicians make the decisions they do.

(B) It is easy for me to understand why politicians do the things they do.

SC 23. (A) Although sometimes it is difficult, I can always willfully restrain my immediate behavior.

E (B) Something I cannot do is have complete mastery over all my behavioral tendencies.

Fatalism 24. (A) In the long run people receive the respect and good outcomes they worked for.

E (B) Unfortunately, because of misfortune or bad luck, the average guy's worth often passes unrecognized no matter how hard he tries.

SSC 25. (A) With enough effort people can wipe out political corruption.

E (B) It is difficult for people to have much control over the things politicians do in office.

26. (A) Letting your friends down is not so bad because you cannot do good all the time for everybody.

(B) I feel very bad when I have failed to finish a job I promised I would do.

SSC   27. (A) By active participation in the appropriate political organizations people can do a lot to keep the cost of living from going higher.

E   (B) There is very little people can do to keep the cost of living from going higher.

SC E 28. (A) It is possible for me to behave in a manner very different from the way I would want to behave.

           (B) It would be very difficult for me to not have mastery over the way I behave.

SSC E 29. (A) In this world I am affected by social forces which I neither control nor understand.

           (B) It is easy for me to avoid and function independently of any social forces that may attempt to have control over me.

      30. (A) It hurts more to lose money than to lose a friend.

           (B) The people are the most important thing in this world of ours.

Fatalism   31. (A) What people get out of life is always a function of how much effort they put into it.

E   (B) Quite often one finds that what happens to people has no relation to what they do, what happens just happens.

SSC   32. (A) Generally speaking, my behavior is not governed by others.

E   (B) My behavior is frequently determined by other influential people.

SSC   33. (A) People can and should do what they want to do both now and in the future.

E   (B) There is no point in people planning their lives too far in advance because other groups of people in our society will invariably upset their plans.

      34. (A) Happiness is having your own house and car.

           (B) Happiness to most people is having their own close friends.

Fatalism   35. (A) There is no such thing as luck, what happens to me is a result of my own behavior.

E   (B) Sometimes I do not understand how I can have such poor luck.

36. (A) More emphasis should be placed on teaching the principles of Christianity in public school.
    (B) Christianity should not be included in a school curriculum; it can be taught in church.

Fatalism E 37. (A) Many of the unhappy things in people's lives are at least partly due to bad luck.
    (B) People's misfortunes result from the mistakes they make.

SC 38. (A) Self-regulation of one's behavior is always possible.
E (B) I frequently find that when certain things happen to me I cannot restrain my reaction.

SSC 39. (A) The average man can have an influence in government decisions.
E (B) This world is run by a few people in power and there is not much the little guy can do about it.

SC 40. (A) When I make up my mind, I can always resist temptation and keep control of my behavior.
E (B) Even if I try not to submit, I often find I cannot control myself from some of the enticements in life such as over-eating or drinking.

Fatalism E 41. (A) My getting a good job or promotion in the future will depend a lot on my getting the right turn of fate.
    (B) When I get a good job, it is always a direct result of my own ability and/or motivation.

42. (A) Successful people are mostly honest and good.
    (B) One should not always associate achievement with integrity and honor.

SSC E 43. (A) Most people do not understand why politicians behave the way they do.
    (B) In the long run people are responsible for bad government on a national as well as on a local level.

Fatalism E 44. (A) I often realize that despite my best efforts some outcomes seem to happen as if fate planned it that way.
    (B) The misfortunes and successes I have had were the direct result of my own behavior.

45. (A) Most people are kind and good.
    (B) People will not help others unless circumstances force them to.

Norms for the Reid–Ware Three-Factor
Internal–External Scale

Subjects	N	Mean	SD
Undergrads (Reid & Ware, 1973)			
Males			
Self-control factor	55	4.25	2.29
Social systems control		6.65	2.98
Fatalism factor		4.09	2.88
Females			
Self-control factor	44	5.52	1.91
Social systems control		6.84	2.75
Fatalism		4.47	2.88
Undergrads: Male and Female (Reid & Ware, 1973)	167		
Self-control factor		4.77	2.25
Social systems control		6.53	2.82
Fatalism factor		3.99	2.86

APPENDIX VII: THE ROTTER
INTERNAL–EXTERNAL LOCUS OF CONTROL*

The Rotter internal–external locus of control scale is a 23-item forced choice questionnaire with 6 filler items adapted from the 60-item James scale. It is scored in the external direction, that is, the higher the score the more external the individual.

Social Reaction Inventory

This is a questionnaire to find out the way in which certain important events in our society affect different people. Each item consists of a pair of alternatives lettered a or b. Please select the one statement of each pair (and only one) which you more strongly *believe* to be the case as far as you're concerned. Be sure to select the one you actually believe to be more true rather than the one you think you should choose or the one you would like to be true. This is a measure of personal belief; obviously there are no right or wrong answers.

Your answer, either a or b to each question on this inventory, is to be reported beside the question. Print your name and any other information requested by the examiner on the bottom of page 4, then finish reading these directions. Do not begin until you are told to do so.

*From Rotter (1966).

Please answer these items *carefully* but do not spend too much time on any one item. Be sure to find an answer for *every* choice. For each numbered question make an X on the line beside either the *a* or *b*, whichever you choose as the statement most true.

In some instances you may discover that you believe both statements or neither one. In such cases, be sure to select the one you more strongly believe to be the case as far as you're concerned. Also try to respond to each item *independently* when making your choice; do not be influenced by your previous choices.

Remember

Select that alternative which you *personally believe to be more true.*

I more strongly believe that:

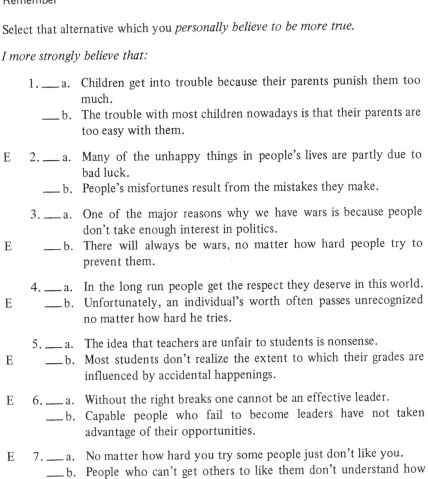

1. ___ a. Children get into trouble because their parents punish them too much.
   ___ b. The trouble with most children nowadays is that their parents are too easy with them.

E 2. ___ a. Many of the unhappy things in people's lives are partly due to bad luck.
   ___ b. People's misfortunes result from the mistakes they make.

3. ___ a. One of the major reasons why we have wars is because people don't take enough interest in politics.
E ___ b. There will always be wars, no matter how hard people try to prevent them.

4. ___ a. In the long run people get the respect they deserve in this world.
E ___ b. Unfortunately, an individual's worth often passes unrecognized no matter how hard he tries.

5. ___ a. The idea that teachers are unfair to students is nonsense.
E ___ b. Most students don't realize the extent to which their grades are influenced by accidental happenings.

E 6. ___ a. Without the right breaks one cannot be an effective leader.
   ___ b. Capable people who fail to become leaders have not taken advantage of their opportunities.

E 7. ___ a. No matter how hard you try some people just don't like you.
   ___ b. People who can't get others to like them don't understand how to get along with others.

8. ___ a. Heredity plays the major role in determining one's personality.
   ___ b. It is one's experiences in life which determine what they're like.

E   9. ___ a. I have often found that what is going to happen will happen.
   ___ b. Trusting to fate has never turned out as well for me as making a decision to take a definite course of action.

10. ___ a. In the case of the well prepared student there is rarely if ever such a thing as an unfair test.
E   ___ b. Many times exam questions tend to be so unrelated to course work that studying is really useless.

11. ___ a. Becoming a success is a matter of hard work, luck has little or nothing to do with it.
E   ___ b. Getting a good job depends mainly on being in the right place at the right time.

12. ___ a. The average citizen can have an influence in government decisions.
E   ___ b. This world is run by the few people in power, and there is not much the little guy can do about it.

13. ___ a. When I make plans, I am almost certain that I can make them work.
E   ___ b. It is not always wise to plan too far ahead because many things turn out to be a matter of good or bad fortune anyhow.

14. ___ a. There are certain people who are just no good.
   ___ b. There is some good in everybody.

15. ___ a. In my case getting what I want has little or nothing to do with luck.
E   ___ b. Many times we might just as well decide what to do by flipping a coin.

E   16. ___ a. Who gets to be the boss often depends on who was lucky enough to be in the right place first.
   ___ b. Getting people to do the right thing depends upon ability; luck has little or nothing to do with it.

E   17. ___ a. As far as world affairs are concerned, most of us are the victims of forces we can neither understand, nor control.
   ___ b. By taking an active part in political and social affairs the people can control world events.

E   18. ___ a. Most people can't realize the extent to which their lives are controlled by accidental happenings.

___ b. There really is no such thing as "luck."

19. ___ a. One should always be willing to admit his mistakes.
    ___ b. It is usually best to cover up one's mistakes.

E 20. ___ a. It is hard to know whether or not a person really likes you.
      ___ b. How many friends you have depends upon how nice a person you are.

E 21. ___ a. In the long run the bad things that happen to us are balanced by the good ones.
      ___ b. Most misfortunes are the result of lack of ability, ignorance, laziness, or all three.

22. ___ a. With enough effort we can wipe out political corruption.
E   ___ b. It is difficult for people to have much control over the things politicians do in office.

E 23. ___ a. Sometimes I can't understand how teachers arrive at the grades they give.
      ___ b. There is a direct connection between how hard I study and the grades I get.

24. ___ a. A good leader expects people to decide for themselves what they should do.
    ___ b. A good leader makes it clear to everybody what their jobs are.

E 25. ___ a. Many times I feel that I have little influence over the things that happen to me.
      ___ b. It is impossible for me to believe that chance or luck plays an important role in my life.

26. ___ a. People are lonely because they don't try to be friendly.
E   ___ b. There's not much use in trying too hard to please people, if they like you, they like you.

27. ___ a. There is too much emphasis on athletics in high school.
    ___ b. Team sports are an excellent way to build character.

28. ___ a. What happens to me is my own doing.
E   ___ b. Sometimes I feel that I don't have enough control over the direction my life is taking.

E 29. ___ a. Most of the time I can't understand why politicians behave the way they do.
      ___ b. In the long run the people are responsible for bad government on a national as well as on a local level.

Norms for the Rotter Internal–External
Locus of Control Scale

Scores are in the external direction, the higher the score the more external.

Subjects	N	Mean	SD
Students at a Southern Negro college	62M		
involved in protest movements	54F		
(Gore & Rotter, 1963)			
1. Attend rally for civil rights		10.3	3.1
2. Sign petition		9.2	3.4
3. Join a silent march		7.4	2.9
4. Join Freedom Riders		8.1	3.8
5. None of the above		10.0	3.9
Inmates of correctional institution			
(Lefcourt & Ladwig, 1965a)			
1. Negro	60	8.97	2.97
2. White	60	7.87	3.03
Negro college students—male and female			
(Strickland, 1965)			
1. Active—engaged in civil rights			
groups	53	7.49	3.49
2. Inactive	105	9.64	3.70
1. 1964 Service Corps	72F	7.92	3.84
	27M	8.00	3.97
2. 1965 Service Corps	68F	8.26	3.49
	34M	8.00	3.08
3. 1965 Control Group	46F	9.37	3.76
	49M	8.67	3.89
4. 1966 Service Corps	79F	9.54	4.20
	21M	7.38	4.73
5. 1966 Control Group	47F	8.79	3.76
(Hersch & Scheibe, 1967)			
	38M	8.84	3.70

(Service Corps were college students attending chronic wards of mental institutions.) (Control Groups were college students attending summer school.)

Subjects	N	Mean	SD
Undergrads (Levy, 1967):	24M		
	& 24F	9.77	4.11
Male & female smokers—mean age	213	7.0	3.50
of 40.1; average of 13.4 years of	95M	6.59	3.65
education (Lichtenstein & Keutzer, 1967)	118F	7.42	3.44
College males (Zytowski, 1967)	62	6.82	2.49
Undergrads in introductory psychology	46M	9.8	1.42
(Feather, 1968)	88F	11.44	1.69

continued

Norms for the Rotter Scale — *Continued*

Subjects	N	Mean	SD
Undergrads (Hamsher, Geller, & Rotter, 1968)	60M	10.1	3.95
	113F	11.0	3.96
Undergrads–male and female; males made up 70% of sample with no significant sex differences (Julian & Katz, 1968)	1338	8.4	4.12
High school students (Hsieh, Shybut & Lotsof, 1969)			
1. Anglo-American	131M	8.58	3.89
	108F		
2. American-born Chinese	38M	9.79	3.07
	42F		
3. Hong Kong students	241M	12.07	3.96
	102F		
Male addict patients–Negro and white (Berzins & Ross, 1973)	97	6.79	3.90
Female undergrads (Crego, 1970)	99	7.97	3.8
First year female undergrads unable to relate in interpersonal situations (Dua, 1970)			
1. Pretest	30	14.03	4.27
2. Posttest	30	9.66	3.59
Female student nurses (Lefcourt & Steffy, 1970)	37	7.14	3.28
Female undergrads (Strickland, 1970)	180	8.34	3.85
Undergrads enrolled in introductory psychology, male and female (Biondo & MacDonald, 1971)	198	9.56	
Male soldiers (Cone, 1971)			
1. Mental clinic outpatients–all male soldiers	102	12.64	8.33
2. Stockade prisoners–soldiers	110	12.20	7.84
3. Same as 2 but tested 2 months later	98	12.87	7.76
Administrators (Harvey, 1971)			
1–5 years	14	7.57	2.88
6–10 years	7	6.43	2.52
11 years	27	5.41	3.15
1–10 years	21	7.19	2.75
Male VA psychiatric patients (Kish, Solberg, & Uecker, 1971)	169	8.1	4.2
Male undergrads (Lefcourt & Telegdi, 1971)	90	8.16	4.38

continued

Norms for the Rotter Scale — *Continued*

Subjects	N	Mean	SD
Hospitalized male veterans (Palmer, 1971)			
1. Psychiatric	89	5.0	2.77
2. Nonpsychiatric	88	4.0	2.70
Males in introductory psychology classes (Phares, 1971)	646	9.2	3.48
Undergrads in psychology or social science classes (Schneider & Parsons, 1970)			
Males:			
United States	95	9.76	
West Germans	44	9.75	
Denmark	124	9.83	
Japan	67	13.45	
Females:			
United States	74	10.38	
West Germans	24	10.96	
Denmark	147	9.94	
Japan	41	14.40	

APPENDIX VIII: THE STANFORD PRESCHOOL INTERNAL–EXTERNAL SCALE*

The SPIES measures preschool children's expectancies about whether events occur as a consequence of their own action (internal control) or as a consequence of external forces (external control). A forced choice format elicits expectancies about locus of control separately for positive and negative events. The SPIES is scored in the internal direction; scores obtained are expectancies for internal control of positive events (I^+) and negative events (I^-) and a sum of these two (total I).

The Stanford Preschool Internal–External Scale (I)

1. When you are happy, are you happy
   I^+(a) because you did something fun, or
   (b) because somebody was nice to you?

2. When somebody tells you that you are good, is that
   I^+(a) because you really have been good, or
   (b) because he is a nice person?

---

*From Mischel, Zeiss, and Zeiss (1974).

3. Do you think I brought you to the surprise room (experimental room)
   I^+(a) because you have been good today, or
   (b) because I'm just a nice guy (lady)?

4. When your mother gives you a cookie, is that
   I^+(a) because you need a cookie, or
   (b) because she has too many cookies?

5. When somebody brings you a present, is that
   I^+(a) because you are a good boy (girl), or
   (b) because they like to give people presents?

6. When you draw a whole picture without breaking your crayon is that
   I^+(a) because you were very careful, or
   (b) because it was a good crayon?

7. If you had a shiny new penny and lost it, would that be
   I^-(a) because you dropped it, or
   (b) because there was a hole in your pocket?

8. When you are sad and unhappy, are you sad and unhappy
   I^-(a) because you did something sad, or
   (b) because somebody wasn't very nice to you?

9. When you play a game and lose, do you lose
   I^-(a) because you just didn't play well, or
   (b) because the game was hard?

10. When somebody stops playing with you, is that
    I^-(a) because he doesn't like the way you play, or
    (b) because he is tired?

11. When you get a hole in your pants, is that
    I^-(a) because you tore them or
    (b) because they wore out?

12. If you had a pet turtle and he ran away, do you think that would be
    I^-(a) because you did something to make him leave, or
    (b) because there was a hole in his cage?

13. When you are drawing a picture and your crayon breaks, is that
    I^-(a) because you pushed too hard, or
    (b) because it was a bad crayon?

14. When you can't find one of your toys, is that
    I^-(a) because you lost it, or
    (b) because somebody took it?

The Stanford Preschool Internal–External Scale (II)

1. When you're playing at a friend's house and his mother gives you a piece of candy, is that
    I^+(a) because you want some candy, or
    (b) because she wants to be nice?

2. When your father reads a book to you, is that
    I^+(a) because you want to hear the story, or
    (b) because he likes to read?

3. If you put a hard puzzle together, is that
    I^+(a) because you knew how, or
    (b) because your teacher helped you?

4. If you walk into the room and your mother smiles, is that
    I^+(a) because you did something to make her smile, or
    (b) because she likes to smile a lot?

5. If you wake up from a nap and your mother lets you get up, is that
    I^+(a) because you slept enough, or
    (b) because she thinks it's time to get up?

6. If you're good and eat all your dinner, are you good
    I^+(a) because you're hungry, or
    (b) because the food is good?

7. If you pet a dog and he's happy and wags his tail, is that
    I^+(a) because you were friendly and nice to him, or
    (b) because he likes all children?

8. If you pet a dog and he runs away, is that
    I^-(a) because you scared him or
    (b) because he doesn't like any children?

9. If you're playing and your friend throws you a ball and it goes out into the street, is that
    I^-(a) because you missed it, or
    (b) because he threw it too hard?

10. When you fall down and hurt yourself, is that
    I^-(a) because you weren't careful, or
    (b) because somebody was in your way?

11. If you wake up early from a nap and your mother tells you to stay in bed longer, did you wake up
    I^-(a) because you weren't trying hard enough to sleep, or
    (b) because your mother made too much noise?

Norms for the SPIES
(Mischel, Zeiss, & Zeiss, 1974)

Subjects	N	Mean	SD
Males:	98		
1. I^+		2.24	1.20
2. I^-		2.55	1.41
3. Total I		5.80	1.88
Females	113		
1. I^+		3.31	1.19
2. I^-		2.71	1.52
3. Total I		6.02	1.87
Combined	211		
1. I^+		3.28	1.19
2. I^-		2.64	1.47
3. Total I		5.91	1.87

12. If you're bad and play with your food and don't eat your dinner, are you bad
    I^-(a) because you're not hungry, or
    (b) because the food is not good?

13. If you had a toy that was broken and didn't work, would that be
    I^-(a) because you dropped it, or
    (b) because it wore out?

14. When your mother scolds you, is that
    I^-(a) because you did something wrong, or
    (b) because she was just mad?

APPENDIX IX: LEFCOURT, REID, AND WARE INTERVIEW QUESTIONS FOR ASSESSING VALUES, EXPECTANCIES, AND LOCUS OF CONTROL

This newly developed questionnaire has been designed to be administered either as an interview or as an extensive, open-ended questionnaire. It has the benefit of allowing for causal attributions to success and failure for valued goals. It is hoped that this device will encourage others to invent more goal-specific methods such as these for their own purposes.

1. For one, what about your present life is of the greatest importance to you? Or, to put it another way, what essentials are there in your present life which you would find most distressing to lose?

2. What about your life would change if this (these) loss (losses) were to occur? That is, what would this (these) loss (losses) mean to you?
3. Of the essentials in your life that you have described, which is *the* most important for you?
4. What chance do you feel there is of losing this "essential" in the near future? (Check one point.)

—	—	—	—	—
highly unlikely	unlikely	possibly	likely	highly likely

5. What would contribute to the successful continuation of this major concern of yours?
6. If you were to lose out with regard to this "essential" what would be the most likely causes of this loss?
7. What things do you most look forward to in your own future?
8. Which of these ambitions is of most concern to you?
9. What's important about it for you?
10. How likely is it that your hopes will be met? (Check one point.)

—	—	—	—	—
very unlikely	unlikely	possibly	likely	very likely

11. If you were to succeed in your ambitions, to what would you attribute your success? What would be the most prominent of these causes?
12. If you were to fail to realize your ambitions, what would be the likely causes? Which would be the most important cause?
13. How important would it be to you to know that you were largely responsible for attaining success with your major concerns? Why?
14. And, how important would it be for you to know that you were largely responsible for failure with regard to your major concerns? Why?

References

Abramowitz, S. I. Locus of control and self-reported depression among college students. *Psychological Reports*, 1969, *25*, 149–150.

Abramowitz, S. I. Internal-external control and social political activism: A test of the dimensionality of Rotter's internal-external scale. *Journal of Consulting and Clinical Psychology*, 1973, *40*, 196–201.

Abramowitz, C. V., Abramowitz, S. I., Roback, H. B., & Jackson, C. Differential effectiveness of directive and nondirective group therapies as a function of client internal-external control. *Journal of Consulting and Clinical Psychology*, 1974, *42*, 849–853.

Abramson, L. Y., Garber, J., & Seligman, M. E. P. Learned helplessness in humans: an attributional analysis. In J. Garber & M. E. P. Seligman (Eds.), *Human helplessness: Theory and applications.* New York: Academic Press, 1980.

Abramson, L. Y., Seligman, M. E. P., & Teasdale, J. D. Learned helplessness in humans: Critique and Reformulation. *Journal of Abnormal Psychology*, 1978, *87*, 49–74.

Alegre, C. & Murray, E. J. Locus of control, behavioral intention, and verbal conditioning. *Journal of Personality*, 1974, *42*, 668–681.

Alker, H. A., & Poppin, P. J. Personality and ideology in university students. *Journal of Personality*, 1973, *11*, 653–671.

Alpert, R., & Haber, R. N. Anxiety in academic achievement situations. *Journal of Abnormal and Social Psychology*, 1960, *61*, 207–215.

Anderson, C. R. Locus of control, coping behaviors and performance in a stress setting: a longitudinal study. *Journal of Applied Psychology*, 1977, *62*, 446–451.

Andreyev, L. *The seven that were hanged.* New York: Boni & Liveright, 1918.

Ansbacher, H. & Ansbacher, R. *The individual psychology of Alfred Adler.* New York: Basic Books, 1956.

Antrobus, P. M. *Internality, pride and humility.* Unpublished doctoral dissertation, University of Waterloo, 1973.

Arendt, H. *Adolph Eichmann in Jerusalem: A report on the banality of evil.* New York: Viking Press, 1963.

Arlin, M. The interaction of locus of control, classroom structure, and pupil satisfaction. *Psychology in the Schools*, 1975, *12*, 279-286.

Averill, J. R. Personal control over aversive stimuli and its relationship to stress. *Psychological Bulletin*, 1973, *80*, 286-303.

Bandura, A., Adams, N. E., Hardy, A. B., & Howells, G. N. Tests of the generality of self-efficacy theory. *Cognitive Therapy and Research*, 1980, *4*, 39-66.

Baron, R. M., Cowan, G., Ganz, R. L., & McDonald, M. Interaction of locus of control and type of performance feedback: considerations of external validity. *Journal of Personality and Social Psychology*, 1974, *30*, 285-292.

Baron, R. M., & Ganz, R. L. Effects of locus of control and type of feedback on the task performance of lower class black children. *Journal of Personality and Social Psychology*, 1972, *21*, 124-130.

Bar-Tal, D., & Bar-Zohar, Y. The relationship between perception of locus control and academic achievement. *Contemporary Educational Psychology*, 1977, *2*, 181-199.

Bar-Tal, D., Kfir, D., Bar-Zohar, Y., & Chen, M. The relationship between locus of control and academic achievement anxiety and level of aspiration. *British Journal of Educational Psychology*, 1980, *50*, 53-60.

Batlis, N. C. Relationships between locus of control and instrumentality theory predictors of academic performance. *Psychological Reports*, 1978, *43*, 239-245.

Batlis, N. C., & Waters, L. K. Locus of control and achievement motivation as moderators of the expectancy-academic performance relationship. *Educational and Psychological Measurement*, 1973, *33*, 895-902.

Battle, E., & Rotter, J. B. Children's feelings of personal control as related to social class and ethnic groups. *Journal of Personality*, 1963, *31*, 482-490.

Baum, A., Aiello, J. R., & Calesnick, L. E. Crowding and personal control: social density and the development of learned helplessness. *Journal of Personality and Social Psychology*, 1978, *36*, 1000-1011.

Bax, J. C. *Internal-external control and field dependence.* Unpublished honor's thesis, University of Waterloo, 1966.

Beck, A. T. *Depression: Causes and treatment.* Philadelphia: University of Pennsylvania Press, 1967.

Berzins, J. I., & Ross, W. F. Locus of control among opiate addicts. *Journal of Consulting and Clinical Psychology*, 1973, *40*, 84-91.

Best, J. A. Tailoring smoking withdrawal procedures to personality and motivational differences. *Journal of Consulting and Clinical Psychology*, 1975, *43*, 1-8.

Best, J. A., & Steffy, R. A. Smoking modification procedures for internal and external locus of control clients. *Canadian Journal of Behavioral Science*, 1975, *7*, 155-165.

Bettelheim, B. Individual and mass behavior in extreme situations. *Journal of abnormal and social psychology*, 1943, *38*, 417-452.

Bialer, I. Conceptualization of success and failure in mentally retarded and normal children. *Journal of Personality*, 1961, *29*, 303-320.

Bibring, E. The mechanism of depression. In P. Greenacre (Ed.), *Affective Disorders*. New York: International Universities Press, 1953.

Binik, Y., & Seligman, M. E. P. Sudden swimming deaths. *American Psychologist*, 1979, *34*, 270-272.

Binik, Y. M., Theriault, G., & Shistack, B. Sudden death in the laboratory rat: cardiac function, sensory, and experiental factors in swimming deaths. *Psychosomatic Medicine*, 1977, *39*, 82-92.

Biondo, J. & MacDonald, A. P. Internal-external locus of control and response to influence attempts. *Journal of Personality*, 1971, *39*, 407-419.

Blechman, E. A., & Dannemiller, E. A. Effects on performance of perceived control over noxious noise. *Journal of Consulting and Clinical Psychology*, 1976, *44*, 601–607.

Bloomberg, M. On the relationship between internal-external control and morality. *Psychological Reports*, 1974, *35*, 1077–1078.

Bloomberg, M., & Soneson, S. The effects of locus of control and field independence-dependence on moral reasoning. *Journal of Genetic Psychology*, 1976, *128*, 59–66.

Boor, M. Relationship of internal-external control and national suicide rates. *The Journal of Social Psychology*, 1976, *100*, 143–144.

Bowers, K. S. Pain, anxiety, and perceived control. *Journal of Consulting and Clinical Psychology*, 1968, *32*, 596–602.

Brady, J. V., Porter, R. W., Conrad, D. G., & Mason, J. W. Avoidance behavior and the development of gastroduodenal ulcers. *Journal of Experimental Analyses of Behavior*, 1958, *1*, 69–72.

Brecher, M. & Denmark, F. L. Internal-external locus of control and verbal fluency. *Psychological Reports*. 1969, *25*, 707–710.

Bruch, H. *Learning Psychotherapy*. Cambridge, Mass: Harvard Univ. Press, 1974.

Bryant, B. K., & Trockel, J. F. Personal history of psychological stress related to locus of control orientation among college women. *Journal of Consulting and Clinical Psychology*, 1976, *44*, 266–271.

Burnes, K., Brown, W. A., & Keating, G. W. Dimensions of control: correlations between MMPI and I-E scores. *Journal of Consulting and Clinical Psychology*, 1971, *36*, 301.

Buss, A. H. *Psychopathology*. New York: John Wiley & Sons, 1966.

Butterfield, E. C. Locus of control, test anxiety, reactions to frustration, and achievement attitudes. *Journal of Personality*, 1964, *32*, 298–311.

Butterfield, E. C. The role of competence motivation in interrupted task recall and repetition choice. *Journal of Experimental Child Psychology*, 1965, *2*, 354–370.

Butts, S. V., & Chotlos, J. A. A comparison of alcoholics and nonalcoholics on perceived locus of control. *Quarterly Journal of Studies on Alcohol*, 1973, *34*, 1327–1332.

Calhoun, L. G., Cheney, T., & Dawes, A. S. Locus of control, self-reported depression and perceived causes of depression. *Journal of Consulting and Clinical Psychology*, 1974, *42*, 736.

Calicchia, J. P. Narcotic addiction and perceived locus of control. *Journal of Clinical Psychology*, 1974, *30*, 499–504.

Cash, T. F., & Stack, J. J. Locus of control among schizophrenics and other hospitalized psychiatric patients. *Genetic Psychology Monographs*, 1973, *87*, 105–122.

Chance, J. E. *Internal control of reinforcements and the school learning process*. Paper presented at Society for Research in Child Development Convention, Minneapolis, 1965.

Chance, J. E., & Goldstein, A. G. *Locus of control and performance on embedded figures*. Paper presented at the Midwestern Psychological Association Convention, Chicago, 1967. Also in *Perception and Psychophysics*, 1971, *9*, 33–34.

Chandler, T. A., Wolf, F. M., Cook, B., & Dugovics, D. A. Parental correlates of locus of control in fifth graders: an attempt at experimentation in the home. *Merrill-Palmer Quarterly*, 1980, *26*, 183–195.

Chess, S. B., Neuringer, C., & Goldstein, G. Arousal and field dependency in alcoholics. *Journal of General Psychology*, 1971, *85*, 93–102.

Coddington, R. D. The significance of life events as etiologic factors in the diseases of children. *Journal of Psychosomatic Research*, 1972, *16*, 7–18.

Cohen, S. Aftereffects of stress on human performance and social behavior: A review of research and theory. *Psychological Bulletin*, 1980, *88*, 82–108.

Coleman, J. S. *Resources for social change: Race in the United States*. Toronto: Wiley (Interscience), 1971.

Coleman, J. S. Campbell, E. Q., Hobson, C. J., McPartland, J., Mood, A. M., Weinfeld, F. D., &

York, R. L. *Equality of educational opportunity.* Washington, D. C.: United States Government Printing Office, 1966.

Collins, B. E. Four separate components of the Rotter I-E Scale: Belief in a difficult world, a just world, a predictable world and a politically responsive world. *Journal of Personality and Social Psychology,* 1974, *29,* 381–391.

Collins, B. E., Martin, J. C., Ashmore, R. D., & Ross, L. Some dimensions of the internal-external metaphor in theories of personality. *Journal of Personality,* 1973, *41,* 471–492.

Cone, J. D. Locus of control and social desirability. *Journal of Consulting and Clinical Psychology,* 1971, *36,* 449.

Connolly, J., & McCarrey, M. The relationship between levels of moral judgment maturity and locus of control. *Canadian Journal of Behavioral Science,* 1978, *10,* 162–175.

Cook, T. M., Novaco, R. W., & Sarason, I. G. *Generalized expectancy, life experience, and adaptation to Marine Corps recruit training (AR-002).* Seattle, Washington: University of Washington, April, 1980.

Cooper, J. F. *The deerslayer.* Boston: Ginn & Co., 1910.

Corah, J. L., & Boffa, J. Perceived control, self-observation and response to aversive stimulation. *Journal of Personality and Social Psychology,* 1970, *16,* 1–14.

Crandall, V. C. *Differences in parental antecedents of internal-external control in children and in young adulthood.* Paper presented at the American Psychological Association Convention, Montreal, 1973.

Crandall, V. C., Katkovsky, W., & Crandall, V. J. Children's beliefs in their control of reinforcements in intellectual academic achievement behaviors. *Child Development,* 1965, *36,* 91–109.

Crandall, V. J., Katkovsky, W., & Preston, A. Motivational and ability determinants of young children's intellectual academic achievement situations. *Child Development,* 1962, *33,* 643–661.

Crandall, V. C., & Lacey, B. W. Children's perception of internal-external control in intellectual-academic situations and their Embedded Figures Test performance. *Child Development,* 1972, *43,* 1123–1134.

Cravens, R. W., & Worchel, P. The differential effects of rewarding and coercive leaders on group members differing in locus of control. *Journal of Personality,* 1977, *45,* 150–168.

Crego, C. A. A pattern analytic approach to the measure of modes of expression of psychological differentiation. *Journal of Abnormal Psychology,* 1970, *76,* 194–198.

Cromwell, R. L., Butterfield, E. C., Brayfield, F. M., & Curry, J. J. *Acute Myocardial Infarction.* St. Louis: Mosby, 1977.

Cromwell, R. L., Rosenthal, D., Shakow, D., & Zahn, T. P. Reaction time, locus of control, choice behavior, and description of parental behavior in schizophrenic and normal subjects. *Journal of Personality,* 1961, *29,* 363–379.

Crowne, D. P., & Liverant, S. Conformity under varying conditions of personal commitment. *Journal of Abnormal and Social Psychology,* 1963, *66,* 547–555.

Davis, W. L., & Davis, D. E. Internal-external control and attribution of responsibility for success and failure. *Journal of Personality,* 1972, *40,* 123–136.

Davis, W. L., & Phares, E. J. Internal-external control as a determinant of information seeking in a social influence situation. *Journal of Personality,* 1967, *35,* 547–561.

Davis, W. L., & Phares, E. J. Parental antecedents of internal-external control of reinforcement. *Psychological Reports,* 1969, *24,* 427–436.

Dean, D. G. *Dynamic social psychology: Toward appreciation and replication.* New York: Random House, 1969.

deCharms, R. *Personal causation: The internal affective determinants of behavior.* New York: Academic Press, 1968.

deCharms, R. Personal causation training in the schools. *Journal of Applied Social Psychology,* 1972, *2,* 95–113.

deCharms, R. Personal causation and locus of control: Two different traditions and two uncorrelated measures. In H. M. Lefcourt (Ed.), *Research with the Locus of Control Construct* (Vol. 1). New York: Academic Press, 1981.

Deever, S. G. Ratings of task oriented expectancy for success as a function of internal control and field independence. *Dissertation Abstracts, Section B.*, 1968, *29*, (1), 365.

DesPres, T. *The Survivor*. New York: Oxford University Press, 1976.

Diamond, M. J. & Shapiro, J. L. Changes in locus of control as a function of encounter group experiences. *Journal of Abnormal Psychology*, 1973, *82*, 514-518.

Diener, C. I., & Dweck, C. S. An analysis of learned helplessness: Continuous changes in performance, strategy, and achievement cognitions following failure *Journal of Personality & Social Psychology*, 1978, *36*, 451-462.

DiNardo, P. A., & Raymond, J. B. Locus of control and differences in attention during meditation. *Journal of Consulting and Clinical Psychology*, 1979, *47*, 1136-1137.

Doctor, R. Locus of control of reinforcement and responsiveness to social influence. *Journal of Personality*, 1971, *39*, 542-551.

Dohrenwend, B. S., & Martin, J. L. Personal versus situational determination of anticipation and control of the occurrence of stressful life events. *American Journal of Community Psychology*, 1979, *7*, 453-468.

Dolgun, A., & Watson, P. *Alexander Dolgun's story: an american in the Gulag*. New York: Knopf, 1975.

Dollinger, S. J., & Taub, S. I. The interaction of locus of control expectancies and providing purpose on children's motivation. *Journal of Research in Personality*, 1977, *11*, 118-127.

Donovan, D. M., & O'Leary, M. R. Comparison of perceived and experienced control among alcoholics and nonalcoholics. *Journal of Abnormal Psychology*, 1975, *84*, 726-728.

Donovan, D. M., & O'Leary, M. R. The drinking-related locus of control scale. *Journal of Studies on Alcohol*, 1978, *39*, 759-784.

Dua, P. S. Comparison of the effects of behaviorally oriented action and psychotherapy reeducation on introversion-extraversion, emotionality, and internal-external control. *Journal of Counseling Psychology*, 1970, *17*, 567-572.

DuCette, J. & Wolk, S. Locus of control and extreme behavior. *Journal of Consulting and Clinical Psychology*, 1972, *39*, 253-258.

DuCette, J. & Wolk, S. Cognitive and motivational correlates of generalized expectancies for control. *Journal of Personality and Social Psychology*, 1973, *26*, 420-426.

DuCette, J., Wolk, S., & Soucar, E. Atypical pattern in locus of control and nonadaptive behavior. *Journal of Personality*, 1972, *40*, 287-297.

Duke, M., Johnson, T. C., & Nowicki, S. Effects of sports fitness camp experience on locus of control orientation in children, ages 6 to 14. *The Research Quarterly*, *1977*, *48*, 280-283.

Duke, M. P., & Lancaster, W. A note on locus of control as a function of father absence. *The Journal of Genetic Psychology*, 1976, *129*, 335-336.

Duke, M. P., & Lewis, G. The measurement of locus of control in black preschool and primary school. *Journal of Personality Assessment*, 1979, *43*, 351-355.

Duke, M. P., & Nowicki, S. Locus of control and achievement—the confirmation of a theoretical expectation. *Journal of Psychology*, 1974, *87*, 263-267.

Dweck, C. S. The role of expectations and attributions on the alleviation of learned helplessness. *Journal of Personality and Social Psychology*, 1975, *31*, 674-685.

Dweck, C. S., & Bush, E. S. Sex differences in learned helplessness: (I) differential debilitation with peer and adult evaluators. *Developmental Psychology*, 1976, *12*, 147-156.

Dweck, C. S., & Goetz, T. E. Attributions and learned helplessness. In J. H. Harvey, W. Ickes, & R. F. Kidd (Eds), *New Directions in Attribution Research* (Vol. 2). Hillsdale, N.J.: Lawrence Erlbaum Associates, 1978.

Dweck, C. S. & Reppucci, N. D. Learned helplessness and reinforcement responsibility in children. *Journal of Personality and Social Psychology*, 1973, *25*, 109-116.

Efran, J. *Some personality determinants of memory for success and failure.* Unpublished doctoral dissertation, Ohio State University, 1963.

Elkins, S. Slavery and personality. In B. Kaplan (Ed.), *Studying personality cross-culturally.* New York: Harper & Row, 1961.

Ericksen, R. V., & Roberts, A. H. Some ego functions associated with delay of gratification in male delinquents. *Journal of Consulting and Clinical Psychology*, 1971, *36*, 378-382.

Erickson, R. C., Smyth, L., Donovan, D. M., & O'Leary, M. R. Psychopathic and defensive style of alcoholics as a function of congruence—incongruence between psychological differentiation and locus of control. *Psychological Reports*, 1976, *39*, 51-54.

Feather, N. T. Some personality correlates of external control. *Australian Journal of Psychology*, 1967, *19*, 253-260.

Feather, N. T. Valence of outcome and expectation of success in relation to task difficulty and perceived locus of control. *Journal of Personality and Social Psychology*, 1968, *7*, 372-386.

Felton, G. S. The experimenter expectancy effect examined as a function of task ambiguity and internal-external control. *Journal of Experimental Research in Personality*, 1971, *5*, 286-294.

Ferster, C. B. A functional analysis of depression. *American Psychologist*, 1973, *28*, 857-870.

Fink, H. C., & Hjelle, L. A. Internal-external control and ideology. *Psychological Reports*, 1973, *33*, 967-974.

Finkelman, J. M., & Glass, D. C. Reappraisal of the relationship between noise and human performance by means of a subsidiary task measure. *Journal of Applied Psychology*, 1970, *54*, 211-213.

Fish, B., & Karabenick, S. A. Relationship between self-esteem and locus of control. *Psychological Reports*, 1971, *29*, 784.

Fitz, R. J. The differential effects of praise and censure on serial learning as dependent on locus of control and field-dependency. *Dissertation Abstracts International*, 1971, *31*, 4310.

Fontana, A. F., Hughes, L. A., Marcus, J. L., Dowds, B. N. Subjective evaluation of life events. *Journal of Consulting and Clinical Psychology*, 1979, *47*, 906-911.

Foulds, M. L. Changes in locus of internal-external control. *Comparative Group Studies*, 1971, *2*, 293-300.

Foulds, M. L. Guinan, J. F., & Warehime, R. G. Marathon group: changes in perceived locus of control. *Journal of College Student Personnel*, 1974, *15*, 8-11.

Frank, J. D. Psychotherapy and the sense of mastery. In R. L. Spitzer & D. F. Klein (Eds.), *Evaluation of Psychological Therapies.* Baltimore: John Hopkins University Press, 1976.

Franklin, R. D. Youth's expectancies about internal versus external control of reinforcement related to N variables. *Dissertation Abstracts*, 1963, *24*, 1684.

Frazier, E. F. *Black bourgeosie.* New York: Collier Books, 1962.

Friedman, M. L., & Dies, R. R. Reactions of internal and external test-anxious students to counseling and behavior therapies. *Journal of Consulting and Clinical Psychology*, 1974, *42*, 921.

Fromm, E. *The Art of Loving.* New York: Harper & Row, 1956.

Garber, J., & Seligman, M. E. P. (Eds.). *Human helplessness: theory and applications.* New York: Academic Press, 1980.

Gardner, G. E. Aggression and violence—the enemies of precision learning in children. *American Journal of Psychiatry*, 1971, *128*, 77-82.

Geer, J. H., Davison, G. C., & Gatchel, R. I. Reduction in stress in humans through nonveridical perceived control of aversive stimulation. *Journal of Personality and Social Psychology*, 1970, *16*, 731-738.

Getter, H. A personality determinant of verbal conditioning. *Journal of Personality*, 1966, *34*, 397-405.

Gillis, J. S., & Jessor, R. Effects of brief psychotherapy on belief in internal control: an exploratory study. *Psychotherapy: Theory Research, and Practice*, 1970, *7*, 135-137.

Gilmor, T. M. Locus of control as a mediator of adaptive behavior in children and adolescents. *Canadian Psychological Review*, 1978, *19*, 1-26.

Gilmor, T. M., & Minton, H. L. Internal versus external attribution of task performance as a function of locus of control, initial confidence and success-failure outcome. *Journal of Personality*, 1974, *42*, 159-174.

Glass, D. C., Reim, B., & Singer, J. E. Behavioral consequences of adaptation to controllable and uncontrollable noise. *Journal of Experimental Social Psychology*, 1971, *7*, 244-257.

Glass, D. C., & Singer, J. E. *Urban stress*. New York: Academic Press, 1972.

Glass, D. C., Singer, J. E., & Friedman, L. N. Psychic cost of adaptation to an environmental stressor. *Journal of Personality and Social Psychology*, 1969, *12*, 200-210.

Glass, D. C., Singer, J. E., Leonard, H. S., Krantz, D., Cohen, S., & Cummings, H. Perceived control of aversive stimulation and the reduction of stress responses. *Journal of Personality*, 1973, *41*, 577-595.

Goldberg, S. Social competence in infancy: a model of parent-infant interaction. *Merrill-Palmer Quarterly*, 1977, *23*, 163-177.

Golin, S. The effects of stress on the performance of normal and high anxious subjects under chance and skill conditions. *Journal of Abnormal Psychology*, 1974, *83*, 466-472.

Gordon, D. A. Children's beliefs in internal-external control and self esteem as related to academic achievement. *Journal of Personality Assessment*, 1977, *41*, 383-386.

Gore, P. S. *Individual differences in the prediction of subject compliance to experimenter bias*. Unpublished doctoral dissertation, Ohio State University, 1962.

Gore, P. S. & Rotter, J. B. A personality correlate of social action. *Journal of Personality*, 1963, *31*, 58-64.

Gorman, B. S. An observation of altered locus of control following political disappointment. *Psychological Reports*, 1968, *23*, 1094.

Gorman, B. S. *A multivariate study of the relationship of cognitive control and cognitive principles to reported daily mood experiences*. Unpublished doctoral dissertation, City University of New York, 1971.

Gorsuch, R. L., Henighan, R. P., & Barnard, C. Locus of control: an example of dangers in using children's scales with children. *Child Development*, 1972, *43*, 579-590.

Goss, A., & Morosko, T. E. Relation between a dimension of internal-external control and the MMPI with an alcoholic population. *Journal of Consulting and Clinical Psychology*, 1970, *34*, 189-192.

Gottesfeld, H., & Dozier, G. Changes in feelings of powerlessness in a community action program. *Psychological Reports*, 1966, *19*, 978.

Gozali, J., & Bialer, I. Children's locus of control scale. *American Journal of Mental Deficiency*, 1968, *72*, 622-625.

Gozali, J., Cleary, T. A., Walster, G. W., & Gozali, J. Relationship between the internal-external construct and achievement. *Journal of Educational Psychology*, 1973, *64*, 9-14.

Gozali, J., & Sloan, J. Control orientation as a personality dimension among alcoholics. *Quarterly Journal of Studies on Alcohol*, 1971, *32*, 159-161.

Gregory, W. L. Locus of control for positive and negative outcomes. *Journal of Personality and Social Psychology*, 1978, *36*, 840-849.

Gregory, W. L. Expectancies for controllability, performance attributions, and behavior. In H. M. Lefcourt (Ed.), *Research with the locus of control construct* (Vol. 1). New York: Academic Press, 1981.

Gregory, W. L., Chartier, G. M., & Wright, M. H. Learned helplessness and learned effectiveness: Effects of explicit response cues on individuals differing in personal control expectancies. *Journal of Personality and Social Psychology*, 1979, *37*, 1982–1992.

Gregory, W. L., & Nelson, D. V. Locus of control and cue explication. *Personality and Social Psychology Bulletin*, 1978, *4*, 248–251.

Griffin, J. H. *Black like me*. Boston: Houghton–Mifflin, 1962.

Gross, W. F., & Nerviano, V. J. Note on the control orientation of alcoholics. *Psychological Reports*, 1972, *31*, 406.

Gurin, G., & Gurin, P. Expectancy theory in the study of poverty. *Journal of Social Issues*, 1970, *26*, 83–104.

Gurin, P., Gurin, G., Lao, R. C., & Beattie, M. Internal-external control in the motivational dynamics of Negro youth. *Journal of Social Issues*, 1969, *25*, 29–53.

Haggard, E. A. Experimental studies in affective processes. *Journal of Experimental Psychology*, 1943, *33*, 257–284.

Haley, W. E., & Strickland, B. R. *Locus of control and depression.* Paper presented at Eastern Psychological Association Convention, Boston, 1977.

Halpin, B., & Ottinger, D. *Children's locus of control scales. A reappraisal of reliability characteristics.* Unpublished manuscript, 1981.

Hamsher, J. H., Geller, J. D., & Rotter, J. B. Interpersonal trust, internal-external control and the Warren Commission Report. *Journal of Personality and Social Psychology*, 1968, *9*, 210–215.

Harpin, P. M. *Individual variability in behavior within a person-environment interactional design.* Unpublished dissertation, Arizona State University, 1980.

Harpin, P. M., & Sandler, I. N. Interaction of sex, locus of control, and teacher control: Toward a student-classroom match. *American Journal of Community Psychology*, 1979, *7*, 621–632.

Harrison, F. I. Relationship between home background, school success, and adolescent attitudes. *Merrill-Palmer Quarterly of Behavior and Development*, 1968, *14*, 331–344.

Harrow, M., & Ferrante, A. Locus of control in psychiatric patients. *Journal of Consulting and Clinical Psychology*, 1969, *33*, 582–589.

Harvey, J. M. Locus of control shift in administrators. *Perceptual and Motor Skills*, 1971, *33*, 980–982.

Hersch, P. D., & Scheibe, K. E. On the reliability and validity of internal-external control as a personality dimension. *Journal of Consulting Psychology*, 1967, *31*, 609–613.

Hetherington, E. M. Effects of father absence on personality development in adolescent daughters. *Developmental Psychology*, 1972, *7*, 313–326.

Hill, D. J., & Bale, R. M. Measuring beliefs about where psychological pain originates and who is responsible for its alleviation: Two new scales for clinical researchers. In H. M. Lefcourt (Ed.), *Research with the locus of control construct* (Vol. 1). New York: Academic Press, 1981.

Hiroto, D. S. *Validation of the learned helplessness hypothesis with humans.* Paper presented at the American Psychological Association Convention, Honolulu, 1972.

Hiroto, D. S. Locus of control and learned helplessness. *Journal of Experimental Psychology*, 1974, *102*, 187–193.

Hiroto, D. S., & Seligman, M. E. P. Genrality of learned helplessness in man. *Journal of Personality and Social Psychology*, 1975, *31*, 311–327.

Hjelle, L. A. Social desirability as a variable in the locus of control scale. *Psychological Reports*, 1971, *28*, 807–816.

Hokanson, J. E., DeGood, D. E., Forrest, M. S., & Brittain, T. M. Availability of avoidance behaviors in modulating vascular stress responses. *Journal of Personality and Social Psychology*, 1971, *19*, 60–68.

Holmes, T. H., & Rahe, R. H. The social readjustment scale. *Journal of Psychosomatic Research,* 1967, *11,* 213–218.

Houston, B. K. Control over stress, locus of control and response to stress. *Journal of Personality and Social Psychology,* 1972, *21,* 249–255.

Hsieh, T. T., Shybut, J., & Lotsof, E. J. Internal versus external control and ethnic group membership. *Journal of Consulting and Clinical Psychology,* 1969, *33,* 122–124.

Hughes, C. W., & Lynch, J. J. A reconsideration of psychological precursors of sudden death in infrahuman animals. *American Psychologist,* 1978, *33,* 419–429.

Hughes, C. W., Stein, E. A., & Lynch, J. J. Hopelessness-induced sudden death in rats. *The Journal of Nervous and Mental Disease,* 1978, *166,* 387–401.

Hunsley, J. *Stressful life events and moods: moderating effects of locus of control and coping styles.* Unpublished honor's thesis, University of Waterloo, 1981.

Husaini, B. A., & Neff, J. A. Characteristics of life events and psychiatric impairment in rural communities. *Journal of Nervous and Mental Disease,* 1980, *168,* 159–166.

James, W. H. *Internal versus external control of reinforcement as a basic variable in learning theory.* Unpublished doctoral dissertation, Ohio State University, 1957.

James, W. H. *The application of social learning theory to educational processes.* Paper presented at a meeting of the Society for Research in Child Development, Minneapolis, 1965.

James, W. H., & Rotter, J. B. Partial and 100 percent reinforcement under chance and skill conditions. *Journal of Experimental Psychology,* 1958, *55,* 397–403.

James, W. H., Woodruff, A. B., & Werner, W. Effect of internal and external control upon changes in smoking behavior. *Journal of Consulting Psychology,* 1965, *29,* 127–129.

Jessor, R., Graves, T. D., Hanson, R. C., & Jessor, S. *Society, Personality and Deviant Behavior.* New York: Holt, Rinehart & Winston, 1968.

Joe, V. C. A review of the internal-external control construct as a personality variable. *Psychological Reports,* 1971, *28,* 619–640.

Joe, V. C. Social desirability and the I-E scale. *Psychological Reports,* 1972, *30,* 44–46.

Joe, V. C., & Jahn, J. C. Factor structure of the Rotter I-E scale. *Journal of Clinical Psychology,* 1973, *29,* 66–68.

Johnson, B. L., & Kilmann, P. R. The relationship between recalled parental attitudes and internal-external control. *Journal of Clinical Psychology,* 1975, *31,* 40–42. (a)

Johnson, B. L., & Kilmann, P. R. Locus of control and perceived confidence in problem solving abilities. *Journal of Clinical Psychology,* 1975, *31,* 54–55. (b)

Johnson, C. D., & Gormly, J. Academic cheating: The contribution of sex, personality and situational variables. *Developmental Psychology,* 1972, *6,* 320–325.

Johnson, J. H., & Sarason, I. G. Life stress, depression and anxiety: Internal-external control as a moderator variable. *Journal of Psychosomatic Research,* 1978, *22,* 205–208.

Johnson, R. C., Ackerman, J. M., Frank, H., & Fionda, A. J. Resistance to temptation and guilt following yielding and psychotherapy. *Journal of Consulting and Clinical Psychology,* 1968, *32,* 169–175.

Jolley, M. T., & Spielberger, C. D. The effects of locus of control and anxiety on verbal conditioning. *Journal of Personality,* 1973, *41,* 443–456.

Jorgenson, D. O. Locus of control and the perceived causal influence of the lunar cycle. *Perceptual and Motor Skills,* 1981, *52,* 864.

Julian, J. W., & Katz, S. B. Internal versus external control and the value of reinforcement. *Journal of Personality and Social Psychology,* 1968, *76,* 43–48.

Kahn, R. L., Wolfe, D. M., Quinn, R. P., Snoek, J. C., & Rosenthal, R. A. *Organizational stress: Study in role conflict and ambiguity.* New York: Wiley, 1964.

Karabenick, S. A. Valence of success and failure as a function of achievement motives and locus of control. *Journal of Personality and Social Psychology,* 1972, *21,* 101–110.

Karabenick, S. A., & Srull, T. K. Effects of personality and situational variation in locus of control on cheating: Determinants of the "congruence effect". *Journal of Personality,* 1978, *46,* 72-95.

Katkovsky, W., Crandall, V. C., & Good, S. Parental antecedents of children's beliefs in internal-external control of reinforcement in intellectual achievement situations. *Child Development.* 1967, *28,* 765-776.

Katz, I. The socialization of academic motivation in minority group children. In D. Levine (Ed.), *Nebraska Symposium on Motivation.* Lincoln, Nebr.: University of Nebraska Press, 1967.

Kazantzakis, N. *Zorba the Greek,* N.Y.: Simon & Schuster, 1959.

Kelman, H. C., & Lawrence, L. H. Assignment of responsibility in the case of Lt. Calley. *Journal of Social Issues,* 1972, *28,* 177-212.

Kiehlbauch, J. B. *Selected changes over time in internal-external control expectancies in a reformatory population.* Unpublished doctoral dissertation, Kansas State University, 1968.

Kilmann, P. R., Albert, B. M., & Sotile, W. M. Relationship between locus of control, structure of therapy, and outcome. *Journal of Consulting and Clinical Psychology,* 1975, *43,* 588.

Kilpatrick, D. G., Dubin, W. R., & Marcotte, D. B. Personality, stress of the medical education process, and changes in affective mood state. *Psychological Reports,* 1974, *34,* 1215-1223.

Kirscht, J. P. Perception of control and health beliefs. *Canadian Journal of Behavioral Sciences,* 1972, *4,* 225-237.

Kish, G. B., Solberg, K. B., & Uecker, A. E. Locus of control as a factor influencing patients' perceptions of ward atmosphere. *Journal of Clinical Psychology,* 1971, *27,* 287-289.

Kleiber, D., Veldman, D. J. & Menaker, S. L. *The multidimensionality of locus of control.* Paper presented at Eastern Psychological Association Convention, Washington, D.C., 1973.

Knauth, P. *A season in hell.* New York: Harper & Row, 1975.

Kobasa, S. C. Personality and resistance to illness. *American Journal of Community Psychology,* 1979, *7,* 413-423. (a)

Kobasa, S. C. Stressful life events, personality, and health: An inquiry into hardiness. *Journal of Personality and Social Psychology,* 1979, *37,* 1-11. (b)

Kobasa, S. C., Maddi, S. R., & Kahn, S. Hardiness and health: A prospective study. *Journal of Personality and Social Psychology,* 1982, *42,* 168-177.

Kobler, A. L., & Stotland, E. *The end of hope.* New York: Free Press, 1964.

Koenigs, S. S., Fiedler, M. L., & deCharms, R. Teacher beliefs, classroom interaction and personal causation. *Journal of Applied Social Psychology,* 1977, *7,* 95-114.

Koestler, A. *The ghost in the machine.* New York: Macmillan, 1967.

Lao, R. Internal-external control and competent and innovative behavior among Negro college students. *Journal of Personality and Social Psychology,* 1970, *14,* 263-270.

Lefcourt, H. M. Risk taking in Negro and white adults. *Journal of Personality and Social Psychology,* 1965, *2,* 765-770.

Lefcourt, H. M. Internal-external control of reinforcement: A review. *Psychological Bulletin.* 1966, *65,* 206-220. (a)

Lefcourt, H. M. Belief in personal control: a goal for psychotherapy. *Journal of Individual Psychology,* 1966, *22,* 185-195. (b)

Lefcourt, H. M. The effects of cue explication upon persons maintaining external control expectancies. *Journal of Personality and Social Psychology,* 1967, *5,* 372-378.

Lefcourt, H. M. Recent developments in the study of locus of control. In B. A. Maher (Ed.), *Progress in experimental research in personality* (Vol. 6). New York: Academic Press, 1972.

Lefcourt, H. M. The function of the illusions of control and freedom. *American Psychologist,* 1973, *28,* 417-425.

Lefcourt, H. M. *Locus of control and the acceptance of one's reinforcement experience.* Paper presented at the World Congress of Sociology, Toronto, 1974.

Lefcourt, H. M. *Locus of control: current trends in theory and research*. Hillsdale, N.J.: Lawrence Erlbaum Associates, 1976.

Lefcourt, H. M. Locus of control for specific goals. In L. C. Perlmutter & R. A. Monty (Eds.), *Choice and Perceived Control*. Hillsdale, N.J.: Lawrence Erlbaum Associates, 1979.

Lefcourt, H. M. Locus of control and coping with life's events. In E. Staub (Ed.), *Personality*. New York: Prentice-Hall, 1980.

Lefcourt, H. M. The construction and development of the multidimensional-multiattributional causality scales. In H. M. Lefcourt (Ed.), *Research with the locus of control construct* (Vol. 1). New York: Academic Press, 1981. (a)

Lefcourt, H. M. (Ed.) *Research with the locus of control construct* (Vol. 1). New York: Academic Press, 1981. (b)

Lefcourt, H. M., Antrobus, P., & Hogg, E. Humor response and humor production as a function of locus of control, field dependence and type of reinforcements. *Journal of Personality*, 1974, *42*, 632-651.

Lefcourt, H. M., Gronnerud, P., & McDonald, P. Cognitive activity and hypothesis formation during a double entendre word association test as a function of locus of control and field dependence. *Canadian Journal of Behavioral Science*, 1973, *5*, 161-173.

Lefcourt, H. M., Hogg, E., & Sordoni, C. Locus of control, field dependence, and conditions arousing objective versus subjective self-awareness. *Journal of Research in Personality*, 1975, *9*, 21-36.

Lefcourt, H. M., Hogg, E., Struthers, S. & Holmes, C. Causal attributions as a function of locus of control, initial confidence and performance outcomes. *Journal of Personality & Social Psychology*, 1975, *32*, 391-397.

Lefcourt, H. M. & Ladwig, G. W. The American Negro: A problem in expectancies. *Journal of Personality and Social Psychology*, 1965, *1*, 377-380. (a)

Lefcourt, H. M., & Ladwig, G. W. The effect of reference group upon Negroes' task persistence in a biracial competitive game. *Journal of Personality and Social Psychology*, 1965, *1*, 668-671. (b)

Lefcourt, H. M., & Ladwig, G. W. Alienation in Negro and white reformatory inmates. *Journal of Social Psychology*, 1966, *68*, 152-157.

Lefcourt, H. M., Lewis, L. E., & Silverman, I. W. Internal versus external control of reinforcement and attention in decision making tasks. *Journal of Personality*, 1968, *36*, 663-682.

Lefcourt, H. M. Miller, R. S., Ware, E. E., & Sherk, D. Locus of control as a modifier of the relationship between stressors and moods. *Journal of Personality and Social Psychology*, 1981, *41*, 357-369.

Lefcourt, H. M. & Siegel, J. Reaction time behavior as a function of internal-external control of reinforcement and control of test administration. *Canadian Journal of Behavioral Science*, 1970, *2*, 253-266. (a)

Lefcourt, H. M. & Siegel, J. Reaction time performance as a function of field dependence and autonomy in test administration. *Journal of Abnormal Psychology*, 1970, *76*, 475-481. (b)

Lefcourt, H. M., Sordoni, Carl, & Sordoni, Carol. Locus of control, field dependence and the expression of humor, *Journal of Personality*, 1974, *42*, 130-143.

Lefcourt, H. M., & Steffy, R. A. Level of aspiration, risk-taking behavior, and projection test performance: A search for coherence. *Journal of Consulting and Clinical Psychology*, 1970, *34*, 193-198.

Lefcourt, H. M., & Telegdi, M. Perceived locus of control and field dependence as predictors of cognitive activity. *Journal of Consulting and Clinical Psychology*, 1971, *37*, 53-56.

Lefcourt, H. M., VonBaeyer, C. L., Ware, E. E., & Cox, D. J. The multidimensional-multiattributional Causality Scale: The development of a goal specific locus of control scale. *Canadian Journal of Behavioral Science*, 1979, *11*, 286-304.

Lefcourt, H. M., & Wine, J. Internal versus external control of reinforcement and the deployment of attention in experimental situations. *Canadian Journal of Behavioral Science* 1969, *1*, 167–181.

Lessing, E. E. Racial differences in indices of ego functioning relevant to academic achievement. *Journal of Genetic Psychology*, 1969, *115*, 153–167.

Levenson, H. *Distinctions within the concept of internal-external control.* Paper presented at the American Psychological Association Convention, Washington, D.C., 1972.

Levenson, H. Multidimensional locus of control in psychiatric patients. *Journal of Consulting and Clinical Psychology*, 1973, *41*, 397–404. (a)

Levenson, H. Perceived parental antecedents of internal, powerful others and chance locus of control orientations. *Developmental Psychology*, 1973, *9*, 268–274. (b)

Levenson, H. Activism and powerful others: Distinctions with the concept of internal-external control. *Journal of Personality Assessment.* 1974, *38*, 377–383.

Levenson, H. Differentiating among internality, powerful others, and chance. In H. M. Lefcourt (Ed.), *Research with the locus of control construct* (Vol. 1). New York: Academic Press, 1981.

Lewandowski, A. An investigation of cognitive and attitudinal correlates of the coronary-prone behavior pattern. Unpublished doctoral dissertation, University of Waterloo, 1979.

Lewin, K. Psycho-sociological problems of a minority group. *Character and Personality*, 1940, *8*, 176–187.

Lewinsohn, P. *Clinical and theoretical aspects of depression.* Paper presented at the Georgia Symposium in Experimental Clinical Psychology, 1972.

Lewis, O. *Children of Sanchez.* New York: Random House, 1961.

Liberman, B. L. The role of mastery in psychotherapy: Maintenance of improvement and prescriptive change. In J. D. Frank, R. Hoehn-Saric, S. D. Imber, B. L. Liberman, & A. R. Stone, *Effective Ingredients of Successful Psychotherapy.* New York: Brunner/Mazel, 1978.

Lichtenstein, E., & Keutzer, C. S. Further normative and correlational data on the internal-external (I.E.) control of reinforcement scale. *Psychological Reports*, 1967, *21*, 1014–1016.

Lipp, L., Kolstoe, R., James, W., & Randall, H. Denial of disability and internal control of reinforcement: A study using a perceptual defense paradigm. *Journal of Consulting and Clinical Psychology*, 1968, *32*, 72–75.

Little, V. L., & Kendall, P. C. Note on locus of control and academic achievement in institutionalized delinquents. *Journal of Abnormal Child Psychology*, 1978, *6*, 281–283.

Loeb, R. C. Concomitants of boys' locus of control examined in parent-child interactions. *Developmental Psychology*, 1975, *11*, 353–358.

Lotsof, E. J., James, W. H., Drucker, R., & Blount, W. Perceptual discrimination, task structure, and locus of control. Paper presented at Midwestern Psychological Association, St. Louis, 1964.

Lottman, T. J., & DeWolfe, A. S. Internal versus external control in reactive and process schizophrenia. *Journal of Consulting and Clinical Psychology*, 1972, *39*, 344.

Ludwigsen, K., & Rollins, H. *Recognition of random forms as a function of source of cue, perceived locus of control, and socioeconomic level.* Paper presented at Southeastern Psychological Association Convention, Miami Beach, 1971.

Lynch, M. L., Ogg, W. D., & Christensen, M. G. Impact of a life planning workshop on perceived locus on control. *Psychological Reports*, 1975, *37*, 1219–1222.

MacDonald, A. P., & Hall, J. Internal-external locus of control and perception of disability. *Journal of Consulting and Clinical Psychology*, 1971, *36*, 338–343.

MacDonald, A. P. & Tseng, M. S. Dimensions of internal versus external control revisited. Unpublished manuscript, West Virginia University, 1971.

Maher, B. *Principles of Psychopathology.* New York: McGraw Hill, 1966.

Mahrer, A. R. The role of expectancy in delayed reinforcement. *Journal of Experimental Psychology*, 1956, *52*, 101–105.

Manuck, S. B., Hinrichsen, J. J., & Ross, E. O. Life stress, locus of control, and state and trait anxiety. *Psychological Reports*, 1975, *36*, 413-414. (a)

Manuck, S. B., Hinrichsen, J. J., & Ross, E. O. Life stress, locus of control and treatment seeking. *Psychological Reports*, 1975, *37*, 589-590. (b)

Martin, R. D., & Shepel, L. F. Locus of control and discrimination ability with lay counselors. *Journal of Consulting and Clinical Psychology*, 1974, *42*, 741.

Maslow, A. H. *Motivation and personality*. New York: Harper, & Row, 1954.

Massari, D. V., & Rosenblum, D. C. Locus of control, interpersonal trust and academic achievement. *Psychological Reports*, 1972, *31*, 355-360.

Masters, J. C. Treatment of adolescent rebellion by the reconstrual of stimuli. *Journal of Consulting Psychology*, 1970, *35*, 213-216.

Mausner, B., & Platt, E. S. *Smoking: a behavioral analysis*. Elmsford, New York: Pergamon Press, 1971.

May, R. *Love and will*. New York: Norton, 1969.

McArthur, L. A. Luck is alive and well in New Haven. *Journal of Personality and Social Psychology*, 1970, *16*, 316-318.

McClelland, D. C., Atkinson, J. W., Clark, R. A., & Lowell, E. L. *The achievement motive*. New York: Appleton-Century-Crofts, 1953.

McFarlane, A. H., Norman, G. R., Streiner, D. L., Roy, R., & Scott, D. J. A longitudinal study of the influence of the psychosocial environment on health status: A preliminary report. *Journal of Health and Social Behavior*. 1980, *21*, 124-133.

McGhee, P. E. & Crandall, V. C. Beliefs in internal-external control of reinforcement and academic performance. *Child Development*, 1968, *39*, 91-102.

McGinnies, E., Nordholm, L. A., Ward, C. D., & Bhanthumnavin, D. L. Sex and cultural differences in perceived locus of control among students in five countries. *Journal of Consulting and Clinical Psychology*, 1974, *42*, 451-455.

McGinnies, E., & Ward, C. D. Persuasibility as a function of source credibility and locus of control: Five cross-cultural experiments. *Journal of Personality*, 1974, *42*, 360-371.

McIntire, W. G., & Dryer, A. S. Relationship of cognitive style to locus of control. *Perceptual and Motor Skills*, 1973, *37*, 553-554.

McKinney, J. P. The development of values: A perceptual interpretation. *Journal of Personality and Social Psychology*, 1975, *31*, 801-807.

McNair, D. M. Lorr, M., & Droppleman, L. *The profile of mood status*. Educational and Industrial Testing Service, San Diego, 1971.

Melges, F. T., & Weisz, A. E. The personal future and suicidal ideation. *Journal of Nervous and Mental Disease*, 1971, *153*, 244-250.

Menninger, K. *The vital balance*. New York: Viking, 1963.

Messer, S. B. The relation of internal-external control to academic performance. *Child Development*, 1972, *43*, 1456-1462.

Meyer, W. U. *Selbstverantwortlichkeit und Leistungs motivation*. Unpublished doctoral dissertation, Ruhr University, Bochum, Germany, 1970.

Midlarski, E. Aiding under stress: The effects of competence, dependency, visibility, and fatalism. *Journal of Personality*, 1971, *39*, 132-149.

Midlarski, E., & Midlarski, M. Some determinants of aiding under experimentally induced stress. *Journal of Personality*, 1973, *41*, 305-327.

Milgram, S. Behavioral study of obedience. *Journal of Abnormal and Social Psychology*, 1963, *67*, 371-378.

Milgram, S. Some conditions of obedience and disobedience to authority. In I. D. Steiner & M. Fishbein (Eds.), *Current studies in social psychology*. New York: Holt, Rinehart & Winston, 1965.

Miller, A. G., & Minton, H. Machiavelliansm, internal-external control and the violation of experimental instructions. *Psychological Record*, 1969, *19*, 369-380.

Miller, P. C. *The construction and development of the Marital Locus of Control Scale*. Unpublished Master's Thesis, University of Waterloo, 1981.

Mirels, H. L. Dimensions of internal versus external control. *Journal of Consulting and Clinical Psychology*, 1970, *34*, 226-228.

Mirels, H. L., & Garrett, J. B. The Protestant ethic as a personality variable. *Journal of Consulting and Clinical Psychology*, 1971, *36*, 40-44.

Mischel, W. Preference for delayed reinforcement and social responsibility. *Journal of Abnormal and Social Psychology*, 1961, *62*, 1-7.

Mischel, W. Theory and research on the antecedents of self-imposed delay of reward. In B. A. Maher (Ed.), *Progress in experimental personality research* (Vol. 3). New York: Academic Press, 1966.

Mischel, W. Towards a cognitive social learning reconceptualization of personality. *Psychological Review*, 1973, *80*, 252-283.

Mischel, W. Personal communication, 1975.

Mischel, W., Zeiss, R. & Zeiss, A. An internal-external control test for young children. *Journal of Personality and Social Psychology*, 1974, *29*, 265-278.

Moos, R. H., Insel, P. M., & Humphrey, B. *Family, work and group environment scales: combined preliminary manual*. Palo Alto, California: Consulting Psychologists Press, 1974.

Moos, R. H., & Trichett, E. J. *Classroom environment scale manual*. Palo Alto, Calif.: Consulting Psychologist Press, 1974.

Morelli, G., Krotinger, H., & Moore, S. Neuroticism and Levenson's locus of control scale. *Psychological Reports*, 1979, *44*, 153-154.

Mowrer, O. H. *Learning theory and personality dynamics*. New York: Ronald Press, 1950.

Mowrer, O. H., & Viek, P. An experimental analogue of fear from a sense of helplessness. *Journal of Abnormal and Social Psychology*, 1948, *43*, 193-200.

Myrdal, G. *An American dilemma*. New York: Harper & Row, 1944.

Naditch, M. P. *Putting the value back into expectancy X value theory*. Paper presented at Eastern Psychological Association Convention, Washington, D.C., 1973.

Naditch, M. P. *Acute adverse reactions to psychoactive drugs, locus of control, the discrepancy between aspirations and achievements, and hypochondriasis*. Unpublished manuscript, 1974.

Naditch, M. P. Locus of control and drinking behavior in a sample of men in army basic training. *Journal of Consulting and Clinical Psychology*, 1975, *43*, 96.

Naditch, M. P., & DeMaio, T. Locus of control and competence. *Journal of Personality*, 1975, *43*, 541-559.

Naditch, M. P., Gargan, M., & Michael, L. Denial, anxiety, locus of control, and the discrepancy between aspirations and achievements as components of depression. *Journal of Abnormal Psychology*, 1975, *84*, 1-9.

Nelsen, H. M., & Frost, E. Residence, anomie, and receptivity to education among southern Appalachian Presbyterians. *Rural Sociology*, 1971, *36*, 521-532.

Nisbett, R. E., & Temoshok, L. Is there an "external" cognitive style? *Journal of Personality and Social Psychology*, 1976, *33*, 36-47.

Nord, W. R., Connelly, F., & Daignault, G. Locus of control and aptitude test scores as predictors of academic success in graduate school. *Journal of Educational Psychology*, 1974, *66*, 956-961.

Novaco, R. W., Stokols, D., Campbell, J., & Stokols, J. Transportation, stress, and community psychology. *American Journal of Community Psychology*, 1979, *7*, 361-380.

Nowicki, S. *Predicting academic achievement of females from locus of control orientation: Some problems and some solutions*. Paper presented at American Psychological Association Convention, Montreal, 1973.

Nowicki, S. Reported stressful events during developmental periods and their relation to locus of control orientation in college students. *Journal of Consulting and Clinical Psychology*, 1978, *6*, 1552-1553.

Nowicki, S. Competition-cooperation as a mediator of locus of control and achievement. *Journal of Research in Personality*, 1982, in press.

Nowicki, S. & Barnes, J. Effects of a structured camp experience on locus of control orientation. *Journal of Genetic Psychology*, 1973, *122*, 247-252.

Nowicki, S., & Duke, M. P. Sex differences in locus of control and performance under competitive and cooperative conditions. *Journal of Educational Psychology*, 1978, *70*, 482-486.

Nowicki, S., & Hopper, A. E. Locus of control correlates in an alcoholic population. *Journal of Consulting and Clinical Psychology*, 1974, *42*, 735.

Nowicki, S., & Roundtree, J. *Correlates of locus of control in secondary school age students.* Unpublished manuscript, Emory University, 1971.

Nowicki, S., & Segal, W. Perceived parental characteristics, locus of control orientation and behavioral correlates of locus of control. *Developmental Psychology*, 1974, *10*, 33-37.

Nowicki, S. & Strickland, B. A locus of control scale for children. *Journal of Consulting and Clinical Psychology*, 1973, *40*, 148-154.

Odell, M. *Personality correlates of independence and conformity.* Unpublished master's thesis, Ohio State University, 1959.

O'Leary, M. R., Donovan, D. M., Cysewski, B., & Chaney, E. F. Perceived locus of control, experienced control, and depression: A trait description of the learned helplessness model of depression. *Journal of Clinical Psychology*, 1977, *33*, 164-168.

O'Leary, M. R., Donovan, D. M., & Hague, W. H. Interpersonal differentiation, locus of control and cognitive style among alcoholics. *Perceptual and Motor Skills*, 1974, *39*, 997-998.

Ollendick, D. G. Parental locus of control and the assessment of children's personality characteristics. *Journal of Personality Assessment*, 1979, *43*, 401-405.

Otten, M. W. Inventory and expressive measures of locus of control and academic performance: A 5 year outcome study. *Journal of Personality Assessment*, 1977, *41*, 644-649.

Overmier, J. B., & Seligman, M. E. P. Effects of inescapable shock upon subsequent escape and avoidance responding. *Journal of Comparative and Physiological Psychology*, 1967, *31*, 570-585.

Owens, M. W. *Disability-minority and social learning.* Unpublished master's thesis, West Virginia University, 1969.

Palmer, R. D. Parental perception and perceived locus of control in psychopathology. *Journal of Personality*, 1971, *3*, 420-431.

Parent, J., Forward, J., Canter, R., & Mohling, J. Interactive effects of teaching strategy and personal locus of control on student performance and satisfaction. *Journal of Educational Psychology*, 1975, *67*, 764-769.

Parks, C., Becker, W. N., Chamberlain, J. M., & Crandall, J. M. Eliminating self-defeating behaviors and change in locus of control. *Journal of Psychology*, 1975, *91*, 115-120.

Parsons, O. A., & Schneider, J. M. Locus of control in university students from Eastern and Western societies. *Journal of Consulting and Clinical Psychology*, 1974, *42*, 456-461.

Paulhus, D., & Christie, R. Spheres of control: An interactionist approach to assessment of perceived control. In H. M. Lefcourt (Ed.), *Research with the locus of control construct* (Vol. 1). New York: Academic Press, 1981.

Penk, W. Age changes and correlates of internal-external locus of control scales. *Psychological Reports*, 1969, *25*, 856.

Pervin, L. A. The need to predict and control under conditions of threat. *Journal of Personality*, 1963, *31*, 570-585.

Pettigrew, T. F. Social evaluation theory: convergences and applications. In D. Levine (Ed.), *Nebraska Symposium on Motivation.* Lincoln, Neb.: U. of Nebraska Press, 1967.

Phares, E. J. Expectancy changes in skill and chance situations. *Journal of Abnormal and Social Psychology*, 1957, *54*, 339–342.

Phares, E. J. Differential utilization of information as a function of internal-external control. *Journal of Personality*, 1968, *36*, 649–662.

Phares, E. J. Internal-external control and the reduction of reinforcement value after failure. *Journal of Consulting and Clinical Psychology*, 1971, *37*, 386–390.

Phares, E. J. *Locus of control: a peronality determinant of behavior.* Morristown, N.J.: General Learning Press, 1973.

Phares, E. J. *Locus of control in personality.* Morristown, N.J.: General Learning Press, 1976.

Phares, E. J., Ritchie, D. E., & Davis, W. L. Internal-external control and reaction to threat. *Journal of Personality and Social Psychology*, 1968, *10*, 402–405.

Phares, E. J., Wilson, K. G., & Klyver, N.W. Internal-external control and the attribution of blame under neutral and distractive conditions. *Journal of Personality and Social Psychology*, 1971, *18*, 285–288.

Pines, H. A. An attributional analysis of locus of control orientation and source of informational dependence. *Journal of Personality and Social Psychology*, 1973, *26*, 262–272.

Pines, H. A., & Julian, J. W. Effects of task and social demands on locus of control differences in information processing. *Journal of Personality*, 1972, *40*, 407–416.

Platt, E. S. *Internal-external control and changes in expected utility as predictors of the change in cigarette smoking following role playing.* Paper presented at Eastern Psychological Association Convention, Philadelphia, 1969.

Platt, J. J., & Eisenman, R. Internal-external control of reinforcement, time perspective, adjustment, and anxiety. *Journal of General Psychology*, 1968, *79*, 121–128.

Powell, A. & Vega, M. Correlates of adult locus of control. *Psychological Reports*, 1972, *30*, 455–460.

Prociuk, T. J., & Breen, L. J. Defensive externality and academic performance. *Journal of Personality and Social Psychology*, 1975, *31*, 549–556.

Propst, L. R. Efforts of personality and loss of anonymity on aggression: A re-evaluation of deindividuation. *Journal of Personality*, 1979, *47*, 531–545.

Ramey, C. T. Starr, R. H., Pallas, J., Whitten, C. F., & Reed, V. Nutrition, response-contingent stimulation and the mineral deprivation syndrome: Results of an early intervention program. *Merrill-Palmer Quarterly*, 1975, *21*, 45–53.

Randall, T. M., & Desrosiers, M. Measurement of supernatural belief: Sex differences and locus of control. *Journal of Personality Assessment*, 1980, *44*, 493–498.

Ray, W. J., & Katahn, M. Relation of anxiety to locus of control. *Psychological Reports*, 1968, *23*, 1196.

Read, P. P. *Alive.* New York: Lippincott, 1974.

Reid, D., & Ware, E. E. Multidimensionality of internal-external control: implications for past and future research. *Canadian Journal of Behavioral Science*, 1973, *5*, 264–271.

Reid, D., & Ware, E. E. Multidimensionality of internal versus external control: addition of a third dimension and non-distinction of self versus others. *Canadian Journal of Behavioral Science*, 1974, *6*, 131–142.

Reid, D. W., Hass, G., & Hawkings, D. Locus of desired control and positive self-concept of the elderly. *Journal of Gerontology*, 1977, *32*, 441–450.

Reid, D. W., & Ziegler, M. A survey of the reinforcements and activities elderly citizens feel are important for their general happiness. *Essence*, 1977, *2*, 5–24.

Reid, D. W., & Ziegler, M. The desired control measure and adjustment among the elderly. In H. M. Lefcourt (Ed.), *Research with the locus of control construct* (Vol. 1). New York: Academic Press, 1981.

Reim, B., Glass, D. C., & Singer, J. E. Behavioral consequences of exposure to uncontrollable and unpredictable noise. *Journal of Applied Social Psychology*, 1971, *1*, 44–56.

Reimanis, G. *Effects of experimental IE modification techniques and home environment variables on IE.* Paper presented at the American Psychological Association Convention, Washington, D.C., 1971.

Reimanis, G. School performance, intelligence, and locus of reinforcement control scales. *Psychology in the Schools,* 1973, *10,* 207–211.

Reimanis, G. Locus of control in American and Northeastern Nigerian students. *The Journal of Social Psychology,* 1977, *103,* 309–310.

Rest, J. B. New approaches in the assessment of moral judgment. In T. Lickona (Ed.), *Morality: Theory, research, and social issues.* New York: Holt, Rinehart, & Winston, 1976.

Richter, C. P. The phenomenon of unexplained sudden death in animals and man. In H. Feifel (Ed.), *The meaning of death.* New York: McGraw-Hill, 1959.

Riessman, F. *The culturally deprived child.* New York: Harper & Row, 1962.

Ritchie, E., & Phares, E. J. Attitude change as a function of internal-external control and communicator status. *Journal of Personality,* 1969, *37,* 429–443.

Rohner, E. C., Chaille, C., & Rohner, R. P. Perceived parental acceptance-rejection and the development of children's locus of control. *Journal of Psychology,* 1980, *104,* 83–86.

Rohsenow, D. J., & O'Leary, M. R. Locus of control research in alcoholic populations: A review. I. Development, Scales, & Treatment. *International Journal of the Addictions,* 1978, *13,* 55–78. (a)

Rohsenow, D. J., & O'Leary, M. R. Locus of control research in alcoholic populations: A review. II. Relationship to other measures. *International Journal of the Addictions,* 1978, *13,* 213–226. (b)

Roodin, P. A., Broughton, A., & Vaught, G. M. Effects of birth order, sex, and family size on field dependence and locus of control. *Perceptual and Motor Skills,* 1974, *39,* 671–676.

Rose, A. *The Negro in America.* New York: Harper & Row, 1948.

Rosenzweig, S. The picture association method and its application in a study of reactions to frustration. *Journal of Personality,* 1945, *14,* 3–23.

Rotter, J. B. *Social learning and clinical psychology.* Englewood Cliffs, N.J.: Prentice-Hall, 1954.

Rotter, J. B. The role of the psychological situation in determining the direction of human behavior. In M. R. Jones (Ed.), *Nebraska Symposium on Motivation,* Lincoln, Nebr.: University of Nebraska Press, 1955.

Rotter, J. B. Some implications of a social learning theory for the prediction of goal directed behavior from testing procedures. *Psychological Review,* 1960, 67, 301–316.

Rotter, J. B. *Clinical Psychology.* Englewood Cliffs, N.J.: Prentice Hall, 1964.

Rotter, J. B. Generalized expectancies for internal versus external control of reinforcement. *Psychological Monographs,* 1966, *80* (Whole No. 609).

Rotter, J. B. External control and internal control. *Psychology Today,* 1971, *5,* 37–59.

Rotter, J. B. Some problems and misconceptions related to the construct of internal vs. external control of reinforcement. *Journal of Consulting and Clinical Psychology,* 1975, *48,* 56–67.

Rotter, J. B., Chance, J. E., & Phares, E. J. *Applications of a social learning theory of personality.* New York: Holt, Rinehart & Winston, 1972.

Rotter, J. B., Liverant, S., & Crowne, D. P. The growth and extinction of expectancies in chance controlled and skilled tasks. *Journal of Psychology,* 1961, *52,* 161–177.

Rotter, J. B., & Mulry, R. C. Internal versus external control of reinforcements and decision time. *Journal of Personality and Social Psychology,* 1965, *2,* 598–604.

Rotter, J. B., Seeman, M., & Liverant, S. Internal versus external control of reinforcement: A major variable in behavior theory. In N. F. Washburne (Ed.), *Decisions, values and groups* (Vol. 2). London: Pergamon Press, 1962.

Rotter, J. B., Simmons, W. L., & Holden, K. B. *Some correlates of a general attitude towards the locus of control of reinforcement.* Unpublished manuscript, Ohio State University, 1962.

Rupp, M., & Nowicki, S. Locus of control among Hungarian children. *Journal of Cross Cultural Psychology*, 1978, *9*, 359-366.

Ryckman, R. M., Rodda, W. C., & Sherman, M. F. Locus of control and expertise relevance as determinants of changes in opinion about student activism. *The Journal of Social Psychology*, 1972, *88*, 107-114.

Saltzer, E. B. Locus of control and the intention to lose weight. *Health Education Monographs*, 1978, *6*, 118-128.

Saltzer, E. B. Cognitive moderators of the relationship between behavioral intentions and behavior. *Journal of Personality and Social Psychology*, 1981, *41*, 260-271.

Sandler, I. N., & Lakey, B. Locus of control as a stress moderator: The role of control perceptions and social support. *American Journal of Community Psychology*, in press.

Sarason, I. G., Johnson, J. H., & Siegel, J. M. Assessing the impact of life changes: Development of the life experiences survey. *Journal of Consulting and Clinical Psychology*, 1978, *46*, 932-946.

Sauber, S. R. Locus of control and task categorization: A study using the perceptual defense paradigm. *Journal of Social Issues*, 1971, *85*, 311-312.

Schaefer, E. S., & Bell, R. Q. Development of a parental attitude research instrument. *Child Development*, 1958, *29*, 339-361.

Scheidt, R. J. Belief in supernatural phenomena and locus of control. *Psychological Reports*, 1973, *32*, 1159-1162.

Schneider, J. M., & Parsons, O. A. Categories of the locus of control scale and cross-cultural comparisons in Denmark and the United States. *Journal of Cross-Cultural Psychology*, 1970, *1*, 131-138.

Schultz, R. Effects of control and predictability on the physical and psychological well-being of the institutionalized aged. *Journal of Personality and Social Psychology*, 1976, *33*, 563-573.

Scott, D. The Negro and the enlisted man: An analogy. *Harper's Magazine*, 1962, *225*, 16-21.

Seeman, M. Alienation and social learning in a reformatory. *American Journal of Sociology*, 1963, *69*, 270-284.

Seeman, M., & Evans, J. W. Alienation and learning in a hospital setting. *American Sociological Review*, 1962, *27*, 772-783.

Seligman, M. E. P. Chronic fear produced by unpredictable shock. *Journal of Comparative and Physiological Psychology*, 1968, *66*, 402-411.

Seligman, M. E. P. *Helplessness*. San Francisco: W. H. Freeman, 1975.

Seligman, M. E. P., & Maier, S. F. Failure to escape traumatic shock. *Journal of Experimental Psychology*, 1967, *74*, 1-9.

Seligman, M. E. P., Maier, S. F., & Geer, J. The alleviation of learned helplessness in the dog. *Journal of Abnormal and Social Psychology*, 1968, *73*, 256-262.

Seligman, M. E. P., Maier, S. F., & Solomon, R. L. Unpredictable and uncontrollable aversive events. In F. R. Brush (Ed.), *Aversive conditioning and learning*. New York: Academic Press, 1969.

Shaw, R. L., & Uhl, N. P. *Relationship between locus of control scores and reading achievement of black and white second grade children from two socioeconomic levels*. Paper presented at Southeastern Psychological Association Convention, New Orleans, 1969.

Shea, D. J., & deCharms, R. Achievement motivation, control of reinforcements and goal setting behavior. In R. deCharms, *Enhancing motivation*. New York: Irvington, 1976.

Sherman, M. R., Pelletier, R. J., & Ryckman, R. M. Replication of the relationship between dogmatism and locus of control. *Psychological Reports*, 1973, *33*, 749-750.

Sherman, S. Internal-external control and its relationship to attitude change under different social influence techniques. *Journal of Personality and Social Psychology*, 1973, *23*, 23-29.

Sherrod, D. R. Crowding, perceived control, and behavioral aftereffects. *Journal of Applied Social Psychology*, 1974, *4*, 171-186.

Sherrod, D. R., & Cohen, S. Density, perceived control, and design. In J. R. Aiello, and A. Baum (Eds.), *Residential crowding and design*. New York: Plenum, 1978.

Sherrod, D. R., Hage, J. N., Halpern, P. L., & Moore, B. S. Effects of personal causation and perceived control on responses to an adversive environment: The more control the better. *Journal of Experimental Social Psychology*, 1977, *13*, 14–27.

Shipe, D. Impulsivity and locus of control as predictors of achievement and adjustment in mildly retarded and borderline youth. *American Journal of Mental Deficiency*, 1971, *76*, 12–22.

Shore, R. E. *Parental determinants of boys' internal-external control* Unpublished doctoral dissertation, Syracuse University, 1967.

Shybut, J. Time perspective, internal versus external control and severity of psychological disturbance. *Journal of Clinical Psychology*, 1968, *24*, 312–315.

Singer, E. *Key concepts in psychotherapy*. New York: Random House, 1965.

Skinner, B. F. *Beyond Freedom and Dignity*. New York: Knopf, 1971.

Smith, C. E., Pryer, M. W., & Distefano, M. K. Internal-external control and severity of emotional impairment among psychiatric patients. *Journal of Clinical Psychology*, 1971, *27*, 449–450.

Smith, R. E. Changes in locus of control as a function of life crisis resolution. *Journal of Abnormal Psychology*, 1970, *75*, 328–332.

Snyder, C. R., & Larson, G. R. A further look at student acceptances of general personality interpretations. *Journal of Consulting and Clinical Psychology*, 1972, *38*, 384–388.

Solomon, D., Houlihan, K. A., & Parelius, R. Intellectual achievement responsibility in Negro and white children. *Psychological Reports*, 1969, *24*, 479–483.

Sordoni, C. *Experiments in humor: creativity, locus of control and their relationship to two dimensions of humor*. Unpublished doctoral dissertation, University of Waterloo, 1979.

Sroufe, L. A. The coherence of individual development. *American Psychologist*, 1979, *34*, 834–841.

Srull, T. K., & Karabenick, S. A. Effects of personality-situation locus of control congruence. *Journal of Personality and Social Psychology*, 1975, *32*, 617–628.

Staub, E., Tursky, B., and Schwartz, G. E. Self-control and predictability: their effects on reactions to aversive stimulation. *Journal of Personality and Social Psychology*, 1971, *18*, 157–162.

Steiner, I. D. Perceived freedom. In L. Berkowitz (Ed.), *Advances in experimental social psychology* (Vol. 5). New York: Academic Press, 1970.

Stephens, M. W. *Parent behavior antecedents, cognitive correlates and multidimensionality of locus of control in young children*. Paper presented at American Psychological Association Convention, Montreal, 1973.

Stephens, M. W., & Delys, P. A locus of control measure for preschool children. *Developmental Psychology*, 1973, *9*, 55–65. (a)

Stephens, M. W., & Delys, P. External control expectancies among disadvantaged children at preschool age. *Child Development*, 1973, *44*, 670–674. (b)

Stewart, J. E., & Moore, K. P. Time perception as a function of locus of control. *Personality and Social Psychology Bulletin*, 1978, *4*, 56–58.

Strahan, R., & Huth, H. Relations between embedded figures test performance and dimensions of the I-E scale. *Journal of Personality Assessment*, 1975, *39*, 523–524.

Strassberg, D. S., & Robinson, J. S. The relationship between locus of control and other personality measures in drug users. *Journal of Consulting and Clinical Psychology*, 1974, *42*, 744–745.

Strickland, B. R. The prediction of social action from a dimension of internal-external control. *Journal of Social Psychology*, 1965, *66*, 353–358.

Strickland, B. R. Individual differences in verbal conditioning, extinction and awareness. *Journal of Personality*, 1970, *38*, 364–378.

Strickland, B. R. Delay of gratification as a function of race of the experimenter. *Journal of Personality and Social Psychology*, 1972, *22*, 108–112.

Strickland, B. R. Internal-external control of reinforcement. In T. Blass (Ed.), *Personality variables in social behavior*. Hillsdale, N.J.: Lawrence Erlbaum Associates, 1977.

Strodtbeck, F. L. Family interaction, values and achievement. In D. C. McClelland (Ed.), *Talent and society*. New York: Van Nostrand, 1958.

Sullivan, H. S. *The psychiatric interview*. New York: Norton, 1954.

Suomi, S. J. Contingency, perception and social development. In L. R. Sherrod & M. E. Lamb (Eds.), *Infant social cognition: empirical and theoretical considerations*. Hillsdale, N.J.: Lawrence Erlbaum Associates, 1980.

Taub, S. I., & Dollinger, S. V. Reward and purpose as incentives for children differing in locus of control expectancies. *Journal of Personality*, 1975, *43*, 179-195.

Thomas, L. E. The I-E scale, ideological bias and political participation. *Journal of Personality*, 1970, *38*, 273-286.

Thompson, S. C. Will it hurt less if I can control it? A complex answer to a simple question. *Psychologycal Bulletin*, 1981, *90*, 89-101.

Thompson, T. *Lost*. New York: Dell, 1975.

Tiffany, D. W. Mental health: A function of experienced control. *Journal of Clinical Psychology*, 1967, *23*, 311-315.

Time Magazine, Sept. 20, 1971. In *Annual Editions Readings in Psychology*, 1972, Guilford, Conn.: Dushkin Publishing Group, 1972, pp. 6-13.

Tobacyk, J. J., Broughton, A., & Vaught, G. M. Effects of congruence-incongruence between locus of control and field dependence on personality functioning. *Journal of Consulting and Clinical Psychology*, 1975, *43*, 81-85.

Tolor, A., Reznikoff, M. Relation between insight, repression-sensitization, internal-external control, and death anxiety. *Journal of Abnormal Psychology*, 1967, *72*, 426-430.

Tyler, F. B., Gatz, M., & Keenan, K. A constructivist analysis of the Rotter I-E scale. *Journal of Personality*, 1979, *47*, 11-35.

Ubbink, E. M., & Sadava, S. W. Rotter's generalized expectancies as predictors of helping behavior. *Psychological Reports*, 1974, *35*, 865-866.

Valins, S., & Nisbett, R. E. *Some implications of the attribution processes for the development and treatment of emotional disorders*, New York: General Learning Press, 1971.

Viney, L. L. Multidimensionality of perceived locus of control: two replications. *Journal of Consulting and Clinical Psychology*, 1974, *42*, 463-464.

Walls, R. T., & Miller, J. J. Delay of gratification in welfare and rehabilitation clients. *Journal of Counseling Psychology*, 1970, *4*, 383-384.

Walls, R. T., & Smith, T. S. Development of preference for delayed reinforcement in disadvantaged children. *Journal of Educational Psychology*, 1970, *61*, 118-123.

Wallston, K. A., Maides, S. A., & Wallston, B. S. Health-related information seeking as a function of health related locus of control and health value. *Journal of Research in Personality*, 1976, *10*, 215-222.

Wallston, K. A., & Wallston, B. S. Health locus of control scales. In H. M. Lefcourt (Ed.), *Research with the locus of control construct* (Vol. 1). New York: Academic Press, 1981.

Wallston, B. S., Wallston, K. A., Kaplan, G. D., & Maides, S. A. Development and validation of the health locus of control (HLC) scale. *Journal of Consulting and Clinical Psychology*, 1976, *44*, 580-585.

Warhime, R. G., & Woodson, M. Locus of control and immediate affect states. *Journal of Clinical Psychology*, 1971, *27*, 443-444.

Watson, D. Relationship between locus of control and anxiety. *Journal of Personality and Social Psychology*, 1967, *6*, 91-92.

Watson, D., & Baumal, E. Effects of locus of control and expectation of future control upon present performance. *Journal of Personality and Social Psychology*, 1967, *6*, 212-215.

Watson, J. S. The development and generalization of "contingency awareness" in early infancy: Some hypotheses. *Merrill-Palmer Quarterly of Behavior and Development*, 1966, *12*, 123-135.

Watson, J. S. Memory and "contingency analysis" in infant learning. *Merrill-Palmer Quarterly of Behavior and Development*, 1967, *13*, 55-76.

Watson, J. S. Smiling, cooing and "the game". *Merrill-Palmer Quarterly of Behavior and Development*, 1972, *18*, 323-339.

Watson, J. S. Perception of contingency as a determinant of social responsiveness. In E. B. Thoman (Ed.), *The origins of social responsiveness*. Hillsdale, N.J.: Lawrence Erlbaum Associates, 1979.

Watson, J. S., & Ramey, C. T. Reactions to response contingent stimulation in early infancy. *Merrill-Palmer Quarterly of Behavior and Development*, 1972, *18*, 219-227.

Weiner, B. New conceptions in the study of achievement motivation. In B. A. Maher (Ed.), *Progress in experimental personality research* (Vol. 5). New York: Academic Press, 1970.

Weiner, B. *Theories of motivation: from mechanism to cognition*. Chicago: Markham, 1972.

Weiner, B. Achievement motivation as conceptualized by an attribution theorist. In B. Weiner (Ed.), *Attribution theory, achievement motivation*. New York: General Learning Press, 1974.

Weiner, B. A theory of motivation for some classroom experiences. *Journal of Educational Psychology*, 1979, *71*, 3-25.

Weiner, B., Heckhausen, H., Meyer, W. U., & Cook, R. E. Causal ascriptions and achievement motivation. *Journal of Personality and Social Psychology*, 1972, *21*, 239-248.

Weiner, B., Nierenberg, R., & Goldstein, M. Social learning (locus of control) versus attributional (causal stability) interpretations of expectancy of success. *Journal of Personality*, 1976, *44*, 52-68.

Weiner, B., Russell, D., & Lerman, D. The cognition-emotion process in achievement-related contexts. *Journal of Personality and Social Psychology*, 1979, *37*, 1211-1220.

Weiss, J. M. Effects of coping behavior in different warning signal conditions on stress pathology in rats. *Journal of Comparative and Physiological Psychology*, 1971, *1*, 1-14.

Weiss, J. M. Psychological and behavioral influences on gastrointestinal lesions in animal models. In J. D. Maser & M. E. P. Seligman (Eds.), *Psychopathology: experimental models*. San Francisco: W. H. Freeman, 1977.

Weisz, J. R., & Stipek, D. Developmental change in perceived control: Review, critique, and proposed agenda. *Human Development*, in press.

Wheeler, R. W., & Davis, J. M. Decision making as a function of locus of control and cognitive dissonance. *Psychological Reports*, 1979, *44*, 499-502.

White, R. W. The experience of efficacy in schizophrenia. *Psychiatry: Journal for the study of interpersonal processes*, 1965, *28*, 199-211.

Wichern, F., Gordon, D., & Nowicki, S. Observed maternal and child behaviors in a dependence producing task as a function of children's locus of control orientation *Merrill-Palmer Quarterly*, 1981, *27*, 43-51.

Wichern, F., & Nowicki, S. Independence training practices and locus of control orientation in children and adolescents. *Developmental Psychology*, 1976, *12*, 1977.

Williams, J. G., & Stack, J. J. Internal-external control as a situational variable in determining information-seeking by Negro students. *Journal of Consulting and Clinical Psychology*, 1972, *39*, 187-193.

Witkin, H., Dyk, R. B., Faterson, G. E., Goodenough, D. R., & Karp, S. A. *Psychological differentiation*. New York: Wiley, 1962.

Wolfgang, A., & Potvin, R. *Internality as a determinant of classroom participation and academic performance among elementary students*. Paper presented at American Psychological Association Convention, Montreal, 1973.

Wolk, S., & DuCette, J. The moderating effect of locus of control in relation to achievement-motivation variables. *Journal of Personality*, 1973, *41*, 59-70.

Wolk, S., & DuCette, J. Intentional performance and incidental learning as a function of personality and task directions. *Journal of Personality and Social Psychology,* 1974, *29,* 90–101.

Wong, P. T. P., Watters, D. A., & Sproule, C. F. Initial validity and reliability of the Trent Attribution Profile as a measure of attribution schema and locus of control. *Educational and Psychological Measurement,* 1978, *38,* 1129–1134.

Worell, L., & Tumilty, T. N. The measurement of locus of control among alcoholics. In H. M. Lefcourt (Ed.), *Research with the locus of control construct* (Vol. 1). New York: Academic Press, 1981.

Wortman, C. B., & Brehm, J. W. Responses to uncontrollable outcomes: an integration of reactance theory and the learned helplessness model. In L. Berkowitz (Ed.), *Advances in experimental social psychology* (Vol. 8) New York: Academic Press, 1975.

Wright, R. J., & DuCette, J. P. *Locus of control and academic achievement in traditional and non-traditional settings.* Paper presented at American Education Research Association Convention, San Francisco, 1976.

Yates, R., Kennelly, K., & Cox, S. H. Perceived contingency of parental reinforcements, parent-child relations and locus of control. *Psychological Reports,* 1975, *36,* 139–146.

Ziegler, M., & Reid, D. W. Correlates of locus of desired control in two samples of elderly persons. Community residents and hospitalized patients. *Journal of Consulting and Clinical Psychology,* 1979, *47,* 977–979.

Zytkoskee, A., Strickland, B. R., & Watson, J. Delay of gratification and internal versus external control among adolescents of low socioeconomic status. *Developmental Psychology,* 1971, *4,* 93–98.

Zytowski, D. B. Internal-external control of reinforcement and the Strong Vocational Interest Blank. *Journal of Consulting Psychology,* 1967, *14,* 177–179.

Author Index

243

Subject Index